BF575 .G7 A29

Acute grief

P9-DGG-643

DATE DUE

JUN 03 1995		
MAY 1 3 1998		
AUG 1 5 05		

DEMCO 38-297

Acute Grief

Acute Grief
Counseling the Bereaved

Otto S. Margolis, Howard C. Raether,
Austin H. Kutscher, J. Bruce Powers,
Irene B. Seeland, Robert DeBellis,
and Daniel J. Cherico, editors

with the editorial assistance of
Lillian G. Kutscher

Columbia University Press
New York, 1981

Columbia University Press
New York   Guildford, Surrey

Copyright © 1981 by Columbia University Press
All Rights Reserved
Printed in the United States of America

Library of Congress Cataloging in Publication Data
Main entry under title:

Acute grief.

(Foundation of Thanatology series)
Includes bibliographies and index.
1. Bereavement—Psychological aspects.
2. Grief. 3. Counseling. I. Margolis, Otto
Schwarz. [DNLM: 1. Grief. 2. Counseling.
3. Attitude to death. BF575.G7 A1894]
BF575.G7A29   155.9′37   80-21020
ISBN 0-231-04586-7

Acknowledgment

THE EDITORS WISH to acknowledge the support and encouragement of the Foundation of Thanatology in the preparation of this volume. All royalties from the sale of this book are assigned to the Foundation of Thanatology, a tax exempt, not for profit, public scientific and educational foundation.

Thanatology, a new subspecialty of medicine, is involved in scientific and humanistic inquiries and the application of the knowledge derived therefrom to the subjects of the psychological aspects of dying; reactions to loss, death, and grief; and recovery from bereavement.

The Foundation of Thanatology is dedicated to advancing the cause of enlightened health care for the terminally ill patient and his family. The Foundation's orientation is a positive one based on the philosophy of fostering a more mature acceptance and understanding of death and the problems of grief and the more effective and humane management and treatment of the dying patient and his bereaved family members.

Contents

Preface

WHEN DOES GRIEF occur most acutely? Both research and experience indicate that the life crisis referred to as acute grief occurs immediately following the death of a person of significance in the bereaved's life, someone in whom the investment of love had been of a major dimension or on whom the greater share of responsibility for a family's wellbeing had depended. During this time period the threads connecting the past with the present are severed and the weaving of a new fabric of living should begin. Whether drained physically and emotionally by the ordeal of the prolonged illness of the person being mourned or shocked into numbness if death has struck unexpectedly, each survivor must confront stark practicalities and make crucial and painful decisions that may have a profound effect on the restructuring and refocusing of life.

What is the length of the acute grief period? And what is the place of acute grief in the overall continuum from bereavement through its resolution? Most grief counselors or therapists agree that acute grief spans a period of about 14 days and includes as its central event the funeral or other ceremonial observances of a ritualistic or religious nature. Except when the death has been a sudden one, acute grief follows the period of anticipatory grief and precedes the nine-month to two-year period of the normal mourning or grief process. During this period new primary support systems should emerge for survivors. Caregivers, both in professional and societal contexts, come forward to replace those who gave guidance during the acute grief crisis and to assist the bereaved through a "normal" grief recovery, thereby avoiding a lapse into pathological grief.

A concept of "staging" recovery from bereavement has surfaced and includes the stage of acute grief where shock accompanies the impact of the death and the funeral and post-funeral activities are settings for other stages of progress toward a renewal of hope and positive living. Such stages would seem to parallel the stages of anticipatory grief before acute grief, of mourning immediately after acute grief, and resolution of grief following the grieving period.

What are the emotional and physical signs and symptoms of actue grief, merging as it does with anticipatory grief before and "normal" bereavement thereafter? Certainly, these should be considered in at least two categories: those which are exacerbated and those which make their appearance for the first time—to be carried over in reduced or increased intensity into the later periods of bereavement. The collaborating authors in this book document these in great detail from the perspectives of their many disciplines. From professional and personal experiences, they describe the interactions between the dying patient and family members as roles and paths of "command" are relinquished and responsibilities, including many that are difficult to delegate, are passed on to others. The psychosocial aspects of the supportive care to be offered survivors are analyzed to determine from whence the required supportive care should eventually be derived, whether from members of the immediate family, from close friends, or from responsive members of the community.

Who should give guidance or counsel or therapy to those bereaved? Are their credentials for providing this support evaluated —even granted—only on the basis of academic degrees earned in a structured learning process? Or can they also flow naturally from those who have been exposed to a wide range of life and death experiences?

Responses to these questions are given careful consideration by sociologists, nurses, funeral service directors, clergymen, psychiatrists, psychologists, social workers, research scientists, educators, administrators, business executives, physicians from numerous medical specialties, and others. Their experiences and writings offer a global view of acute grief itself and of the techniques of routine caring and crisis intervention known to avert many of the psychological, physical, socioeconomic, and other disabling effects of bereavement. The facilitation of each individual's adjustment to loss and the ability to give guidance, counsel, or other therapeutic support to those who grieve do not fall within the province of any one group, but rather seem to call most ideally for the efforts of a team.

The purpose of this text, then, is to illustrate the generalizations cited above and to offer constructive guidelines for those who give and those who receive counsel, guidance, or therapy during the period of acute grief and throughout the stages of the crises accompanying separation, anxiety, loss, bereavement, grief, and ultimate recovery from grief.

The Editors

Acute Grief

Part I

Overview of Loss, Grief, and Bereavement

Grief as a Cosmic Crisis

James P. Carse

Grief is a profound emotional crisis. It is profound because it is enormously complex and related to a wide array of circumstances. It is a crisis because it brings one to the necessity of decision. Grief does not simply come and go. It must be dealt with, and because it is profoundly complicated, it must be dealt with in a fundamental manner.

I look at the phenomenon of grief in these two ways: as an experience of manifold dimensions and as a crisis.

1

We are most accustomed to viewing grief in psychological categories, indicating our concern with the personal and inward elements of the experience. Thus, we note that bereaved persons are severely disoriented and often incapable of making important judgments. It is customary in many traditions that the bereaved be excused from nearly all the activities by which they sustain themselves. Someone else may cook for them; they may be relieved of any vocational responsibilities and even be expected not to bathe or attend to other matters of personal hygiene. We also commonly observe that grief brings with it the experience of guilt. One is filled with tormenting thoughts of the many things left unsaid or the acts of kindness never performed. More seriously still, in acute grief one may have

serious difficulties in direct reality perception or be incapable of articulate speech.

But there are important nonpsychological aspects to grief. Almost always there is a significant economic impact associated with
death. A long and expensive illness may have preceded the death, or
the family may have lost its chief provider. Along with the other
aspects of loss one may have to deal with an impending relocation or
even the sale of personal possessions.

In addition to its psychological and economic aspects, we may
not overlook what could be considered the social, or even political,
factors in grief. The reaction to the death of someone close inescap-
ably involves a community of other persons. Not only are the
bereaved often dependent on others, particularly in the initial period
of grief, but also the deceased may have been important to the community. There may well be qualities of anger or dismay at the way
the community has responded, or failed to respond, or even shared in
the responsibility of the death. The bereaved often feel their lost
loved ones to have been victims of incompetent health care, or of
society's inability to provide minimal social support, or of personal
pressures that lead to self-destructive behavior.

In considering any single instance of grief one would be ill advised to ignore any one of these aspects. I propose a way of talking
and thinking about grief that holds these many aspects in focus. Instead of regarding grief as a psychological or economic phenomenon,
or looking separately at its social and political aspects, I suggest we
consider it a *cosmic* event. By this I do not mean that we are to
consider it as something that happens in space, or that death is an
event that is felt all about the universe. Rather, I use the word *cosmic*
in a way reflecting on its original Greek meaning. The cosmos for the
ancient philosophers simply meant an ordered world. There is nothing intimidating or overwhelming about the world if we know the
fundamental order by which all worldly events occur. To be human
is, in fact, to be able to discern what that order is and to design a life
that coheres with it.

We all learn in the course of our schooling and our experience as
we move from childhood to adulthood to assemble a view of the
cosmos and clarify our understanding of the place we have in it.
What is most important to us is to recognize that the cosmos, so understood, is not a mere accumulation of lifeless matter in whose
midst we have assembled strategies of protection and survival. *We
live in a personal universe.* The cosmos does not have a meaning or a
structure that is in any way independent of our relation to other per-

sons. It is true that we are often deeply concerned to find ways of protecting ourselves from the extremes of weather and of ensuring a constant food supply—as though our chief adversary were the caprices of the elements. The reason we are concerned, however, is that we are interested not merely in surviving but also in living in a certain style with other human beings.

We can, in fact, have no view of nature that does not express the way we are related to the other persons. Consider the concept of "wilderness," for example. We are in the habit of conceiving the wilderness as a place empty of human habitation and alien to civilization. The wilderness is not simply the point at which civilization ends—it is an uncivilized *place*. In other words, even a conception of nature "in the wild" is distinctly human oriented. The wilderness is impressive because it is a place where we can have a human experience unlike almost all others—but it is always in relation to human experience that we conceive it.

It may seem as though we have wandered far from our subject, but this reference to the wilderness is simply a way of drawing attention to the fact that we live in a personal universe and that we can live in it all only to the degree that it is personal, that is, only to the degree that *our relation to the ordered cosmos is the way we are with others*. This is important to the understanding of grief in the sense that when the death of someone close to us has occurred it has probably disrupted our ordered cosmos. It is not simply that there is one person less to cope with; it is that we live in a universe that makes no sense. The cosmos has lost its fundamental order. As a result, our own lives lose their meaning.

I have drawn attention to the cosmic nature of grief for a definite reason: to emphasize that grief has power in that it drives us to the formidable task of reassembling a new universe. This task is beyond the capacity of many. For this reason some persons are apparently permanently crippled by grief. They are simply overwhelmed by the manifold tasks into which bereavement throws them. Their whole lives take therefore the shape of grief.

2

Grief inevitably brings us to crisis—defined here as a situation in which it is necessary to make a fundamental decision concerning the course and content of our lives.

On the face of it, the death of someone with whom we are intimately connected seems not to bring us to a decision, but rather to take all substantive decisiveness from our hands. Indeed, the very nature of death is that it seems to be a power quite without any rival, and when it strikes close to us we ordinarily experience a terrible impotence.

There is a subtle and yet crucial issue at stake in this experience of impotence. It is evident that one of the discoveries we are likely to make in the initial reaction to the death of another is that our lives are so tightly associated with the other that they scarcely belong to us. When we experience the cosmic shattering we are brought face to face with the realization that the universe we have lived in is not only personal but also assembled in association with others. Indeed, it is habitable only because we can live in it with these particular persons. The cosmos is personal, but strangely it is not our own.

We can exaggerate this point without distorting it. We can say that our universe becomes all the more personal as we enter into more intimate association with others. If we are alienated from other existing human beings, isolated in the human community, lacking any warmth of personal affection, we are living in a forbidding and largely disordered cosmos. If our lives are, on the other hand, rich in shared intimacy, the cosmos takes the dimensions of a vast home. However, it is also true that in this latter case we are much more vulnerable to the disordering of the basic structure of our lives by the death of significant others.

There is something of a formula here: the more ordered and habitable our universe, the more we can be shattered by grief.

But how is this a crisis, and where does decision enter this account? The vulnerability to grief has another side. Just as we cannot assemble a universe, or live in it, by ourselves, neither have others assembled it for us entirely by themselves. There is a profound reciprocity here. It appears that parents provide a home for their children and that if they did not do so the children would be incapable of assuming this task themselves. This is true, but it is also the case that the children must respond. It is not the hot suppers and a rainproof dwelling that make a home; it is rather the parents' caring and relating that permit the children to respond as persons. In thus responding, the children bring something to the home parents are incapable of providing—a free exchange, a subtle but far-reaching interdependency of parents and children on each other.

In other words, the discovery in the initial stages of grief that the universe is personal and can be shattered by death is attended by another, and perhaps even more frightening, discovery: we are free to rebuild it. This is frightening because we learn that the universe has no inner consistency, that it will not stay put, and that it will pass with all other phenomena. What was lost cannot be restored. On the other hand, a new universe can be assembled in its place, quite as the previous was assembled.

Grief is overcome only as this latter aspect is integrated into one's self-understanding. When we see that what has been taken away from us can be built in a new manner because it was something we could only share and not privately possess, we have been healed of our bereavement. There are, however, two consequences of this crucial fact, each worth briefly examining here.

3

We have said that grief is the twofold experience of the fact that the universe is personal—just as it has been assembled in relation with others, the loss of those others presents us with the crisis of deciding whether we will fashion another in its place. If the personal nature of the cosmos owes to our dependence on others, it also exposes our freedom from others.

We can see from this that, *first,* bereavement can become a more or less permanent form of life, even without the close death of another, and, *second,* the healing of grief consists not only in the free decision to create a new order for our personal cosmos but also in our ability to share this creation with others quite as it was shared with us previously. If the present universe has become personal by reciprocal action, all new universes must be just as reciprocal.

First, then, consider the way in which some persons never survive their grief. Principally this takes the form of being unwilling to see that the universe is forever passing. Living in grief means choosing to live in a familiar cosmos with a static order and becoming oblivious to the fact that this order is not something that subsists in itself but is shared with others. Most dramatically this refusal arises with the experience of death, but it need not. It may be a simple recognition that death has power to undo all that is fixed, a recognition taking the form that some students of the phenomenon of grief have referred to as "anticipatory grief."

There is a poignant irony in this refusal. By denying that the universe is endlessly changing as the pattern of our intimacy with others is altered by death and many other significant experiences, we have made it increasingly homeless. By insisting on its changeless order, we have foundered on its disorder, and most probably we hide this dreadful fact from ourselves by insisting all the more on changelessness. The obverse is striking: by accepting the impermanence, the ceaselessly evolving order of things, we find the universe supremely habitable.

This first consequence of the discovery of the crisis of decision in grief necessarily leads us to the second: the cosmos becomes personal and habitable only to the degree that we choose not to live in it alone. Why does this consequence follow from the first?

Because we are mortal, we are historical. That is to say, life is not a state or a condition—it is a passage. It opens and closes in the course of time. For this reason, the quality of our lives at any moment is always deeply affected by the facts that we are in passage, that we are growing older, that we are undergoing what Teilhard de Chardin called life's "passivities": both growth and aging. Neither can be avoided. For this reason, each of our intimate associations is subject to the same inescapable changes. This has the interesting result that to the extent we are truly intimate with one another we shall accept that our relationship will suffer endless change. And, similarly, only as far as we are able to identify the irreversible changes in our lives can we enter into intimacy with others.

We live in a personal universe. It is personal because we have assembled it, and not because it has fashioned us. Further, the universe is reciprocally personal; it can be personal only as it is shared. True sharing is possible only to the degree that we can accept the fact of change, of endless alterability, both in our world and in our relationships. Death is, of course, the very fact that guarantees that change. We cannot choose not to die—but because we die we can choose to live. Indeed, life is possible only in the form of choice. And it is precisely to this choice that the experienced crisis of grief repeatedly brings us.

We cannot heal another of grief—for the healing must be reciprocal. But we can live in such a way that it is evident to others that we are unafraid to accept the ceaseless change death has worked on life. Doing so, we open ourselves to an intimacy healing us of our own grief and restoring us to a meaningful cosmos.

❦ 2

Grief, Grief Therapy and Continuing Education

· Jeannette R. Folta

Thomas Eliot (1930) pronounced one of the initial statements calling for an objective, comparative analysis of grief and bereavement in families. His work catalyzed a series of individuals who became interested and involved in conducting research in grief and bereavement and who added to the body of knowledge about these phenomena. Among this group was Erich Lindemann, who, in his classic study (1944), demonstrated acute grief as a definite syndrome that may appear immediately following bereavement, be delayed, be exaggerated, or be apparently absent. Further, he indicated that a distorted picture representing some aspect of the grief syndrome may be present and that, through the use of appropriate techniques, this dysfunctional reaction can be resolved into a normal grief reaction.

Others have since confirmed Lindemann's observation of the grief syndrome and the accompanying symptoms. George Engel (1964), for example, amplified Lindemann's observations in his conceptualization of six stages of normal grief: (1) shock and disbelief, (2) developing awareness, (3) restitution, (4) resolving loss, (5) idealization, and (6) outcome. In normal grief the first stage may last anywhere from moments to hours or even days. The second stage, the reality of death, begins to penetrate the survivor's consciousness and is followed by feelings of loss, emptiness, and anguish. During the third stage the work of mourning is facilitated by the various religious or secular ceremonies. Resolving the loss is a stage in which the mourner attempts to deal with the pain of the loss, and the fifth stage, idealization of the deceased, follows this. Feeling numb, crying, anguish, a sense of emptiness, anger, guilt, and even acting-out behavior may all be a part of normal grief. The entire process can take about a year and if successful is exemplified by the bereaved individual's ability to remember comfortably and realistically both the pleasures and pains of the relationship.

Patterson (1969, p. 79) amplified Engel's position when he stated that:

> . . . grieving is the gradual process of destroying the intense emotional ties to the dead person. The best example of this process is the intense sad feelings provoked by thinking of the dead person. Each time this happens, it gets the sad person a little closer to being able to think about the dead person without being overwhelmed by the feelings. The other aspect of grieving is making restitution for the loss. If grief work could be accomplished in more people, much chronic unhappiness could be reduced.

Grief is a life crisis, a normal process, not a psychiatric disorder. The grief reaction itself carries with it elements that usually tend to produce its own healing. In most cases no special counseling or therapy is needed for the griever. What is needed is someone to help the person understand what is going on in his or her life, to keep in touch with this person and from time to time, and to ascertain that progress is being made. Unfortunately, since death and grief came "out of the closet," we have seen a movement afoot indicating that some professions believe that grief and grief therapy should become a sub-subspecialty under the multiplicity of already existing subspecialties. There has been some discussion in the U.S. and Europe about whether or not certain professionals (particularly social workers and nurses) ought to have advanced degree programs to prepare them to become grief therapists. Normal grief needs no therapy; it needs no high-powered professional. Grief counseling from the family, from the friends, from the clergy, funeral directors, and self-help groups is more than sufficient. This can be done in a one-to-one relationship or in a group format. Counseling is, of course, vital as a primary preventive mode.

Assigning trained professionals to direct services in the usual case is a costly, inefficient, and poor use of both funds and resources. On the other hand, pathological grief—exemplified by the inability to cry; physical ailments; excessive, prolonged depression; obsessive, self-destructive, or other-destructive behavior—does require highly trained professionals and a one-to-one format of therapy. However, in relation to the total number of individuals experiencing grief, pathological grief is quite rare.

Grief therapy implies treatment toward cure. If we truly believe that grief in the sense of most circumstances is in fact a normal process, then we should not treat it as a pathological disorder, and we should place primary emphasis on counseling as opposed to therapy.

Continuing education is based on the principle that education needs to be an enduring, ceaseless, lifelong endeavor. Implicit in this principle is the assumption that one has basic preparation in a particular area. In the U.S., where death has become an increasingly private phenomenon, we need to begin with an excellent basic educational program on grief and develop a continuing education program that would involve at least three levels.

The first level, the most basic, would be a public education program for both the lay public and professional groups. This program should consist of basic information necessary to understand what loss and stress are, what normal grief reactions are, what to expect in the process of grief, what constitutes inappropriate and/or abnormal grief reactions, what community resources are available, how best to use the referral systems within the community, what impact death and grief have on family structures and relationships, and what changes, if any, loss creates in people's lives.

My experience during a sabbatical year spent in Norway and Africa studying grief reactions cross-culturally impressed me with the differences between the problems caused by death itself as opposed to those caused by grief. In Norway my colleague and I offered a seminar in the evenings for anyone interested. Attending it were physicians and social workers, history majors, students, faculty, community workers—all kinds of people from many disciplines. At one session a young pediatrician came to us and said, "Something you said in class the other day really rang a bell and came in handy in an experience that I had this morning." And she began to relate the experience. She was walking downtown when she met the father of one of her patients who had died some six months earlier. She began to talk to the father about how he was doing and what was happening in his life, when he broke down and began to cry. Finally, he said, "I must talk to you. The grief that is in me is causing our family to break apart. My wife and I are about to get divorced." When she investigated the situation, she found out that the actual problem was not related to grief, but to the circumstances of the death. The child who had died was the third sibling this family had lost from the same genetic disease. When this child died, the family asked the physicians for advice about having more children and were told that the possibility future children would die from the same inherited disease was great. The physicians then advised the parents not to have any more children, but they did not discuss methods of birth control. As a result, for six months this couple practiced abstinence because they knew nothing about available birth control techniques. The problem in their lives was related largely to the problems attendant on the death itself, not the grief. Similarly, when a spouse dies, the survivor may experience financial hardship. This is not a consequence of grief; it is a consequence of death, occurring whether or not one grieves for the lost individual.

Friends pose problems. In the United States, in Norway, and also in Nigeria, the problems that come with grief—mainly psychosomatic illnesses, prolonged, delayed grief, and pathological grief—frequently occur in friends because there is no acceptable way for them to grieve publicly. Included in our basic educational preparation about death and dying ought to be an emphasis on friendship groups, as well as family groups.

This basic program should also educate the public and professionals about the process of dying. What are the problems one encounters as one goes through the experience with the dying? What are the problems that the dying experience as they go through the process? What alternatives are available? What are the consequences of dying at home versus dying in hospital? What is anticipatory grief? How can the dying experience become a growth experience for survivors?

At the second level of continuing education, on the assumption that basic preparation has been provided, there should be a focus on the development of counseling skills. At a minimum, this should provide for the development of techniques of interviewing, listening, and observing and for learning theories of behavior and techniques such as transactional analysis and psychodynamics. Treatment for psychosomatic illnesses and differentiation between normal and abnormal grief might also be included in this second level.

On the third level, perhaps one reserved for professionals in the health fields and, in particular, the mental health fields, intensive programs should be developed on pathological grief and its manifestations. Kaplan (1964) refers to three levels of prevention, and these levels of the continuing education program should be regarded from the same perspective. That is, the first level, basic information and basic preparation, should serve as a first level of defense and prevention of future problems. The second level, counseling, assists in preventing any delayed or untoward reaction that might occur as a consequence of the grief. The third level obviously deals with more serious pathological problems. In this last area we need to develop professionals who are adequately trained to identify the problems related to grief and those related to other circumstances. It is imperative that, during the program, we understand the problems caused by grief and those superimposed on grief. For example, if an individual is already giving evidence of experiencing the beginning of pathological depression, and at the same time suffers an additional bereavement, the question is, has the grief caused pathological depression, or has the grief merely been the straw that broke the camel's back?

As we begin to deal with the pathology, the treatment will differ, depending on whether the depression or the grief is the primary problem. It is also important to distinguish between psychosomatic and physiological illnesses. Problems secondary to grief, such as hypertension, ulcers, and coronaries, require treatment by health care professionals educated to understand that it is not the physical disease per se that is the problem. They need to be aware that success in treating the physical disease depends on the success with which they treat the grief.

In summary, grief is a normal phenomenon, experienced by most of us at some period or other in our lives, and this grief can in fact change our lives and our life-styles. However, all grief is not necessarily pathological. We must differentiate between the normal and the pathological, and, in order to prevent pathology, we must assist people to understand what is happening to them as they go through the grieving process.

References

Eliot, T. D. 1930. "The Adjusted Behavior of Bereaved Families: A New Field of Research." *Social Forces* 8:543–49.

Engel, G. 1964. "Grief and Grieving." *American Journal of Nursing* 64:93–98.

Kaplan, G. 1964. *Principles of Preventive Psychiatry.* New York: Basic Books.

Lindemann, E. 1944. "Symptomatology and the Management of Acute Grief." *American Journal of Psychiatry* 101 (September):141–48.

Patterson, R. 1969. "Grief and Depression in Old People." *Maryland State Medical Journal* 18 (September):75–79.

❦3

Type of Death as a Determinant in Acute Grief

M. L. S. Vachon

A longitudinal study of 162 widows, conducted by staff of the Clarke Institute of Psychiatry, has provided substantiation of certain hypotheses in regard to phenomena observable in individuals during the period of acute grief.* I submit a detailed case study as an introduction to the factors that the research findings appear to delineate and then discuss these in depth, concluding by recommending principles on which grief counseling can be based.

Case Study

Two years ago the Qs† were a perfectly normal Canadian family living in a rural setting. Mr. Q was a 45-year-old policeman; his wife was about the same age and was an artist who worked mostly at home. Their children were Ronnie aged 20 and Susan aged 15. Ronnie had recently married a woman of whom his mother did not approve.

One evening Mrs. Q had a dream that she felt portended death for her-

*Research on a Preventive Intervention for the Newly Bereaved is funded by the Ontario Ministry of Health, Demonstration Model Grant #DM158. Coinvestigators on the project are J. Rogers, W. A. L. Lyall, A. Formo, K. Freedman, and S. J. J. Freeman.

†To preserve the family's anonymity certain details have been changed; others have been omitted for the sake of brevity.

self or her husband. When she told him of the dream and her interpretation, he said she was crazy, but a few days later, as he departed on a business trip, Mr. *Q* calmly announced that he was going to be the one to die. Mrs. *Q* became quite upset at this, for she felt he had more social value than she did, but he calmly repeated his announcement and left on his trip.

Two days later Mrs. *Q* received word that her husband had died suddenly in the middle of a meeting. Needless to say, the family was shocked. Mrs. *Q* and Ronnie visibly entered the stage of acute grief with much weeping alternating with stunned disbelief. Susan appeared to be in a state of shock and refused to go to the ensuing wake or funeral, saying she would rather remember her father as he was.

For several months after the death Susan had visual hallucinations of her father. This troubled Mrs. *Q*, who felt this reflected Susan's unresolved grief and lack of acceptance of her father's death. Mrs. *Q* also had great difficulty in accepting the loss and was depressed and unable to work much of the time. She was angry at her siblings and in-laws, who she felt had not been sufficiently supportive at the time of death. Shortly after her husband's death Mrs. *Q* began to feel physically ill with abdominal pain and edema in her legs, which her family physician assured her were symptoms common to depressed widows.

After several months of increasing physical difficulty Mrs. *Q* decided to come to the city for a more thorough diagnostic workup. Eventually she was found to have advanced ovarian carcinoma and was referred to the cancer treatment center. The staff at the cancer hospital were surprised at Mrs. *Q*'s acceptance of her disease and its prognosis. She said she was ready to die as soon as she could straighten out some problems with her children and requested that the author be called in to help her deal with Susan's unresolved grief about her father's death so that Susan would be unencumbered by old grief as she strove to adjust to her mother's impending death. Mrs. *Q* felt Ronnie had coped well with his father's death; he was now back in university doing well. Before she died, however, she wanted to see his marital situation straightened out.

When asked how she was feeling about her impending death, Mrs. *Q* smiled beatifically and said that, as long as she could straighten out her children's lives, death was no problem. When asked specifically how she felt when she first found out she had cancer, Mrs. *Q* again smiled and admitted that she was quite pleased to hear this, for it meant she could join her husband sooner than expected.

Mrs. *Q* was seen periodically throughout the final stages of her illness. Usually her son accompanied her to the interviews, which were infrequent because she lived several hundred miles from the treatment center and could be seen only when she was in the city. Susan came for a couple of interviews, during which time an attempt was made to help her work through her grief for her father, to make her aware of the fact that her mother was now dying, and to help her with her ensuing grief and future plans.

Significant problems emerged as this family adjusted to what might be considered their second acute grief experience—the realization of Mrs. *Q*'s impending death. First of all, it became obvious that the previous grief experience had not been resolved, especially for Mrs. *Q*. She was quite resistant to breaking through her own unresolved grief for her husband and could speak only of her longing to join him. The repressed hostility toward family members so common in the bereaved was quite striking in Mrs. *Q*. In her dying months she set about in a very pleasant and controlling fashion to have her son dissolve his marriage and made any inheritance contingent on a final divorce. She planned to buy her daughter an expensive cat, saying it would give Susan something to love when her mother was dead. Shortly before her death she told Susan that she thought she should break up with her boyfriend, whom Susan regarded as her only confidant. She expressed the fear that the boy might be attracted to the fairly small inheritance Susan would get when she turned 25. When she discovered that Susan had developed a breast lump, she asked her oncologist to check it and consider doing a hysterectomy on her 17-year-old daughter so that Susan would never have to confront the possibility of ovarian cancer. What all of these other losses might mean to Susan was never comprehended.

Two days before her death Mrs. *Q* extended invitations to certain family members to come to her deathbed; others were sent specific messages to stay away. A list of those to be invited to her funeral was completed shortly before her death. Mrs. *Q*'s dying was quite peaceful and was marred only by the fact that she did not feel her husband's presence as she had expected. She explained that he was always afraid of illness and was probably upset at seeing how sick she was. She died peacefully early one morning, her son by her side. The death occurred two weeks before the second anniversary of her husband's death.

Acute Grief Following Sudden Death

Obviously the story of the *Q*s is unusual in many ways. However, their situation graphically illustrates some of the problems found in acute grief. Note that the period of acute grief following a sudden death is different from that following a lingering illness. With sudden death the loss is unexpected and complete; a state of shock results that then progresses to an alternation between beginning acceptance and denial. In a long-term life-threatening illness, however, there may be several periods of acute grief: at the time of diagnosis, at the time when the family learns death is inevitable, and possibly, but not necessarily, at the time of death if denial has been a predominant coping mechanism during the final illness. The major difference between the two is that with sudden death the person is dead when the period of grief begins, but in life-threatening illness the person may be alive when the family begins grieving for him. Both processes of acute grief are different and are, therefore, treated separately.

The *Q* family illustrates many of the problems associated with sudden death, including the calm premonition that may precede such deaths, the denial of death and the desire to avoid a traditional funeral as a means of maintaining this denial, the difficulty with hallucinations, and the lack of support from other family members.

If one speaks with the families of people who have died suddenly, one often finds that they describe some type of premonition of impending death. This may have been verbalized, as in the *Q* family, or it may have been a less conscious process defined in retrospect as indicating that at some unconscious level the person was preparing for death. Obviously, the latter situation can be construed as an attempt to ascribe meaning to a situation beyond the family's control. Nevertheless, it is noteworthy that this concept of premonitions recurs frequently in discussions of sudden death. In many ways it lends an element of magic and control to an otherwise unexplainable phenomenon. It may also facilitate the grieving process through constructing circumstances in which the individual can be construed as being ready to meet his death. This may, however, cause difficulty, with anger directed toward the deceased if he is then deemed to have participated even unconsciously in his own death. This issue is discussed later.

Denial is a common reaction to sudden death, as any of us who have coped with the newly bereaved are well aware. It does not make sense that the person who was an integral part of one's life and future plans only yesterday is no longer here today. Even during the funeral this denial can persist, as was illustrated to us by a widow who said, "All during my husband's funeral I kept wishing the entire process would be over so that we could resume our normal life." Often this denial leads to a desire to avoid funerals entirely, as though by avoiding the funeral one could avoid the loss. Susan said that she refused to attend her father's funeral because she preferred to think of him as still being alive. She was annoyed that many of her friends attended the wake and saw her father dead when she would have preferred to have kept his death a secret from everyone. Like other adolescents we have seen, Susan had visual hallucinations of her father wherein he would appear to her life-sized. She derived some pleasure from these hallucinations, for they made her feel he was still alive somewhere and was still interested in her. In fact, she did not really accept his death for many months and never grieved openly. She talked to him often in the early days of bereavement and continued to do so during her mother's illness. Mrs. *Q* was concerned about Susan's hallucinations when she first heard of them and was perhaps somewhat ambivalent because she could not feel the same closeness to her husband.

The lack of social support the family felt from relatives was marked. All of them commented that Mr. *Q*'s relatives showed up only shortly before the funeral and left shortly afterward. Mrs. *Q* was angry that her own family stayed for only a few days following the death. They were all angry that at a family wedding and holiday festivities, which followed a few months after the death, little acknowledgment was made that Mr. *Q* was no longer there. They contrasted the way other relatives behaved with how they might have handled similar situations.

Problems Associated with Unresolved Grief

Many authors, including Parkes (1964), Maddison and Viola (1968), and Glick, Weiss, and Parkes (1979), have reported that bereavement can lead to physical and psychological illness, a finding our own study corroborates. Others, including Rees and Lutkins (1967) and Parkes, Benjamin, and Fitzgerald (1969), have spoken of the increased mortality risk following bereavement.

Le Shan and Worthington (1956, 1966); Greene (1966); Greene, Young, and Swisher (1966); and Schmale and Iker (1966) have suggested that loss experiences may, in selected people, predispose one to develop cancer. Whether or not Mr. *Q*'s death precipitated his wife's illness with cancer is not relevant to the present discussion. What is relevant, however, is that in her state of unresolved grief Mrs. *Q* welcomed the cancer as a way of reuniting with her husband. Although she adhered to her prescribed medical regimen, she always seemed pleased on her return visits when she could announce that the treatment was not working and her situation was deteriorating.

In our attempt to categorize dying patients into stages, it would be easy to call Mrs. *Q*'s attitude one of acceptance. However, one must be able to distinguish between true acceptance of death and the hopeless attitude found in unresolved grief reactions wherein death comes to be seen as a way out of an intolerable situation and a means of reuniting with the deceased. The increased mortality risk to which the bereaved are exposed has already been noted. Cox and Ford (1964) found that with widows this risk seems to be greater during the second year of bereavement, the time when Mrs. *Q* became ill and died. Even in our own study of widows we were surprised to note that two previously healthy 50-year-old women died of influenza in the second year of bereavement, and many others developed serious physical and psychological disorders.

Acute Grief in Terminal Illness

All too often we equate acute grief with the time of death and forget that in terminal illness acute grief episodes may have occurred at the time of diagnosis, when the family learns that death is inevitable, or possibly at the time of death if denial has been a predominant coping mechanism during the final illness. With regard to denial, in our study of widows we found that 40 percent of the women whose husbands died of cancer refused to accept the physician's warning that death was inevitable. Therefore, their symptoms of acute grief occurred at the time of death (Vachon et al., 1977). In the case of the Q family, however, acute grief occurred in the children when they learned that their mother was going to die. Ronnie learned this at the time of his mother's diagnosis, and Susan was given the information by the author a few months before her mother's death.

Mrs. Q never grieved openly for her own impending death but demanded that the children express their grief that she was dying. She did this by frequently reminding them that her condition was deteriorating and by urging that they should spend as much time as possible with her, for she would not be with them much longer. She reminded them that they had had no warning of their father's death and had experienced difficulty in grieving because of this. Therefore, she stressed, they should be grateful that with her death they would have the opportunity to grieve ahead of time so that her death would not be as devastating to them as their father's had been. What was never openly acknowledged in these family scenes was the children's grief at losing two parents in quick succession and their ambivalence at mother's obviously welcoming death and preferring reunion with their father to staying with them.

Grief and Anger

Anger is a powerful emotion that is often denied during the period of acute grief, as well as during its later resolution. In the Q family the dynamics of anger were fairly covert, and little anger was ever acknowledged except that directed against relatives who were seen as being nonsupportive and uncaring at the time of Mr. *Q*'s death and during the bereavement period. It was clear, however, that much unresolved and unexpressed anger existed in this family. Mrs. *Q* was angry at her husband for dying and abandoning her. Likewise, she was angry at her children for leading their own lives and being involved with a wife and boyfriend of whom she did not approve. Her need to try to destroy these relationships and her attempt to organize a hysterectomy for Susan give some idea of the level of her repressed hostility and her desire to control her children's future even in death. Coexistent with this need for control was another unconscious desire—that with her death her children might be deprived of all their major sources of social support that might come from love relationships and relatives. If these relationships had all been destroyed, then the children might well have severe difficulty with their bereavement following their mother's death.

A major role for the counselor in this situation was to gently point out some of the dynamics to all concerned. This decreased some of the obligation associated with deathbed promises and at the same time avoided forcing insight about anger onto a family when death was approaching rapidly and the children wanted and needed to be as supportive as possible to their dying mother.

The Role of the Funeral

Recently, thanatologists have begun to point out the need for reexploration of the role of the funeral in today's society. In our study of Toronto widows we found that most of the women had traditional funerals and the overwhelming majority found the funeral director to be quite helpful during the funeral period. Mr. *Q*'s funeral was a traditional one, that had, however, considerable difficulty attached to it. Susan was unable to attend, for she could not confront her father's death. Mrs. *Q* and Ronnie attended but felt angry throughout the ceremony at the lack of grief and caring shown by other relatives. All the family members spoke with anger of the dinner that followed the funeral at which the usual laughing and storytelling took place. They felt this kind of behavior was inappropriate in view of their recent loss.

When it was time to plan her own funeral, Mrs. *Q* decided to have only a minimal ceremony for very close relatives. She hoped to spare her children the pain the previous ceremony had imposed.

However, as we talked, she came to realize that a funeral or memorial ceremony was a painful thing because grief is painful. By severely restricting the attendance at the funeral, she was depriving her children of some of the social support that might be forthcoming from the friends and relatives whom she had not invited. She decided, therefore, to speak to the children about her ideas and leave the actual plans up to them.

Basic Counseling Principles in Acute Grief

Although this case is not necessarily typical, it does demonstrate reactions concomitant with acute grief as these do appear in many individuals. Some basic counseling principles for those in acute grief appear to be appropriate under most acute grief circumstances.

1. The news of sudden death should be broken to family members carefully and supportively, preferably by someone who was with the person when he died.
2. The use of heavy tranquilizers at this point is usually inappropriate.
3. Close family members should be encouraged to see the deceased but not forced to do so.
4. The role of hallucinations in the bereaved can be therapeutic and should not be thought to be indicative of severe emotional disturbance in most cases.
5. When obvious grieving does not occur in the stage of acute grief, future problems may follow.
6. Generalized anger toward one's social support system during the bereavement period may be predictive of later problems.
7. The bereaved are susceptible to physical and psychological illnesses. Symptoms must be assessed carefully and not simply dismissed as being a normal part of bereavement.
8. With terminal illness, family involvement is important; but be aware—there may be covert family dynamics operating in what appears to be an open, loving family.
9. As far as possible, family members should be encouraged to be with the dying person through the final vigil.
10. Follow-up phone calls or visits should be done with the bereaved by the family physician, public health nurse, or concerned funeral director.

In conclusion, this paper has touched on a number of issues associated with acute grief. Perhaps the examination of certain psychodynamic or sociological issues may appear to be too superficial in that the roles of the nurse, physician, clergy, counselor, or funeral director have not been specifically designated and explored. However, from the problems illustrated in this case, professionals from all the involved disciplines should be able to extrapolate general concepts relevant to their own areas of expertise.

References

Cox, P. and J. Ford. 1964. "The Mortality of Widows Shortly After Widowhood." *Lancet* 163.

Glick, I., R. Weiss, and C. M. Parkes. 1974. *The First Year of Bereavement*. New York: Wiley.

Greene, W. 1966. "The Psychosocial Setting of the Development of Leukemia and Lymphoma." *Annals of the New York Academy of Sciences* 125:794.

Greene, W., L. Young, and S. Swisher. 1966. "Psychological Factors and Reticuloendothelial Disease: Two Observations on a Group of Women with Lymphomas and Leukemias." *Psychosomatic Medicine* 28(5):714.

LeShan, L. and R. Worthington. 1956. "Some Recurrent Life History Patterns Observed in Patients with Malignant Disease." *Journal of Nervous and Mental Disease* 124:460.

LeShan, L. and R. Worthington. 1966. "An Emotional Life History Pattern Associated with Neoplastic Disease." *Annals of the New York Academy of Sciences* 125:780.

Maddison, D. and A. Viola. 1968. "The Health of Widows in the Year Following Bereavement." *Journal of Psychosomatic Research* 12:297.

Parkes, C. M. 1964. "Effects of Bereavement on Physical and Mental Health—A Study of the Medical Records of Widows." *British Medical Journal* 2:274.

Parkes, C. M., B. Benjamin, and R. Fitzgerald. 1969. "Broken Heart: A Statistical Study of Increased Mortality Among Widowers." *British Medical Journal* 1:740.

Rees, W. and S. G. Lutkins. 1967. "Mortality of Bereavement." *British Medical Journal* 4:13.

Schmale, A. and H. Iker. 1966. "The Affect of Hopelessness and the Development of Cancer: Identification of Uterine Cervical Cancer in Women with Atypical Cytology." *Psychosomatic Medicine* 28(5):714.

Vachon, M. L. S., et al., 1977. "The Final Illness in Cancer: The Widows Perspective." *Canadian Medical Association Journal* (November 10).

4

Emotional Involvement of the Family During the Period Preceding Death

Colin Murray Parkes

Cancer invades a family in much the same way that it invades a human body. At first its presence may go unnoticed or be suspected only by one or two members who keep their suspicions to themselves. The time comes, however, when its manifestations become obvious and there is a reaction throughout the organism. Just as bodily reserves are called upon in the patient himself, so his family rallies round and willingly calls upon its reserves of strength, time, money, and sympathy to support its damaged member. But just as the patient's bodily and psychological reserves may eventually become exhausted, so may those of his family.

The increased technical efficiency of modern medicine in curing or alleviating the physical aspects of disease has understandably resulted in a tendency for medical care to be seen as a technical exercise. But by focusing attention on cancer in the body, we run the risk of failing to become aware of the effects of cancer on the family. We may then find ourselves and our families in a particularly invidious position when, at length, we have to admit that we have come to the end of our technical resources.

For patients whose illness has reached the point where further radiotherapy, chemotherapy, or surgery is likely to create more problems than it solves, the continuation of active treatment is unjustifiable. Before this happens it is important for medical and nursing staff to take stock, to look honestly at the resources at their disposal, and to prepare to introduce a phase of care whose aims are radically different from those of the earlier phase.

The focus, from now on, will be, not on saving or prolonging life, but on helping patient and family through the transitions occasioned by the patient's coming death. The end of active treatment may or may not be apparent to the patient, but it is likely that the deterioration in his physical condition, despite all that has been done to help him, will be obvious, and he can hardly fail to be apprehensive about the future. Because the reassurance he is given by doctors and nurses is likely to be growing a bit thin by this time, it is understandable that the trust he has put in them may be replaced by disappointment and mistrust. At this point he most needs the comfort and support of a loving family. And it is at this point that the caregivers may need to be prepared to take a back seat and to recognize that the best way they can help the patient is by themselves helping to support the family. But there is another and more important reason for us to support the family: they are going to survive. The patient will soon have died and his troubles will be over, but to the family bereavement may lead to consequences that will be damaging to health and happiness for many years to come.

There is now copious evidence from a variety of studies indicating that bereavement can have detrimental effects on physical and mental health and can give rise to unhealthy changes in family structure that will bring trouble in the future (Parkes, 1972). Among the conditions reported with increased frequency after bereavement are depressive illnesses, anxiety states, personality disorders, suicide, rheumatic and arthritic conditions, disturbances of autonomic function, ulcerative colitis, and a range of other psychosomatic conditions. Even the mortality rate from coronary thrombosis and arteriosclerotic heart disease has been shown to be increased in bereaved people. The bereaved have been shown to make more use of medical resources than nonbereaved people. They tend to visit their physicians more frequently, are admitted more often to hospital, and undergo more surgical operations. Furthermore, they sometimes react to their loss in such a way that their behavior has damaging effects on the lives of their dependents. Thus, a mother who has suffered a major loss may become overprotective toward her surviving children or attempt to force them to live up to the idealized memory of a dead brother or sister.

Despite all this evidence most doctors and nurses do not see themselves as having any responsibility for the care of the patient's family, especially once their patient has died. I became strongly aware of this while working on a cancer ward. Within the course of a few months, two suicides took place. In one case, a cancer patient died. He had been admitted from another hospital in a depressed state and managed to throw himself from a hospital window within a few hours of admission. The other case was the wife of a patient who had died on the ward a few weeks previously. She had been very dependent on her husband and after his death had found her grief intolerable. When one of the nurses from the ward visited her home eight weeks after bereavement, she learned that the widow had died from an overdose of drugs a few days previously.

Both of these deaths were tragedies, but of the two the latter is more regrettable. Our cancer patient was simply anticipating events by a few days or weeks, and there are some who would argue that he had a right to take this way out if the cancer had made life so painful that he wanted to end it. The widow, on the other hand, was a young woman. She had a 14-year-old daughter, and there was every chance that she would eventually have come through her grief and found a new life for herself and her family.

Yet it was the death of the patient that most upset the staff. Visiting the hospital a few days later, I was repeatedly told the details of what had happened, and blame was either assigned or denied. Each member of the hospital staff was inclined to see the incident as evidence of failure and to share in a feeling of communal guilt. The findings of the inquest were discussed widely, measures were initiated to minimize the risk of recurrence, and staff became, if anything, overconcerned about the danger of further suicides.

The suicide of the widow gave rise to much less distress. Those who learned what had happened recognized that it was a shame she had died, but the news did not excite enough interest to get widely circulated. It was particularly striking that the question of blame hardly ever arose. Although people agreed that the suicide might have been prevented if the widow had been visited sooner, it was not thought to be the duty of any one person or group of people to give such support.

This is hardly surprising and is not mentioned here as a reproach to the people concerned. After all, hospitals have no formal responsibility for the care of the families of patients' who are alive, let alone those who are dead. It is not part of the traditional role of the nurse to prevent suicide in the families of her patients by helping them to prepare for bereavement or by supporting them after this has taken place.

What evidence is there that preparation for bereavement does, in fact, make any difference to the course of grief and the subsequent adjustment the bereaved person will make to life? The Harvard Bereavement Study, set up to answer questions such as this, showed quite clearly how the opportunity to anticipate coming death can affect the life of surviving widows and widowers two to four years later. In that study men and women under the age of 45, whose bereavement was therefore untimely, were divided into two groups. One group had suffered bereavement by reason of an illness (or injury) of less than two weeks' duration or a period of terminal deterioration of three days or less; the second group had had a longer warning of coming bereavement.

After bereavement the "short-preparation" group had much more difficulty than the "long-preparation" group in coming to terms with what had happened. Two-thirds reported an initial reaction of outright disbelief, and they became significantly more anxious, depressed, and self-reproachful than the others. Two to four years later they were still significantly more anxious and lonely than the long-preparation group. They still tended to feel that what had happened was unreal and that they would one day wake up and find that their spouse had not died; alternatively, they felt that they should somehow have prevented the death, although just how was not apparent. They continued to behave as they thought their spouse would have wanted them to and to cultivate a sense of his presence near at hand. They were less likely than the long-preparation group to go out with friends and relatives or to remarry, and they had more difficulty in coping with their roles and responsibilities. Consequently, many of them found themselves in financial difficulties and, hence, set on a course that was creating more problems rather than fewer (Parkes, 1975).

If knowledge of a coming bereavement can make such a difference to the course of grief, it seems reasonable to suppose that anything that helps people to anticipate and to begin to prepare themselves for a loss is likely to prevent consequences of this type from occurring. Since doctors, nurses, and other members of the caregiving professions are at hand at such time, it would seem that they have an important role to play in helping people to anticipate bereavement.

In the case of the cancer patient it is, of course, unusual for the patient's spouse to be completely unaware of the probable outcome, and the trajectory of the illness is such that the death is seldom unexpected. Consequently, in the Harvard Bereavement Study the spouses of cancer patients made a better adjustment to bereavement than those whose spouses had died from some other cause. Even so, there were a number of cases in which cancer deaths did come as a shock to the family, and very often this seemed to reflect the inadequacy of the information they had been given as much as inability on the doctor's part to make reliable predictions.

Lack of preparation tends to produce a shock reaction with the establishment of unhealthy defensive processes. These leave the survivor bound to the dead person in a manner that may interfere with his prospects of self-realization.

It also deprives the individual of the opportunity to make restitution to the dying person for any real or imagined deficiencies or failures in their relationship. As Freud (1912) has pointed out, no relationship is quite without ambivalence, and we all have something for which to say "Sorry." Just as the dying patient needs to set his affairs in order and make peace with God and Man, so too, his wife needs to make her peace with him if she is to avoid self-destructive guilt at a later date.

Anticipation of loss, then, diminishes shock and facilitates restitution. It also provides the family with an opportunity to begin the complex and time-consuming processes of psychosocial change that are bound to occur at last. Much has been written about anticipatory grief. It is sometimes inferred that this is a process that can be gone through before bereavement in much the same way as it can afterward. But this is seldom the case; there is a limit to the amount of anticipation and planning that is safe for family members to undertake prior to the patient's death. The widow-to-be is not free to choose her mourning dress while her husband is still alive, and she tends to avoid thinking too far into the future. A possible reason for this can be inferred from the similarity between a plan and a wish. If a person begins to plan too soon for a new life after bereavement, there is always a danger that he or she might begin to want it. Such wishes are tantamount to a wish for the partner to die, and the death becomes, in one sense, a "murder"—such is the magical power attributed to death wishes.

This means that, although family members want and need to confront the fact that their relative is going to die, there is a limit to the amount of anticipatory preparation possible in advance of the death itself. Anticipatory grief, though it may be initiated, can rarely be completed before the patient's death. Sad exceptions to this general rule do sometimes occur when the patient has undergone severe mental deterioration or has been unconscious for long periods before his death. Here he may be treated as socially dead before he is physically dead, a situation that itself may lead to later recriminations: "Should I have stayed by him? Might he have known what was going on?" By and large, however, family members are much more reluctant than doctors and nurses to treat the patient as dead before his time, and one never ceases to be amazed at the sacrifices that families make to maintain their vigil at the side of an unconscious patient.

These considerations explain why there is a limit to the amount of help we can give to family members before a bereavement. Their need is to maintain a picture of themselves as strong and capable of supporting the patient to the end. Any admission of weakness threatens this self-image, and there is a strong tendency for family members to deny that they have any needs at all. "Don't you worry about me, doctor, I'll be all right. He's the one you should be concerned for." Remarks such as this are likely to follow any expression of concern from the doctors and nurses.

When it is clear that family members are not capable of providing adequate care, it can be very hard for them to admit defeat, and we must be aware of and do our best to counteract their sense of failure. When a patient can no longer be nursed at home but must enter the hospital, the family does not want to "leave it all to the nurses." They need to be told that they still have an important role to play and that their support will be more important than ever now that the patient is entering a strange and frightening phase of his illness.

What of the patient himself? Like the family members, he is in transition; like them he will probably find it hard to accept the reality of what is happening to him; like them he is also finding it increasingly hard to avoid this reality. For both partners there is a problem of "distancing"—each needs to find out what, for him or her, at this moment of time is the optimal distance from which aspects of the situation can be viewed without giving rise to ungovernable fear. One is reminded of the small child who is faced with an unknown stranger; on the one hand he is strongly motivated to run away; at the same time, he is tempted to get as close as he dares so that he can begin to explore the possibility of a relationship. Death, the "dark stranger," is a phenomenon from which we all tend to retreat, yet it is also an object of fascination, and there are ways of relating to death that can make the act of dying a triumph, rather than a defeat. Just as the young child is much less likely to run away if his mother is present to greet the stranger, so the approach to death is facilitated if family members and professional caregivers are secure in its presence. Conversely, situations of panic can arise when it is fear that is communicated.

Panicky feelings are particularly difficult for the dying patient to tolerate because there is nowhere for him to run. Consequently, some patients run toward death in much the same way that the terrified chicken runs toward the fox. This occurred in a 53-year-old patient whom I was asked to see on account of increasing depression. James Grant had a particularly unsightly and painful cancer that was eroding the lower part of his face, and his fear was such that he had said that he wished he could die and "get it over with." Looking at him one could understand his point of view, and I was tempted to recommend a rapid buildup of drugs that soon would have rendered him insensible.

This was before meeting his wife. Mr. and Mrs. Grant had been married only six years and were very close to each other. Mrs. Grant gave an impression of helplessness and wept when I first met her, saying she was dreading his death. Although she was well aware of her husband's wish for death, she was quite unable to accept the thought that she would soon be without him and was clearly not yet ready for him to die.

Fortunately, there was quite a lot that could be done to relieve Mr. Grant's pain and to make him more comfortable. A judicious combination of tranquilizing and narcotic drugs made life less intolerable, and the close support of nurses and doctors who were not horrified by his appearance or apprehensive about his future helped him to relax. At the same time his wife was given similar support and began to face up to the situation.

Two weeks later Mr. Grant's general condition was much worse, but both he and his wife were calm and had enjoyed Christmas together. When at this point he developed pneumonia, his wife agreed that it would be wrong to prolong his life with antibiotics and added, "I'm ready for him to go now." He died, peacefully, the following day.

In this instance, husband and wife had got "out of step" in their progress toward realization. Mr. Grant had looked directly at his life situation, but his courage failed when he found that his wife had been left behind. In other cases it is the patient who is left behind and the family who are the first to confront the situation. Either way, the professionals are the "experts" to whom the family often turn for information and support. The fact that we are capable of giving them information they are not yet ready to receive makes us potentially dangerous, and they may avoid us or treat us with suspicion. If we are sensitive to their feelings, however, and show them we are not going to ride roughshod over their defenses, they will usually accept our help. They may then come to rely on us for an interpretation of the situation that helps them to reach a more accurate view of the world and their place in it.

Both patient and family have important roles to play during the final weeks or months of the patient's life. Unfortunately, this fact is often ignored and in our efforts to care for our patients and to relieve the burden on their families we sometimes push them into a role-less state that is itself another kind of social death. "Don't worry," "Leave it to us," "We'll take care of everything," are the kinds of well-meaning remarks that leave patient and family feeling quite useless. Yet what is the use of a dying patient? He may be physically incapable of feeding himself or controlling his bowels; even communication may be impaired. Surely it would be unfair to expect anything of such a person, except the necessary cooperation with nursing procedures.

I believe this attitude reflects a fundamental misconception of the psychosocial situation of the dying that leads to bad nursing care and consequent discontent among patients, relatives, and nurses. If the only function of the patient is to cooperate with nursing procedures, then what is the function of the nursing procedures—to prolong life so that the patient can continue to cooperate with the nursing procedures? Nursing is not an end in itself but a means to an end.

The importance of the period of dying becomes obvious when we talk to the bereaved. For these people the time before death is recalled with great vividness as a phase of their lives and that of the patient that, for good or ill, continues to occupy their minds. Failure, frustration, and suffering are remembered and dwelt upon; so are successes, satisfactions, and triumphs. If the manner of a man's dying has been bad; if he has suffered unnecessarily, failed to come to terms with his condition and died embittered, or if he has turned his face to the wall and given up, then his death will be seen as a defeat or even a period of horror. If, on the other hand, his passing has been peaceful and free of suffering, if he has accepted the inevitable decline and shared with his family his pleasure in the life that remained to him, this period will be remembered as a fitting and satisfactory ending. It may even come to be seen as a triumph over the forces of chaos, for death challenges the meaning of life.

Looked at in this way, dying is a creative act; only those who are truly alive can make something of dying. The role, then, of the dying patient is not to be a "good" (i.e., conforming) patient, but to make something positive of what would otherwise be a negative event. How he does this is a matter for the individual. The "right way" for one man is not necessarily the "right way" for any other, and we cannot impose our own ideas of the "proper" way to die on anybody else. But we can often help the patient to find his own way of dying.

In the comfortable society in which we live today there are few opportunities for heroism. Yet there are circumstances in which heroism is not at all uncommon, and the cancer ward is one such place. Those who have the privilege of working with cancer patients will often have been impressed by heroic behavior, behavior that leaves us proud of our membership in the human race. But we have no right to expect heroism, and we cannot impose it on others.

On the other hand, we can try to create the circumstances that make it most likely that the dying patient will be able to continue living until he dies. Obviously, we cannot expect much of the person who is either in severe pain or reduced to a state of semicoma by the excessive use of drugs. But let us take it for granted that physical care is good and that the right combination of palliative drugs is being provided at regular intervals. What else remains? It seems to me that the essential thing is for the professional staff to show by their behavior and attitude their intense interest in and respect for the patient and his family. There is a sense in which we almost need to become part of the family if we are to help them effectively. Dying is a social event, and the creative act of dying can be shared. Husband and wife can support each other and find a new meaning in the last phase of their life together. But too often they are cut off from each other at the one time when they most need the other's support. Barriers of fear leave each isolated and afraid to speak of the thoughts that are constantly on their minds. A doctor, nurse, or social worker who is willing to take the time and trouble to get the confidence of the family will often find himself sharing in their struggles. This can be an extraordinarily rewarding type of engagement and a maturing experience for the helper and the helped alike. In a sense we are all dying and to help others to face the prospect of death is to rehearse for one's own demise.

But rewarding though this be, it can also be harrowing work and demands a high level of basic trust and security in the professional. It is hardly surprising, in this case, that the professionals may themselves need the support of a colleague with whom they can discuss their own feelings and work through some of the problems the work imposes upon them.

Like the patient and family members the professional has to discover how close it is safe for him to approach. Appropriate distancing is just as much a problem for him as it is for them, and just as too direct an approach to a fearful problem may overwhelm the patient's capacity to cope with that problem, so the professional who allows himself to become too closely involved will find his own judgment and capacity to help impaired.

Some of these issues are illustrated by the Salmon family. I was first consulted about this couple by their local clergyman, who approached me, somewhat diffidently, to ask what could be done about a cancer patient who was refusing to go into hospital. Because it was clear from his account of the home situation that family care had gone badly wrong, I suggested that he contact the family doctor with the suggestion that I be invited to make a domiciliary visit. This was done, and I visited the home the following day.

Mr. and Mrs. Salmon were a middle-class couple in their middle 60s, living in a nicely furnished flat in south London. The door was opened by Mrs. Salmon, who immediately began to talk in a loud and angry voice about her husband. He was well able to overhear our conversation from the bedroom. She informed me that she was at the end of her tether, that she could not do a thing with him, that he would not take the doctor's advice to go into hospital, and that he kept grumbling at her. Entering the bedroom, I could see that Mr. Salmon was very ill indeed and was also in great pain. He had lost a great deal of weight and was very weak so that his voice was reduced to a whisper. He took little notice of me but gestured toward his abdomen and groaned in the direction of his wife. She bustled round tut-tutting and apologizing to me on his behalf. Clearly, she felt helpless when faced with his pain, and the only way she could deal with her sense of helplessness was to make light of the pain and blame him for complaining. He felt rejected by her refusal to understand and had developed a petulant manner that further aggravated the situation.

I asked Mrs. Salmon to leave us together and tried, gently, to make contact with Mr. Salmon. But it was obvious that he could think of nothing but his pain. When I asked him why he had refused the doctor's suggestion of a hospital bed, he looked so alarmed that I let the matter drop. Physical examination revealed an extremely tender and distended abdomen.

Returning to the living room, I found that the family doctor, a grey-haired lady of similar age to the Salmons, had arrived and was sitting beside Mrs. Salmon on the sofa. Both of them were in tears.

The doctor explained that she had been a close friend of the Salmons, as well as their physician, for many years. Her genuine concern for their well-being was very obvious, as was her sense of helplessness. She explained that she had been reluctant to prescribe narcotic drugs in this case for fear of addiction; when I pointed out that addiction could hardly be a problem in a man as close to death as this, she again began to weep. It was clear that she was no more prepared for him to die than his wife was.

The immediate problem was obviously one of pain relief, and, in consultation with an oncologist, a drug regimen was worked out that effectively controlled Mr. Salmon's pain and other physical symptoms. Consequently, he stopped demanding from his wife relief that she could not give; when he became more tractable, she began to feel safe enough to come closer to him. As a result the vicious circle of fear and estrangement was broken. A week later, Mr. Salmon telephoned to inform me that he had decided that it was time he came into hospital. From the way he spoke it was clear that he regarded this as a gift to his wife—a recognition that she too had needs that he could meet.

He survived for another five days on the ward, lapsing peacefully into coma on the day before his death. During this period, his wife seldom left his side, and a more devoted couple could not be imagined. All the antagonism between them seemed to have disappeared, and they both derived pleasure from each other's company.

A month after her husband's death, Mrs. Salmon was visited in her home. She spoke of the extraordinary way in which her husband had finally come to terms with his own death and of the importance of their final days together after the struggle was over. This had changed what, for her, would have been an awful and guilt-laden experience into one that was a cause for pride.

For me, the most surprising change in this case was in the behavior of Mrs. Salmon herself. My first impression of her had been of a hard-bitten, bossy woman who seemed blind to her husband's suffering; yet to the nurses who met her on the ward she appeared gentle and sensitive to his every need. Which was the correct picture? In the circumstances in which I first met her, Mrs. Salmon was in an impossible position. Faced with the responsibility for coping with her husband's uncontrollable pain, she had two alternatives; either she accepted the awfulness of what was happening to her husband, in which case she would have been overwhelmed with grief and of no use to him, or she found some way of carrying on; denying the full reality of the situation. She chose the latter course, refused to acknowledge that his pain was as bad as he said it was, and tried to force him to do likewise. By so doing, she was, of course, cutting herself off from her husband, and he knew and resented this.

When a person who is sick and frightened sees his dearest relations putting up barriers, avoiding his eye, or refusing to accept the validity of his view of the world, he becomes more frightened and tends to cling more tightly to those relatives. The effect of this clinging is to provoke more panicky attempts by the relatives to escape; they feel sucked into a center of chaos. A pattern of clinging and rejection is set up that, as has been described, can have very bad consequences. In Mr. Salmon's case his refusal to consider going into hospital was a direct consequence of his fear; he clung to his home as he clung to his wife, the only source of security in a world that had become terrifying and painful. Fortunately, the medication and support they were given reduced the anxiety to a level that made it possible for Mrs. Salmon to feel capable of coping again; when she relaxed, she was able to reduce the defensive distance between herself and her husband. Because she was closer, Mr. Salmon felt less need to cling to her, and it was at this point that the circle was broken and he found himself able to let her "off the hook" by accepting the offer of a bed in hospital.

This story illustrates the balance of interacting forces that need to be borne in mind in all our work. Patient and family together constitute the unit of care, and this assumption must underlie all the support we give. It is not enough to support either one of them separately if we ignore the interaction between them.

One other lesson to be learned from this case is apparent. The behavior of Mrs. Salmon was similar to that of certain hospital nurses who regularly belittle their patients and seem blind to the reality of their suffering. Could it be that they too have been forced by the intensity of the suffering they meet to place this barrier between themselves and their patients? If so, maybe they need support and sympathetic understanding from senior nurses and doctors if they are to begin to feel safe enough to let down the barrier.

If relations between staff and patients are difficult, the relations between staff and family members are even more so. The patient, because he is in need, usually accepts our guidance. He hesitates to criticize or object to our ministrations for fear of retaliation. Family members are, however, under no such obligation. They have a duty to protect the patient from harm, and it is right and proper for them to expect us to explain and to justify to them our plans and practices. Naturally, doctors and nurses dislike such critical examination and are put on the defensive when confronted by a questioning family member. Unfortunately, family members are not always capable of being scrupulously fair in their assessments of our work. The woman who is scared that her husband may die may prefer to blame his worsening symptoms on the treatment rather than the illness. Rather than accept the inevitable progression of the disease, she may make accusations of incompetence that undermine our patient's confidence in us. Even our attempts to explain the situation may be misinterpreted and used against us. The words of one doctor or nurse will be quoted against another, trivial differences of opinion used as evidence of mendacity, and our every decision challenged.

Small wonder that we doctors and nurses often feel the need to defend ourselves from the family. We do this in various ways: by limiting visiting hours and avoiding the wards at such times, by delegating contact with the family to our juniors (doctors often expect nurses to cope with the families on the grounds that their time is too valuable to be wasted talking to relatives!); by establishing a strong status hierarchy in which those at the top are accorded magical knowledge and power and all are expected to collude in avoiding any challenge to their protective authority, by establishing territorial rights within the hospital such that family members are allowed in only by ''grace and favor'' rather than by right, and by using technical terms that confuse and mystify the family without communicating information.

Junior staff, who find it less easy to escape from the families, also develop means of defending themselves—the most common one busyness (''I've no time to stop now, dear, I'm run off my feet''), bossiness (''Now don't you trouble your head about that, just let us do the worrying''), ignorance (''They don't tell me anything''), and attempts at upward delegation (''You'll have to ask the doctor''). In the end it is only the most persistent or aggressive family members who find their way through to the top. Once there, they tend to confirm the seniors in their opinion that families are difficult to handle.

In one study conducted by the author, 32 percent of spouses of patients who had died from cancer in London hospitals complained that they had had no contact with a doctor from the end of active treatment until the time of the patient's death, and 88 percent of doctors were said to be ''very busy.''

But this degree of alienation is not inevitable. At St. Christopher's Hospice, Sydenham, where a large proportion of patients are admitted for terminal cancer care, only 9 percent of spouses claimed that they had not seen a doctor (usually when the patient died within a few hours of admission) and only 26 percent of doctors were said to be "very busy" (although the doctors themselves probably would have given a much higher figure).

Furthermore, spouses of patients dying in this hospital were more likely to get to know other members of the staff than were spouses of patients dying elsewhere. (All these differences are statistically significant.)*

These findings certainly seem to indicate that it is possible to improve the situation and justify us in examining how the organization of this particular hospital has brought this about. The first and most obvious answer is by the abolition of visiting hours. Relatives have a right to be on the ward at any time and are encouraged to play a part in the care of the patient. Provided the patient is not near death, they are encouraged to take a "day off" on Mondays, but this is for their own sakes rather than for that of the staff. In fact, 57 percent of spouses spend six hours or more per day on the wards (compared with only 9 percent in other hospitals), and they get to know the staff as well as the other patients and relatives. To emphasize the importance of their place in the hospice and their right to be there they have their own territory, a pleasantly furnished sitting room to which they can withdraw. There is also residential accommodation for families who want to remain close at hand.

For the staff the presence of families on the wards much of the time makes it all the more difficult to avoid contact. In fact, it is clear policy for staff at all levels to try to get to know the families and to make them a part of the ward community. In doing so they lay themselves open to just the hurtful interactions described earlier, and it becomes all the more important to provide a support system for the staff members themselves. This is done in various ways but essentially by the development of a network of colleagues who constitute the Hospice Community. Within that community, hierarchical differences are less marked than in most hospitals in Britain; there is a general acceptance of the notion that the emotions evoked by the job can be shared with one's colleagues. Senior staff keep a "weather eye" open for signs of distress in juniors and spend much of their

---

*The two groups of spouses described here were matched with each other, case for case, by sex, age, socioeconomic status, duration of the patient's illness and the amount of pain he had suffered prior to the terminal period (Parkes, 1979).

time on the wards in a supportive role. Staff can choose from a number of staff groups the one who they think will best meet their needs; these range from groups in which a psychological frame of reference is employed to others where the emphasis is on spiritual guidance.

These two aspects of support, the psychological and the spiritual, are in no sense in opposition. Both psychiatrist and chaplain visit the wards and spend time talking with staff, families, and patients. They also meet with each other to share their insights about particular problems. The distinction between psychological and spiritual problems is not always clear, but since neither professional is motivated to proselytize, collaboration is not difficult.

In the opinion of many staff members it is their religious faith that enables them to accept death as a life transition with a purpose. The saying of ward prayers at morning and evening and the recitation of a prayer at the bedside of a patient who has died help to underline and formalize this faith, and such rituals are often seen as helpful by patients and families. I think it is no coincidence that most of the institutions that specialize in the provision of terminal care are affiliated to religious bodies of one sort or another, and St. Christopher's Hospice is no exception. Nevertheless, patients of all denominations or none at all are accepted for treatment; systematic enquiry has not revealed any complaints of pressure being brought to bear on patients or families to adopt a particular system of belief.

The effect of this type of care on the families is to relieve anxiety without disengaging them from their caregiving roles and to provide them with a network of support similar to that which obtains in a united family. This is shown by the responses of the spouses to a multiple-choice question. They were shown a list of phrases and asked to pick out any that applied to the hospital where their husband or wife had died. The phrase best characterizing St. Christopher's Hospice was "The hospital is like a family," chosen by 70 percent. By contrast, this same phrase was checked by only 15 percent of the comparison group of widows and widowers whose spouses had died elsewhere.

There is still, of course, a large number of people who would rather die at home than in hospital. They do not all get the opportunity to do so. This is hardly surprising in a world in which dying has become so fearful that family members are frightened to accept responsibility for the care of anyone approaching death. We often find ourselves forced to admit a patient to hospital because his wife is afraid that, "He might die on my hands." However irrational we may consider these feelings, they are real enough, and it would be unfair on the patient and the family to refuse admission.

Despite this many families are prepared to accept responsibility for allowing a member to die at home, and others will keep him at home until death is imminent if they are assured that a bed will be made available when needed. This last point carries important implications for the organization of services for the terminally ill. Paradoxically the provision of a direct link with an inpatient unit enabling a family to obtain admission at short notice may reduce the load on scarce in-patient facilities simply because the family then feel safe enough to keep the patient at home. For the patient, too, the assurance that a bed will be available if it is needed may give the reassurance that will make a success of home care.

Home care may take place, then, because the patient feels safe enough at home to prefer to stay there or, as in the case of Mr. Salmon, because he feels too unsafe to go into hospital. Naturally, it is more likely to work out well in the former case than the latter. In either case, however, the family are going to need the support of doctors and nurses.

As long as the patient is at home, he and his family are on their own territory and the family bear the main responsibility for care. It is now the doctors and nurses who are crossing the boundary from their own place into that of the family, and they may find themselves treated as welcome guests or as intruders. When the patient is no longer well enough to come to the clinic for treatment, he will feel more insecure; it becomes all the more important for the doctors and nurses to establish a good working relationship with his family.

At St. Christopher's Hospice, the domiciliary care staff run the outpatient clinic, as well as visit the homes of their patients. They do not take over from the general practitioners and district nurses, who, under Britain's National Health Service, are expected to provide home care, but they act as an added support system to these practitioners and to the families. They are, therefore, able to extend the concept of the Hospice as a caring community into the larger community of which it forms a part.

Thanks to their special experience in terminal care the domiciliary staff are able to give expert advice on the technical aspects of home care. But they also have an important role in providing psychological understanding and support to the family. They do this in the same way as the inpatient staff, by getting to know the principal family members and encouraging them to talk about the situation confronting them. As on the wards, they find themselves close to some frightened and potentially frightening people. Moreover, the fact that they are not on their own territory or even in a position to dictate the treatment means that they often feel especially exposed and helpless.

The need for secure support for all nurses visiting the homes of dying patients is obvious. It is a pity that, in many settings, it is these nurses who are most isolated. Peer-group support, as well as the support of senior colleagues, social workers, and, if possible, a social psychiatrist, is desirable and cannot be left to chance. The need for a support system affects the organization of the work programs and even the design of hospitals or clinics, for geographical separation ensures psychological separation. It is essential to ensure that visiting staff spend a reasonable time each week in interaction with their support network and that the network is truly supportive.

Just as "no man is an island," so no family is an island. The support that can be given by professional caregivers, as well as by the community at large, may go a long way to mitigate the psychosocial effects of cancer or even to turn them to good ends. "Support" in this context seldom requires the application of sophisticated psychodynamic knowledge; it requires something much more demanding. To extend the psychological resources of the family it is necessary to extend the family, that is, to enable the caregivers to share the burden of concern. When this is done, the demands made on the caregivers are great. But in the end the family can be expected to survive, even though the patient dies. Participating in this process of transition and seeing the family come through to a new beginning is a rewarding experience for the community of caregivers, as well as for the family itself.

References

Freud, S. 1912. "The Dynamics of Transference." *Standard Edition*, 10: 106. London: Hogarth Press.

Parkes, C. M. 1972. *Bereavement: Studies of Grief in Adult Life*. New York: Tavistock London and International University Press.

—— 1975. "Unexpected and Untimely Bereavement: A Statistical Study of Young Boston Widows and Widowers." In *Bereavement: Its Psychosocial Aspects*, eds. B. Schoenberg et al., pp. 119–37. New York: Columbia University Press.

—— 1979. "Terminal Care: Evaluation of In-patient Service at St. Christopher's Hospice." *Postgraduate Medical Journal* 55: 517–22.

5

Emotional Care
of the Bereaved

Arthur M. Arkin

What psychological tasks are accomplished in "healthy" grief? What psychiatric measures are available that might maximize the probability of healthy grief?

In acute healthy grief one cannot escape nor does one ordinarily wish to escape from the experience of intense pain and sadness occasioned by the loss of a person to whom one had been emotionally attached. Episodes of weeping and heartfelt sobbing are usual manifestations. It is all accepted as natural and lived through as one of life's inevitabilities. With the passage of time the survivor liberates himself from his strong emotional ties to the deceased and learns to adapt himself to a world from which the deceased is missing. As one mourner reported, in the early days of his grief he had impulses to seek out the deceased and had the illusion of turning to a "statue of invisible silence."

This readjustment entails forming new relationships and patterns of conduct and refurbishing old ones. During this sequence one usually experiences signs and symptoms of somatic distress (sighing respiration, lack of strength and exhaustion, gastrointestinal distress, sleep disturbances, and the like), preoccupation with the image of the deceased, feelings of guilt toward him, inappropriate hostile reactions, and alterations in customary patterns of conduct (Lindemann,

1944). Normally, such phenomena become progressively less intense and sustained and eventually fade.

It is impressive that these features of grief are observable in varying degree in most cases, even though the mourners have had an opportunity to traverse a long preterminal period of anticipatory grief. There is something about the finality of even an anticipated death that is responsible for a further increment of grief.

The family physician, religious counselor, or therapist (the helper)—whoever might be called upon to assist the grief stricken—will do well to inform himself of the details of the terminal illness and the relevant history of the family, both recent and remote, so that he may be alert to deeper psychodynamic and genetic issues. Despite the importance of confining one's explicit interventions and therapeutic comments to areas circumscribed by the *conscious and preconscious* burdens of the mourners, it is vital to guide oneself by cogent working hypotheses regarding their unconscious conflicts and to maintain close empathic contact with them.

In general one attempts to use a supportive, empathic relationship to assist mourners in traversing their grief in the healthiest manner possible. If the deceased is survived by a family, it is reasonable, at the very least, to focus one's efforts on that family member to whom the others spontaneously turn for leadership and support. It is hoped that in this manner, therapeutic influences will filter through to those dependent upon him. Alternatively, if the helper senses that the others would like to join in or receive a direct request along these lines, he should not hesitate to welcome such participation in group fashion.

The following tactics have seemed clinically useful:

1. *Permitting and guiding the mourners to put into detailed words their most intimate thoughts involved in the pain, sorrow, and sense of final loss occasioned by the bereavement and to give free expression to associated affects.*

   An indispensable element is the verbalization of feelings of guilt toward the deceased for both recent and remote transgressions regardless, initially, of whether such guilt is appropriate. For example, one should patiently hear out the details of "if only I'd compelled him to see a doctor sooner," or "if only I had taken her on that European tour," and similar statements.

2. *Guiding the mourner in a review of his lifelong relationship to the deceased.*

   The helper should be alert to important major themes, critical events, and areas of appropriate guilt and of justified self-esteem for acts of devotion, thoughtfulness, authentic love, self-sacrifice, and the like. These will enable the helper to intervene with comments and interventions aimed at promoting healthy grief. For example, if the mourner reproaches himself for a bygone episode of self-indulgence that had been partly at the expense of the deceased, it might be helpful to have on hand historical material that could demonstrate occasions in which he had been thoughtful and generous toward the deceased.

3. *Providing the bereaved with information and understanding regarding the alterations in his emotional reactions.*

Many bereaved feel consternation and alarm from the psychosomatic manifestations of grief and are fearful of becoming ill themselves. It is often reassuring to explain that it is natural that in grief one experiences sleep disturbances, marked heaviness of limbs, difficulty in moving about, disturbances of appetite, other gastrointestinal disturbances, headache, and other problems. Furthermore, mourners are often ashamed of their hostile outbursts and fantasies. Simple comments that this is only to be expected may be all that is necessary to bring amelioration. On the other hand it may be useful to make some further comment to the effect that they are angry because they took the bereavement as a token of being unfairly singled out by a fate personified as cruel rather than indifferent or that paradoxically they feel cruelly abandoned by the deceased.

4. *Assisting the bereaved to formulate an acceptable psychological relationship to the image of the deceased in the future.*

It is important, if feasible, to help the bereaved acquire a future modus vivendi with his psychic representation of the deceased. For example, if the grief reaction is infused with unrealistic remorse, it is valuable to ask repeatedly whether the deceased would have wanted the survivor to live with sustained suffering. Even if the deceased had been a cruel, overly righteous individual, it may still be reasonable to ask whether he might have mellowed if he had lived. Often it is clear that the survivor, despite conscious disclaimers, believes that the deceased is not "really dead" but has continued living in some remote elsewhere. In such cases it has sometimes been useful to assert the possibility that, since death, the deceased may have acquired wisdom, understanding, and compassion for the plight of the mourner. In the event that the bereaved has realistic guilt toward the deceased because of some actual hostile behavior or neglect of him while alive, it may be useful to make tentative suggestions for a memorial, tangible or intangible, purchased or self-created, that might provide the guilt-ridden mourner with some feeling of redemption. The important task is to attempt to arrange for a dignified and compassionate mutual farewell "within the psyche."

5. *Acting as a primer and/or programmer for some of the activities of the bereaved.*

It is usually helpful to the mourner to organize and direct a program of a portion of the day's activities. These activities may include receiving suitable visitors, attending light meals, going to bed, taking short walks, performing religious observances, and the like. The mourner often has marked difficulty in making and executing such plans for himself and is usually grateful and benefited if someone else gently guides him through such tasks.

6. *Assisting the mourner in dealing with difficult reality situations.*

Such assistance includes arranging for temporary care of children, working out legal problems, providing for adequate financial support, shopping for food, and housekeeping.

7. *Formal medical and/or psychiatric measures if the need should arise.*

It is unwise to permit the grief stricken to endure excessive insomnia; not only is it exhausting, but also tossing and turning in the early hours makes the mourner vulnerable to long periods of self-torturing rumination. A physician might prescribe bedtime sedatives for one to two weeks.

Where depression is a major and disabling feature, thought should be given to prescribing a tricyclic antidepressant (doxepin, imipramine, or amitryptiline). This should not, however, be done hastily, for it seems unwise to attempt to shortcircuit the adequate traversal of grief. In general, lower dose schedules, particularly in the elderly, should be employed.

In addition, where hypochondriacal preoccupations are prominent, thorough efforts should be made to rule out the onset of or progress of already existing disease. One should be mindful of the demonstration that elderly people with chronic organic disease comprise a special group of patients possessing a higher degree of postbereavement vulnerability (Wiener et al., 1975).

Certain morbid reactions may be observed and should occasion a consultation with a specialist who is informed about grief and its pathological forms. The three most common forms of pathological grief are:

A. Delayed grief with variable degree of expression at some subsequent date

B. Inhibited grief with minimal or absent indications of "conventional" mourning but with the onset of psychosomatic symptoms and behavior patterns that may be understood as substitutes for or equivalents of the inhibited grief

C. Prolonged and overintense grief (chronic grief), often with intense guilt and self-reproach; other more subtle variants and additional components are described in the specialized literature (Parkes, 1965)

8. *Contraindicated interventions*
   A. Psychological interpretation of key defenses against highly charged, warded off, or unconscious mental content
   B. Excessive solicitude and overprotection of the patient.

In general the baseline attitude of the helper, from which appropriate departures may be made, should be one of compassionate but temperate empathic concern, avoiding sentimentality and overidentification. The therapist should recognize the full extent of the emotional loss but, nevertheless, gently convey to the patient, after subsidence of the acute, initial, intense phase of grief, that it is the normal, expected course that he recover like anyone else, that life must go on, and that the mourner possess the required inner strength to make a new life or to carry on. The helper should make it clear that he would like to make himself available for subsequent sessions on an irregular ad lib basis at a frequency of once weekly or less. Assistance should be offered in making future plans of all types, including possible appropriate changes in occupation, residence, or social life.

Normally, acute grief lasts from one to two months and gradually subsides and recedes by about six months. Reactivation may occur with the anniversary of the death or stimulation of stressful memories involving the deceased. The plans of the helper should take these time factors into account.

References

Lindemann, E. 1944. "Symptomatology and Management of Acute Grief." *American Journal of Psychiatry* 101:141–48.

Parkes, C. M. 1965. "Bereavement and Mental Illness." *British Journal of Medical Psychology* 38(March):1–26.

Wiener, A., et al. 1975. "The Process and Phenomenology of Bereavement," in *Bereavement: Its Psychosocial Aspects,* eds. B. Schoenberg et al., pp. 53–65. New York: Columbia University Press.

♣ 6

Intervention with the Bereaved

Lee H. Suszycki

Feelings of psychic pain, anger, guilt and helplessness can be relieved considerably during bereavement, if prompt and appropriate intervention starts at the time of anticipatory grief and continues through the period of acute grief. The family will still grieve and need support, but the sorrow will be less overwhelming and immobilizing.

To be effective this intervention should ideally commence in the hospital when families are coping with the initial stages of grief. At the same time, support should also be coming from the community, since intervention is aimed at preparation for bereavement. Social work is in a unique position to offer this help and carries a much greater responsibility than is generally recognized because of the continuum of relationships the social worker has with the patient and his family from the first admission to the hospital, through discharge (if this is possible), and, in some circumstances, for many weeks and months thereafter.

To deal with grief and bereavement knowledgeably and effectively, the social worker must be aware of how death and the dying process are being perceived by the patient and the family. The experience is not always viewed with great sorrow and feelings of loss. For some families it can be a relief, a beginning, or an annoyance. The social worker must be sensitive to individual differences without projecting personal views, and treatment goals should be handled accordingly, with full recognition and understanding of the affected individual's needs and wishes.

The grief experience affects not only the bereaved-to-be experiencing grief but also, in most instances, the patient. The degree to which he feels or expresses this varies according to age, temperament, the way he has dealt with traumas and crises in the past, religious and cultural beliefs, and the family's attitudes. Many patients inquire directly about their prognosis, and some wish to participate actively in truthful sharing to the best of their psychic and physical abilities, particularly when they are responsible for the welfare of dependent family members and practical affairs need reorganization. More physicians today are willing to give direct but uncomplicated responses to patients' inquiries. On the other hand some patients wish to deny the grimness of their illness, and this attitude too should be honored and respected.

When necessary, the social worker assumes responsibility for sharing with the patient that he is dying, if the patient is receptive to this, especially if a close and ongoing relationship exists. The challenge of this difficult and painful task can evoke acute emotional pain and anguish in the patient and in the caregiver. Yet, when the task is handled courageously and empathically, the patient can be helped immeasurably during the most critical and vulnerable phase of his life. By encouraging the expression of grief, by listening and showing genuine empathy, the social worker enables the patient to feel less abandoned and tormented by fears of the unknown. Often, the patient can review his life, express concerns or hopes with regard to a family member, request that special funeral arrangements be made, or ask for ongoing support for himself and his family. Whether or not the patient and family can be brought closer together during this period depends on their past and present relationships and on their ability to share effectively and openly with one another. What is most important is that within a nurturing milieu they have been presented with this opportunity to verbalize their mutual sorrow and express feelings of affection that might otherwise have never been voiced. As a consequence the serenity and satisfaction achieved help diminish some of the guilt and despair.

The social worker must be able to tolerate expressions of anger, irritation, and even withdrawal. Comments may imply that the patient fears that no one can help him now and that no one can understand fully his struggles and agony. As a result the social worker may feel rejected. A caregiver should be secure and mature personally and professionally, always indicating that she will remain available to the family and will continue to visit the patient. In essence the social worker may be the indirect recipient of many incongruous, ambivalent, and not so pleasant emotions. The ability to identify those who are pathology ridden as opposed to those who are quite healthy and normal during a period that is psychologically dismembering and shattering to the most rationally functioning of individuals must be cultivated. She, herself, can grieve for the patient's death as long as she is not so overwhelmed that her clinically helpful role is impaired.

Defining grief as acute and felt as such by the family depends on many factors and situations. Generally speaking, such grief appears when it is clear that the patient's days appear to be numbered (and there is no hope), and it reaches its pinnacle during the wake, persisting into the bereavement period in varying degrees.

Acute grief is almost always present as the result of the imminent or sudden deaths of children, young adults, and middle-aged people whose lives and living have been tragically thwarted and whose responsibilities have not been discharged or fulfilled. A death accompanied by extreme physical suffering can also evoke acute grief, with its accompanying feelings of rage and helplessness. When an elderly person dies, usually the family has a profound sense of sadness and loss, rather than acute sorrow, since most can recognize and accept that the individual has lived a long life and done the best he could with it. On the other hand, one can unequivocally state that acute grief is always experienced when very strong and close ties have existed, no matter how old the individual.

Just as the patient needs to be listened to within a stable milieu, so do the family members. They are the ones who have to face the disruption in their lives, reintegrate day-to-day living, reorganize familial roles, and at times readjust future plans. They should be allowed to express their sorrow in the manner and to the degree that is uniquely appropriate to them within an atmosphere that is non-judgemental, uncritical, and comforting. They should feel free to verbalize bitterness, fury, despondency, or just plain relief. If the patient's illness has been chronic, his death has been long anticipated, and the family have rehearsed the final moment and begun to engage in activities without his presence. Hence, their grief will be much less visible, since so much of it has already been worked through. As a result their state of bereavement will be of shorter duration.

It is natural and comforting for the social worker to assume a helpful role with funeral arrangements, if such is the wish of the bereaved. Some wish to escape the painful memories associated with those who were intimately involved with the patient's death and may turn to extended family members, friends, the clergy, or the funeral director for assistance. However, the social worker must determine if such peripheral people are available and, when they are not, offer to get in touch with the funeral home of choice and help to arrange the wake, and even attend it. Her presence will afford the bereaved a continuum of support from someone with whom they feel comfortable and yet who is objective enough to help them review their past lives and refocus on their own hopes, concerns, and fears about the future.

During the wake or shortly thereafter, the social worker can assess how much guidance and support the family requires to manage daily living. Unfortunately, many hospital-based social workers must focus their energies on the inpatient populace, and so they have little time for adequate posthospital counseling. If such is the case and the bereaved need considerable assistance, she can refer them to another resource in the community while encouraging them to keep in touch with her, if only to report on their current doings.

The following case illustrates some of the reactions and concerns of the grief stricken and bereaved and the interventive efforts of the social worker.

Mrs. C, a 34-year-old wife and a mother of a 2-year-old girl, had been initially referred to social service by her next-door neighbor (a social worker) for supportive counseling. Patient was admitted for a bilateral mastectomy. Married for 12 years, she was a writer by profession. Her husband was a 36-year-old lawyer who traveled frequently on business. Her father, a retired physician, lived with his wife in South America. Patient was an Episcopalian, as was husband. Neither had other siblings, and Mr. C's parents were dead. They possessed considerable savings and had adequate hospital insurance coverage. Many good and attentive friends were in the picture.

Mrs. C was a strikingly beautiful, well-groomed, and articulate woman. Prior to surgery, she was distraught, angry, depressed, and resistant to intervention. She subtly indicated her resentment of her neighbor's intrusion into her privacy. "No one can help me now, since I will die anyway. My sister and grandmother had histories of breast cancer and died young. I knew the same thing would happen to me. My husband and I are surrounded by physician friends, and sadly enough, I know the implications of cancer at age 34. For many years, my husband and I tried to have a child. At long last we conceived and a beautiful and healthy baby was born. Now both will be robbed of a family."

Mrs. C indicated that for the present she just wished to be left alone to integrate the entire situation. The social worker acknowledged the painful reality and said that the patient's request was quite understandable. She commented that she would stop by on her daily rounds, if only to say hello. Patient seemed to be amenable to this.

Her physician told the social worker that he was quite direct in answering his patient's queries, apprising her of the possibility of metastases, which radiotherapy and chemotherapy would try to palliate. He felt that the entire family could profit from considerable support.

With subsequent visits Mrs. C grew calmer and less angry as she was helped to recognize that an outpouring of her feelings, no matter how harsh, was appropriate and needed to be expressed and listened to.

During one of the visits the social worker met the patient's husband, whose face and entire being conveyed his sorrow but whose affect, nonetheless, was quite contained and under control. "We will manage somehow. There's a lot of love between us. Laura will be okay." His wife looked at him and started to cry.

Mrs. C's parents came in from South America to stay at their daughter's home and care for Cynthia, the child, while Mr. C was trying to organize a work schedule that would curtail his travels. Both were very visibly shaken. "Why couldn't this have happened to one of us? We have lived." Her father commented how hard it was for him to know that neither he nor any other surgeon could offer his daughter a miraculous cure. They said that, although Cynthia loved them, she missed her mother's presence.

The initial goal was to prepare the patient to face surgery with more equanimity through reduction of anxieties and frustrations that would have their domino effect on the entire family. Both patient and family had many remarkable strengths—cohesiveness, courage, and concern for one another's well-being and comfort. These were fostered to help them cope with and survive their grief while maintaining family stability and competence. The patient needed help in coming to a satisfactory and bearable level of acceptance of her illness and its limitations, and in emotionally integrating her changed physical appearance, since aesthetics meant a lot to her. She required encouragement to fulfill her role of wife and mother to the best of her abilities and to engage in activities that would bring her satisfaction. She half-heartedly resigned herself to accepting a homemaker (five days per week, eight hours per day) who, while her husband was at work, would help care for Cynthia, do some household chores, and escort Mrs. C to and from radiotherapy.

Mr. C needed help to permit him to express his grief without feeling less masculine or protective and to share his feelings with his wife. He had to take a more active role in the care of his daughter, readjust future plans, envision life without his wife, and yet stay very much involved with her and responsive to her needs.

The patient's parents also required recognition of their grief. Their desire to feel useful and helpful had to be placed within an appropriate context of their daughter's and son-in-law's wishes and needs.

Shortly before discharge, Mrs. C started to receive radiotherapy treatments and initially felt nauseous and uncomfortable. Soon, however, she felt almost "joyful" for feeling so much better than she had anticipated. She eagerly awaited going home. "I'll give it the old college try; if it gets too much, I might just give in." The social worker expressed admiration for her courage and determination and emphasized the many fine things she had to live for—no matter how long or short the time.

After a family conference with the social worker present, it was decided that the patient's parents would return to South America with the understanding that they would be called in the event of any emergency. They recognized this to be the best plan, since they did not wish to cause any dissension within an independent and close marriage.

Following the patient's discharge, her husband called the social worker several times from his place of work under the guise of asking for help with practical matters, whereas, in reality, he just wished to share his feelings. "It seems that I'm on a constant seesaw; I vacillate between acceptance of my wife's fatal illness and hope for a miracle, especially when she looks fairly well. I walk around with a heavy heart, but it helps so much to talk. We've grown so much closer to each other than ever before that, when the end finally comes, it will be a heartbreak. I'm so glad there is now." The social worker listened, with empathy, and urged him to call whenever he needed.

Mrs. C would call a few times to express her satisfaction with the homemaker, her family, and the many friends who were so caring and comforting. "I'm so fortunate in so many ways, one could say that I've lived a lifetime."

Patient was readmitted, within eight months of her surgery, with respiratory failure. It was obvious that she was in a terminal condition. Husband and parents were in constant attendance. Although it was difficult for Mrs. C to speak, she seemed to be at peace emotionally. She died four weeks after admission.

Her husband, whom one could never envision as ever having been reduced to tears, wept uncontrollably. "Forgive me, but the pain is too great." Mrs. C's parents were of immense comfort to their son-in-law, as well as to each other. They would help with any and all funeral arrangements. Mrs. C had apparently stipulated that the wake should last one evening only, and they would honor that wish. The social worker indicated that she would like to attend.

The wake was a warm and dignified event with close friends and acquaintances present. The social worker listened to whatever Mr. C and the parents wanted to focus on. Mr. C spoke about how beautiful his wife looked even in death, how proud he would always be of her, how much he loved their child, and the much finer and stronger person he had become through their marital union; his in-laws were grateful to him for giving their daughter so many good and beautiful years: "As soon as Cynthia is old enough to understand, we will tell her just what happened, how much her mother loved her, and how kind her father is."

Mrs. C's parents shared with the social worker that they would encourage their son-in-law to move to South America and live near them, at least for a while. They commented that he always preferred their type of living and had finally convinced his wife to try it when Cynthia got a bit older. The social worker encouraged them to share their thinking with Mr. C and get feedback from him about his plans for the future. She welcomed ongoing contact with all of them.

One month after the burial, Mr. C stoppped by to see the social worker to chat and say goodbye. Yes, his in-law's suggestion sounded fine and practical. He enjoyed South America and hoped that Cynthia would too. In the meantime she would be situated close to her grandparents, whom she loved and who would help care for her while he worked. Mr. C managed to negotiate a promising position in the same line of endeavor. If only he could have made that move with his wife to accompany him! He placed his marriage in what appeared to be a healthy and normal perspective, arranged sound and appropriate plans for the near future for himself and his child and seemed to have a healthy attitude about life. "I will take each day as it comes, and, hopefully, all will turn out fairly well." He expressed appreciation to the social worker for her support and guidance.

It has been well documented and researched that feelings of grief that have not been adequately worked through often disable the individual physically and/or emotionally. Thus, the social worker, within her professional commitment and capabilities, has a unique, humanitarian contribution to offer: to maximize the family's capacity to function as effectively as possible while the patient is dying, through counseling measures and use of suitable community resources that help facilitate the patient's and family's overall comfort. The social worker helps the bereaved go on with a rewarding and meaningful life by addressing their needs herself or by linking them to appropriate community people and groups who can help them to promote their psychosocial well-being.

Many social workers are confronted daily with the complex needs of the dying patient and his family. They must be able to relate to them with confidence and assuredness that their creative skills, knowledge, and methods are indeed effective therapeutic agents that can and do mitigate human crises and despair.

Bibliography

Arndt, H. C. M. and M. Gruber. 1978. "Helping Families Cope with Acute and Anticipatory Grief." In *Social Work with the Dying Patient and Family*, eds., E. Prichard et al., pp. 38–48. New York: Columbia University Press.

Cabot, R. C. 1977. "The Use of Truth and Falsehood in Medicine: An Experimental Study." In *Ethics in Medicine*. Cambridge, Massachusetts and London, England: The MIT Press.

Callahan, D. 1977. "On Defining a Natural Death." In *Hastings Center Report—Institute of Society, Ethics, and the Life Sciences* 7 (3).

Keefe, T. 1976. "Empathy: The Critical Skill." *Social Work* 21 (1) (June).

Kutscher, A. H. 1970. "Practical Aspects of Bereavement." In *Loss and Grief: Psychological Management in Medical Practice*, eds., B. Schoenberg et al., pp. 280–97. New York and London: Columbia University Press.

Lloyd, G. A. 1978. "The Expression of Grief as Deviant Behavior in American Culture." In *Social Work with the Dying Patient and Family*, eds., E. Prichard et al., pp. 12–19. New York: Columbia University Press.

Parkes, C. M. 1972. *Bereavement: Studies of Grief in Adult Life*. New York: International Universities Press.

Pilsecker, C. 1975. "Help for the Dying." *Social Work* 20 (3) (May).

Reeves, R. B. 1970. "The Hospital Chaplain Looks at Grief." In *Loss and Grief: Psychological Management in Medical Practice*, eds., B. Schoenberg at al., pp. 362–72. New York and London: Columbia University Press.

Saunders, C. 1977. "Telling Patients." In *Ethics in Medicine*. Cambridge, Massachusetts and London, England: The MIT Press.

Suszycki, L. H. 1977. "Living, Dying and the Elderly." Unpublished paper presented at the Symposium on Psychosocial Aspects of Radiation Therapy: The Patient, the Family, and the Staff.

❦ 7

Psychosocial Care of the Family after the Patient's Death

Colin Murray Parkes

For the newly bereaved widow the prospect of "coming through to a new beginning" may indeed seem remote, and there will be much pain and much time to pass before she is able to admit that she is "back on course." In traditional medical practice she is likely to receive little help from members of the medical and nursing professions unless she becomes sick and comes to us for help. Even then she may receive no more than physical examination and physical treatment, and her emotional needs may be ignored. The same applies to other members of the bereaved family whose lives have been seriously disrupted by the loss of a key member.

The situation would be less serious if there were others who could be relied upon to give support in bereavement. But there are several reasons why it is particularly hard to be bereaved in present-day western countries. In the first place the small size of the nuclear family unit and the paucity of ties to the extended family mean that ties of kinship no longer provide the long-term support they did in the past. Second, the decline in religious practice and belief means that pastoral care no longer ensures that each bereaved person receives the close support of a clergyman and the church community surrounding him. Third, the relative lack of close links with neighbors in the modern big city means that social isolation is common. And fourth, the taboo on death and death-related behavior in our society is particularly strong. This means that formal mourning is discouraged; expressions of pining, rage, or fear are frowned on; and one's friends and neighbors are embarrassed in the presence of those who show grief.

It is hardly surprising that, once the funeral is over and the friends and family have returned to their homes, the remaining nuclear family members may find themselves lacking close support from any professional, neighborhood, or kinship group. There are, of course, some national and local organizations that offer help to the bereaved (e.g., Parents Without Partners in the United States and Cruse, the organization for widows and their children, in Britain), but these are still limited in their scope and uneven in distribution. Hence, they reach only a very small proportion of those who may need their help.

One reason why bereaved people are often reluctant to seek help from the organizations and individuals available to them is the feeling of distrust or suspicion of strangers that is a natural consequence of bereavement. The newly bereaved person has been forced unwillingly from a familiar world in which he knows his place (however unsatisfactory that place may have been) into an unfamiliar world in which his place is very uncertain, and he has not yet discovered which of his established bases of planning and prediction still remain. Because of this he feels and is vulnerable to exploitation and tends to avoid confronting strange or unfamiliar persons and situations.

On the other hand he is well aware of his need for help and readily accepts it from any of the people around him who are familiar and safe. This means that doctors, nurses, and other caregivers who are known to the bereaved are in a position to give such help or to introduce others who can help!

To understand the types of help needed we must consider the nature of grief, the psychological reaction to bereavement. Grief is not a state but a process. In passing through it the bereaved person passes through a series of phases that tend to follow each other in sequence, although the individual moves back and forth across the sequence so that the transition is by no means smooth. Thus, even years after the bereavement some event that brings the loss strongly to mind, for example, finding a photograph in a drawer or meeting an old friend who knew the dead person, may again precipitate feelings of acute pining similar to those experienced during the first week of bereavement (although less intense).

The process of grieving is a process of learning. In its course the bereaved person gradually abandons one view of the world and learns a new one. At first he is faced with a major discrepancy between the real world—the world as it is—and his view of it—his internal model of the world as he assumes it to be. He finds it hard to take in the reality of what has happened. He recognizes the truth of his bereavement as an intellectual fact, but he cannot appreciate the relevance of that fact to himself; he feels numb, blunted, shocked.

The feeling was described by a 27-year-old American widow, Mrs. O, who viewed her husband's body after his death from cancer. "I, I didn't want to believe it, and yet I saw it right there so it was as though I were torn between what I wanted to believe and what was really there. . . . The following few hours was just, I don't know, it was not me or something, I couldn't . . . I just didn't do anything just, just blank. They gave me his watch and I held it in my hand . . . they wanted to talk to me but I couldn't, I just . . . didn't feel anything, just complete blank."

The phase of numbness is not always as clear-cut as this. In some situations, when the death has been long anticipated and takes place in a peaceful manner, numbness may not occur at all. But in either case, sooner or later the characteristic pangs of grief begin. These are episodes of intense pining for the lost person associated with all the psychological and physiological accompaniments of acute anxiety. The bereaved person has a strong impulse to get back the lost one, to put right the wrong thing that has happened, to make sense of a world that is threatening to become chaotic.

Pangs of grief are brought on by any reminder of the loss, and at first they tend to occur very frequently indeed. They obviously have parallels in the crying and searching of young children when separated from others and seem to represent a struggle to recover the lost person. But the human adult knows very well that any such crying and searching is doomed to failure, and so the cry is stifled to become a sob and the search is replaced by a restless hyperactivity and inability to concentrate for any length of time on anything but the loss. The bereaved person takes up one course of action, drops it, starts another but finds it all pointless and confusing.

Mrs. O was interviewed three weeks after her husband's death. At that time her grief was still at its peak, and she was missing him very strongly. "All of a sudden I miss him, then it hurts. . . . I try to keep my hands very busy, but I haven't been able to do any reading or anything because my mind just wanders away. . . . I have really simple goals," she said, "to make him happy, it seems very simple, and all of a sudden I felt nothing more to do, feel so lost that

I don't know. . . .'' She tried to think of ways to get him back, "I
tried so hard to have dreams so I can see him, but all I end up is
dreaming that I couldn't find him . . . it's especially hard to realize
that he's not there anymore. For a while I felt that I was living in the
past. . . . I wish I (was) not so young so I can join him sooner.''

Fleeting self-destructive thoughts of this kind are not uncommon
and sometimes assume suicidal proportions. Common, too, are intense feelings of anger or guilt that may complicate the course of
grief. But more often, as time passes, the intensity and frequency of
the pangs of grief diminish and the bereaved person enters a phase of
disorganization and despair. At this time the reality of what has happened is recognized, and the individual gives up hope of recovering
the world he has lost. But he has not yet discovered the place that
remains to him. His old plans and hopes are in ruins, but he has not
yet developed new ones to replace them.

This is a time of apathy and dejection. The bereaved person
lives from day to day, without a plan for the future and lacking aims
in life. "I'm still rather confused . . ." said Mrs. O a year after her
husband's death. "What action should I take for my future life and
what do I want? I keep on asking myself and I haven't really come up
with anything.'' She was keeping herself busy to avoid depression
but was well aware of the futility of such activity. "Perhaps it's
because I don't want to feel sad or sorry for myself—which is certainly very difficult. . . .'' She recognized that at 27 she could
hardly expect her life to be at an end, but at the same time, she did
not feel free to regard herself as a single woman. "I'm fighting my
role,'' she said, "I'm not exactly married and not exactly single.
. . . I'm not waiting to die. I feel I have to live my life.'' But she
had little idea how this could be. "I feel I'm very depressed, you
know.''

Only after this phase is reached does the bereaved person begin
to find new beginnings. At first quite unimportant things may begin
to be enjoyed for their own sake, but eventually a new direction
emerges and episodes of pining and depression become less and less
frequent.

That is, if all goes well. But too often there are problems that
complicate and prolong the course of grief. Several studies have
thrown light on these problems, but one in particular, the Harvard
Bereavement Study, has provided us with a set of observations enabling us to identify, at the time of bereavement, those family
members who are likely to get into difficulties later. This means that
we are in a position to know who is in greatest need of support after

bereavement and how the limited time of the professionals can best be spent.

Because earlier work had indicated that widows and widowers were more likely to get into difficulties than other family members and because younger widows and widowers had been found to suffer more than elderly widows and widowers after bereavement, the Harvard Study focused on men and women under the age of 45 who had lost a spouse; 48 widows and 19 widowers were interviewed at 3 weeks and 6 weeks after bereavement and again a year later to ascertain what identifiable characteristics distinguished those who would cope well with the stress of bereavement from those who would cope badly. As a result of this study a predictive questionnaire consisting of eight multiple-choice questions has been derived for use as a predictive instrument. This questionnaire has now been in use for some years in St. Christopher's Hospice (London), where it serves as a means of identifying relatives of cancer patients who are in special need of help. A follow-up of such relatives 20 months after bereavement has now confirmed the predictive value of the questionnaire and enabled some modifications to be made that will make it more suitable for use in Great Britain with a wider age range of bereaved people than the sample originally studied.

Much additional work is needed before we can be sure that the predictive questionnaire is universally valid. At this point it can be recommended only as a starting point for future work. No doubt, a number of similar instruments will come into use in the near future.

What, then, were the factors best predicting a poor outcome for the young widows and widowers of Boston? The first and best single predictor was more an educated guess than a definable characteristic. The coders who had listened to the long tape recordings of the early postbereavement interviews were invited to make their own predictions based on existing knowledge of bereavement reactions. Their answers were not perfect; in fact they were less reliable than predictions made by combining replies to all questions, but they did give a quite good general indication of outcome.

Second there was a measure of the intensity of pining expressed by the respondent three weeks after bereavement. A high score on this was subsequently shown to go along with a close interdependent relationship with the dead person.

The third predictor has already been mentioned, a measure of the extent to which the bereavement had been expected and prepared for. Fourth there was a measure of suicidal ideation reflecting the respondent's attitude to his future life. Those who agreed with statements such as "I wouldn't care if I died tomorrow" were coping less well a year later than those who had no such feelings.

The fifth predictor was a measure of socioeconomic status. This indicated a poor outcome for people from unskilled manual occupations, the lowest social class group. Many of these were black and lived in parts of Boston where civil disturbance was common at this time. Consequently, there was some doubt of the applicability of the finding to other racial and geographic settings. In any event the doubts were unjustified, and low social class has been found to be a significant predictor of depression in a white working-class population in South London.

At borderline levels of significance were measures of anger and self-reproach. These were not strong predictors of outcome in either Boston or London, but the frequency with which strong, persistent feelings of guilt and anger have been reported in studies of bereaved psychiatric patients justifies their inclusion.

The first version of the predictive questionnaire derived from this study was used at St. Christopher's Hospice for 4 years. It is shown in the Table 7.1. This was completed by the senior nurse on the ward where the patient died and applied to the person most affected by the bereavement (the "Key Person" or KP). Unlike the Harvard Study, it relied on observations made *before* the patient's death, but this did not necessitate much rewording of the questionnaire. Because of the findings of earlier studies a question about age was included in this version but dropped from a later modification after research had thrown doubt on its validity in the hospital. A question about the presence or absence of a supportive family was also included, but this too is of doubtful value. In any event nurses found little difficulty in completing the questionnaire and in only one in ten families (when the patient died within a few hours of admission or was not visited in hospital) was it not possible to obtain a predictive score.

Predictive scores were obtained by adding together the score for each question. A score of 18 or more placed the key person in the "high-risk" group. In addition, whenever the nurses felt that there was so urgent a need for support that it would be unethical to withhold it, they scored 4 or 5 on the final question, and this was taken as an overriding score regardless of the total.*

This questionnaire has been completed with respect to 1656

---

* Further support for the predictive validity of the questionnaire comes from the finding that, among five key persons who have, since bereavement, attempted or committed suicide, everyone had a predictive score greater than 18.

Table 7.1. Predictive Questionnaire

Questionnaire: (Ring one item in each section. Leave blank if not known.)
Check here if Key Person (KP) not well enough known to enable these questions to be answered.

A. *Age of KP*
(applies only if K.P. is
spouse)
1. 75+
2. 66–75
3. 56–65
4. 46–55
5. 15–45

B. *Occupation of principal
wage earner of key
person's family*
1. Professional & executive
2. Semiprofessional
3. Office & clerk
4. Skilled manual
5. Semiskilled manual
6. Unskilled manual

C. *Length of KP's
preparation for patient's
death*
1. Fully prepared for long
period
2. Fully prepared for less
than 2 weeks
3. Partially prepared
4. Totally unprepared

D. *Clinging or pining*
1. Never
2. Seldom
3. Moderate
4. Frequent
5. Constant
6. Constant and intense

E. *Anger*
1. None (or normal)
2. Mild irritation
3. Moderate—occasional
outbursts
4. Severe—spoiling
relationships
5. Extreme—always bitter

F. *Self-reproach*
1. None
2. Mild—vague & general
3. Moderate—some clear
self-reproach
4. Severe—preoccupation,
self-blame
5. Extreme—major problem

G. *Family*
1. Warm, will give full
support
2. Doubtful
3. Family supportive but
live distance
4. Family not supportive
5. No family

H. *How will key person cope?*
1. *Well,* normal grief and recovery without special help
2. *Fair,* probably get by without special help
3. *Doubtful,* may need special help
4. *Badly,* requires special help
5. *Very badly,* requires urgent help

All scoring 4–5 on H will be followed up.

key persons; 22 percent scored more than 18 and therefore fell into the high-risk group. With the exception of a subgroup, who were not included, for reasons of research still in progress, the high-risk group have been provided with a special service aiming to support them through their first year of bereavement. This service provides an example of one way of caring for the bereaved families of cancer patients. It is obviously not the only possible approach, but it has turned out to be economical in terms of staff time, and it enables a good service to be given to those who are most in need of it.

Visiting is undertaken, where possible, by a member of staff who is known to the family. This may be a nurse from the ward, one of the domiciliary nurses who visited the family prior to the patient's admission, the hospital social worker or the chaplain or assistant chaplain. If there is no person known to the family, a volunteer will call. The visit is normally made in the key person's house about a week or 10 days after the funeral, this being the time when most bereaved people seem to become aware of their need for support. The funeral over, family and friends have departed and the mourners are discovering what it means to be alone. A visit at this time is almost always welcomed, and visitors find themselves faced with a spate of talk about the loss and the events leading up to it that may last for several hours. The aims of the first visit are to establish a helping relationship, to provide an opportunity for the expression of grief, to assess any suicidal risk, to steer the bereaved person toward other sources of help that may be needed, to discuss problems that are emerging, and to assess how soon a further visit is likely to be required. The visitor is not expected to be an expert on the social and other services; in fact it is better to avoid too "professional" an image. What the bereaved person needs most at this time is an understanding person.

Feelings of anger and bitterness may need to find expression, as well as feelings of sadness, and it is important for the visitor to avoid taking sides or getting drawn into arguments. This is particularly the case when the visitor or his own establishment are attacked. Doctors, clergy, nurses, even "God," may become the objects of irrational anger, and we fail to understand the nature of this anger if we think that it can be met by rational argument. It is usually quite possible to indicate to the bereaved one's understanding of his feelings without conniving with them in condemning its object. When this is done it often happens that the bereaved person, having "blown his top," is able to revise his assessment of the situation and adopt a more rational viewpoint. The fact that the visitor has remained unperturbed reassures him that this anger is not as destructive as he fears it to be.

Suicidal impulses need careful assessment. If ever he is in the slightest doubt, the visitor should ask, "Has it been so bad that you have thought of killing yourself?" This question will usually produce an honest reply, and if there is a real suicidal risk the bereaved person will be able to go on to discuss the means of killing himself. Visitors are often deterred from asking this question for fear of putting the idea into the person's head. But such ideas are in everyone's head at times of bereavement. There is a much greater danger of missing a suicide than of precipitating one.

Mrs. F was 45 years of age at the time her husband died. They had been married for only 13 years but had become very interdependent and cut themselves off from family and friends. The ward staff thought her an emotional and rather inadequate person; the predictive questionnaire gave her a score of 28. Consequently, she was visited by one of the domiciliary nurses three weeks after her loss. The nurse telephoned me the same evening, saying she feared there might be a suicidal risk. Mrs. F had seemed strange, and our nurse felt that the dilapidated state of her flat might reflect an equally disordered frame of mind. This was hardly the evidence on which conclusions could be drawn, and so I asked her to go back the following day to ask Mrs. F outright if she had thought of killing herself. The nurse went back but now found Mrs. F "relatively peaceful and content," and so she did not ask the crucial question. In fact she telephoned me back the same day to reassure me that her anxiety had been unjustified. Seven days later Mrs. F was found dead from an overdose of sleeping tablets.

Having established that a real suicidal risk exists, the visitor must ensure that the bereaved person is not left alone until the risk is past. Psychiatric advice should, in my opinion, always be sought and in some cases admission to an inpatient psychiatric unit arranged. This will permit intensive support to be given during the period of maximum need and will provide time to rally the family and other sources of communal support that will be needed when the crisis is over. Unfortunately, there are some people whose feelings of despair drop away when they are in the psychiatric unit but return as soon as they get back to the home that holds so many memories of the past. Visitors who remain in touch through the period of hospitalization and resume acquaintance afterward can be a valuable adjunct to the psychiatric services and may reduce the danger of a subsequent successful suicide.

The risk of suicide is greatest during the first few weeks of bereavement and declines thereafter. This means that the first visit is of crucial importance and should not be delayed too long. As director of the family service at St. Christopher's Hospice, I meet each month with all the staff members and volunteers who have made home visits during the preceding month. Each new case is reviewed and a plan for future support worked out. When a person has been referred elsewhere for support, there is, of course, no need to duplicate services, but in such cases we have learned that we must always check that the service is being given. In one case we passed responsibility for supporting a widow to a local clergyman who had assured us that he would visit her and give all the help she needed. When, some months later, our research interviewer attempted to locate the widow, she was found to have died from an overdose of sleeping tablets. On inquiry, we discovered that the clergyman who had promised to visit had been rebuffed at the time of his first visit and had made no further attempt to contact her or to find others who could take over. Since this widow had a high score on our questionnaire, we would undoubtedly have attempted to contact her if informed of his difficulties. It is now routine for the service organizer to make a note in her diary to remind her to telephone for a progress report on all family members who are referred to others.

Not that we can force our attention on those who refuse us. It would be an intrusion on personal liberty to attempt to do so, and we need to be aware that the people we contact have not asked for our help. For the same reason it is essential that all questionnaire assessments and notes be treated as highly confidential and revealed to no person who is not either a professional caregiver or a part of the family service.

The frequency and function of later visits can be decided only after the initial assessment. When all is well, the bereaved people are found to be expressing their grief in a normal manner and the family are clearly going to provide adequate support. There may be no need to do more than call back once or twice at a later time to ensure that all is well. Such visits are not likely to be resented by the bereaved, who appreciate the fact that they have not been forgotten. A simple card is sent to every bereaved family from St. Christopher's Hospice on the first anniversary of the death. On it are the words "We are remembering you at St. Christopher's." These cards are appreciated by the family and sometimes result in a visit to the Hospice.

Usually, the high-risk group of relatives are found to need rather more support than this. Irregular visits throughout the first few months of bereavement provide them with the security that enables them to begin to work through the numerous problems with which they are confronted. There may be a need to allow the mourner to go over the same story again and again. Memories of the death and the dead person will be brought up and considered in an attempt to provide what Marris (1974) calls a "structure of meaning" for what has happened. As time passes, however, the visitor will usually discern a change in the pattern of communication. The amount of crying and overt pining will diminish, and the time spent in looking back at the past will grow less. Problems of current living and fears for the future become issues for discussion, and the visitor is often able to help the person to talk them through and to make realistic plans. Again, he should avoid giving too much advice and should not feel that he is failing to help if he lacks solutions to these problems. The mere fact of being present to share in the other's frustrations helps. Of course, it is often possible to assure people that their fears are unrealistic. Thus the death of one family member can make those who survive excessively anxious about their health and that of their children. Trivial symptoms may be treated with exaggerated importance, and quite unrealistic foreboding may build up. In such a case, one seldom needs to do more than point out to the bereaved person the reason for concern and help him to reach a more realistic perception of it.

An extreme form of this type of problem is seen in those who develop a hypochondriacal illness closely resembling the physical illness from which a loved person has died. These conditions often reflect an unusually strong identification with the dead person. In my own experience they respond well to an approach that focuses on the attachment to the dead person and helps the bereaved to gain insight into the origins of the symptoms.

When, as sometimes happens, the bereaved person appears to be "stuck," that is, when expressions of grief seem to be stereotyped and repetitive and the person has lost the feeling of movement toward a greater acceptance of reality, it may be necessary to take stock.

One explanation for such fixation may be a conscious or unconscious wish to make restitution to the dead person by mourning him forever. Mourning is seen as a duty to the dead and as evidence of devotion. If there were defects in the relationship during the final illness or, worse, if the illness itself gave rise to fresh grounds for self-reproach, the survivor is left with a load of guilt that he finds hard to relieve. His self-esteem has dwindled to the point where he can restore it only by a ritual of self-abasement and self-punishment that carries within it the seeds of self-aggrandizement. By exalting the image of the dead person the survivor exalts his own grief and becomes a model of faithfulness. Examples of devoted mourning are a commonplace of poetry and literature, and the esteem in which such perpetual mourners are held by their families and by society at large seems to reflect our own need to let others do our mourning for us. Take, for example, the unfortunate dog Hatchi. He is said to have returned daily to the railway station (in Japan) at which he had formerly met his master. This behavior continued for 10 years after the latter's death. So great was the admiration of the Japanese people for this example of fidelity that a postage stamp was issued to commemorate the dog and a statue raised in his honor.

Widows who continue to grieve for an abnormal length of time are not treated with quite the same honor, but they do expect and sometimes receive tributes to their devotion. The children, while pitying their sad mother, may do little to get her to look outward, and one suspects that they get some secret gratification from the evidence, which is now exhibited, that the relationship between their parents was worth mourning.

In other cases the persistence of grief seems to reflect a need to take advantage of mourning to avoid reengagement with a potentially hostile world. For the socially inadequate person marriage may have provided a haven of safety. Now that this haven is gone, the bereaved person may withdraw from contact with others and justify this by emphasizing the extent of grief.

Related to this problem and overlapping with it is that of the person whose experience of life is of a long series of deprivations and losses. Lacking any sense of "basic trust" (to use Erikson's term), the mourner feels that bereavement has simply confirmed his conviction that life is an empty and purposeless thing and that any pleasure to be gained from relationships with others is evanescent and outweighed by the pain of separation and loss. He mourns, not only for the dead person, but also for life itself.

In all of these cases the presence of a person who understands the problem is a great help. Someone who can point out that the mourner has done his duty to the dead and that endless mourning is self-defeating, who will show concern without elevating the mourning itself, who can act as a bridge to others and provide more rewarding ways of relating, and who insists on treating the bereaved person as a significant person with every hope of a rich and rewarding life ahead will stand a good chance of breaking the vicious circle of withdrawal and grief.

At times it may be necessary to prescribe or arrange to have prescribed a tranquilizer or antidepressant drug to help the bereaved person face the world again. But it is important that the medication be seen as a means of getting the bereaved person out of a rut rather than of providing a permanent crutch. Too often drugs are prescribed as an alternative to personal support and guidance; there is then a danger of the bereaved person's being left with yet another problem, drug dependence.

In cases such as this the visitor must have a clear picture of what his own limitations are, as well as of what may be needed. If it seems clear that this person needs more personal support than the visitor is able to give, then he must attempt to draw in family members and others to share the burden.

Another problem is that of finding the appropriate distance that must be maintained if the visitor is to be effective. Just as the nurse or doctor needs to discover the optimal distance from the cancer patient that will permit effective help, so the family visitor needs to be willing to get close to the bereaved without becoming so over-involved that his or her judgment is impaired. It is easy for an over-sympathetic visitor to get "sucked in" to a form of support that not only discourages autonomous development in the bereaved person but also may interfere with the private life and freedom of the helper. This can happen to the best of us if we are not ourselves supported by a team who are capable of criticizing as well as caring.

Mrs. M was only 19 when her husband was found to have a thymoma with secondary spread. She had three young children of less than school age, and after her husband's discharge from the hospital, she became increasingly irritable toward them and depressed. Lacking either a supportive family or the intelligence and ability to cope without one, she was brought to our notice by her general practitioner. Although her husband was in fairly good shape, it was necessary to admit him to St. Christopher's Hospice to give his wife a rest.

Once he was on the ward the situation improved greatly. Mrs. M brought her children with her each day, and she and her husband spent time with them on the ward and in the garden of the hospice. Fortunately, we were able to find places for the children in the hospice crèche, and this meant that the parents could spend more time together.

Mr. M's condition deteriorated steadily, and he died peacefully 4 months after admission. The predictive questionnaire gave his wife a score of 25, placing her in the high-risk group. Although both the social worker and the chaplain had been giving her support during her husband's illness, the obvious visitor in this case was a nurse of her own age who had befriended her and who had children of the same age.

Mrs. M's reaction to her husband's death was severe. She shut herself up at home, cried a great deal, and seemed desperately depressed. At the nurse's first visit she was very distressed and talked for 2 hours about her husband, his illness, and his death. She was glad of the opportunity to do this, remarking, "No one gives me a chance to talk." When the situation was discussed in our reporting session 2 weeks later, two more disquieting facts emerged; on the one hand, our visiting nurse was going in almost every day and was hardly able to call her life her own; on the other hand, the local social service department had complained that Mrs. M had refused to visit them and it was inferred that perhaps our nurse, by providing an alternative source of help, was unwittingly preventing her from getting the support of a social worker. Our nurse explained that Mrs. M was refusing to visit the social worker because she was afraid that her children would be "taken away." Our own social worker explained to the nurse that, in fact, this was not the case. The social service department had no wish to separate a mother from her children but were anxious to keep them together and would help to make this possible. Sharing the load with the social service department lessened the pressure on our nurse, and she found it easier to withdraw from a position of overinvolvement.

Our nurse persuaded Mrs. M to visit the social service department and accompanied her on her first visit. Subsequently, she was able to decrease the frequency of her visits. Others from the Hospice played a part in care from time to time, but Mrs. M eventually came through the period of disorganization caused by her husband's death, found places for the children in a local nursery school, and got herself a part-time job. Life is still hard for her, but she is "making it," and her relationship with her children is, on the whole, a good one.

Support given to a bereaved mother is, perhaps, more important then most forms of support if only because it is so easy for the grief of the mother to be passed on to the children. (For this reason extra weight is being given to the scores of mothers with young children in the latest modification of the predictive questionnaire.) There is a danger that Mrs. M would have "broken down" in some way if she had not been supported by the hospice staff during the first few weeks of her bereavement. She had, in fact, developed psychosomatic symptoms at that time, and there had been a suggestion that she should receive inpatient psychiatric care. In this event the children would have been taken into a residential institution and a process of separation and alienation would have set in that might have done permanent damage. The cost of this damage in human terms, as well as the economic cost to the community, would have been large.

By comparison the cost of running a family service of this kind is not great. Because St. Christopher's Hospice specializes in terminal care, it has a high death rate, about 500 deaths per annum from four wards of around 20 beds each. By use of the method of identifying the high-risk family member that has been described, numbers are kept down to about 100 cases per annum. Most of the visiting is now done by volunteers. The exceptions are the members of the domiciliary nursing team, who make no distinction between home visits made before and after bereavement. The hospital social worker spends a small amount of her time in running the service, and I, as social psychiatrist, occasionally take over when a family member is in need of psychiatric help, but this does not seem to occur more than two to three times a year. The reporting sessions take place monthly and require about 1½ hours of the time of the three to four staff members and six to eight volunteers who attend.

Systematic evaluation of the bereavement service has demonstrated beneficial effects persisting 20 months after bereavement (Parks, 1979).

Even when no system of selecting bereaved people for follow-up is employed it may be possible to offer support to those who ask for it. The success of self-selection depends on those who need the service's being aware of its existence. It is sometimes possible to link a bereavement support service to an existing body that is seen as trustworthy. In Great Britain, the Camden Bereavement Service operates from the offices of a local Citizens' Advice Bureau. The latter are well known as a responsible voluntary organization in the neighborhood.

Information is sent in a letter with an accompanying leaflet describing the service to all persons registering a death. About 12 percent of the leaflets produce a request for help from the volunteer visitors who run the service. The cost of this service is also very small, since it depends mainly on voluntary help and makes use of a minimum of paid secretarial and social work time. The volunteers meet monthly with an experienced psychiatric social worker to report on recent visits.

Routine visiting of all persons who suffer a bereavement is a rather more expensive use of resources but is a practical reality in some areas. In some parts of Great Britain "health visitors," who are trained nurses with an educational role, make routine visits to bereaved people under the supervision of a general practitioner. In Boston the Widow-to-Widow Project, started by Dr. Phyllis Silverman, employed widows who had come through their own grief and made a new start in life to reach out to newly bereaved widows. This project was of particular interest because of the way in which experience of bereavement was turned to good account. Unfortunately it was a relatively costly project because the "widow aides" were paid fees for their services, and it came to an end when the federal funds that had set it up ran out.

On the whole it seems that the care of the bereaved is not one of the higher priorities of our caring community; only those projects that are run on a shoestring have much chance of succeeding. This may reflect the taboo on all aspects of death and dying. In a society that has succeeded in controlling most of the causes of untimely death and alienating itself from its older generation for whom death is predictable, death can be ignored. Even the uncomfortable awareness that there are still many exceptions to this rule can be partially warded off by life insurance: "Even if I die the little woman will be *all right.*"

The research of recent years has called into question this comforting belief and faced society with the observation that financial security is not the sole or even the principal determinant of the success with which a person meets the stress of bereavement. Let us hope that, by focusing attention on some alternative approaches to the problem, this book will help to reduce the temptation to avoid it.

Reference

Marris, P. 1974. *Loss and Change.* London: Routledge & Kegan Paul.
Parkes, C. M. 1979. "Evaluation of a Bereavement Service." In *The Dying Human,* eds., A. de Vries and A. Carusi. Ramatgan. Israel: Turtledove.

Part II

Experiences of Grief and Bereavement

8

Facilitation of Mourning after a Natural Disaster

Ann S. Kliman

What we have learned about intervention following a natural disaster is readily applicable to what we have learned in the facilitation of mourning with individuals, families, extended families, and communities. Lindemann (1944) was the first investigator to systematically study grief reactions to a mass disaster, following the Cocoanut Grove fire in Boston in 1940. Hundreds of people were killed or hurt and thousands suddenly and unexpectedly became horrified bereaved mourners. Two groups of victims were defined: the direct victims—those who were burned, trampled, and killed—and indirect victims—the families and friends of the direct victims.

When our soldiers entered the concentration camps of Europe in 1945, we learned more about the concept of victimization than any of us have been able to integrate, even today. Then, more than at any other time, we learned that, perhaps, there is a third set of victims. These victims, whom I have learned to designate as the "hidden victims," are all of us. Included among them, of course, are the community caregivers—those who, by training, discipline, and experience, provide human service. When a natural disaster strikes, these hidden victims become visible.

When Hurricane Agnes struck Corning, New York, a 40-foot-high flood swept through the city, killing 18 people, hospitalizing hundreds of others, displacing thousands, and causing several hundred million dollars worth of damage. When a triple-funneled tornado swept through Xenia, Ohio, in 1974, a swath of land 1 mile wide and 7 miles long was devastated. Studying what occurred at these scenes and on the actual locations of these phenomena, I found that a natural disaster, despite the minutes, hours, or even days of warning preceding it, is rarely confronted as a reality by those who have survived it. This kind of denial is present even in those communities where disasters recur approximately every 20 years, such as in Corning, New York; the floodlands throughout the United States; or the hurricane zones along the Gulf of Mexico. Natural disasters occur frequently and predictably, but people are not prepared for them.

I went both to Corning and to Xenia to introduce therapeutic measures that would facilitate the recovery of those who had survived. Corning represented a massively extended family. The community was essentially intact, productive, and well organized. Although it spanned many social, economic, and educational levels, it was unique in that most of the population was employed by the Corning Corporation, in contrast to the Appalachian mountain folk who lived on the outskirts of the city proper. Quite a few hours of warning had preceded the disaster, for the hurricane had already been reported elsewhere, and flood waters were building up. However, the dams, dikes, and levies, which had been examined by Army engineers six months before and found to be intact, were, in fact, not. When the flood waters hit Corning, no one was prepared. Everyone acted as if an unpredictable and inescapable bolt of lightning had struck.

In Xenia it was quite different; there were only a few moments of warning. Xenia, unlike Corning, was a thoroughly integrated community racially. An extraordinary number of well-educated people lived there. Seven colleges and universities circled the city itself, ranging in attitudes from those at Antioch, which was still considered to be a radical college, to those at a number of basically fundamentalist and conservative religious colleges.

I was called on for crisis intervention in both instances. A college student, my son was studying sociology and had Toffler's book *Future Shock*. Toffler stated that there should be a center for preventive psychiatry in every community and that not one existed in the entire 50 states. Outraged, because our center had existed since 1965, my son called us and said, "You'd better write a note to Toffler."

We agreed.

When he came home for his summer vacation, he discovered that neither his father nor I had written that note to Toffler, and so he did so. Toffler received it four days later—one day before the disaster. When the hurricane and flood hit Corning, on June 23, the chief pyschologist at the Corning Glassworks called Toffler and asked, "You wrote a book on 'future shock,' but what do you know about after shock?" Toffler responded, "Not much, but I received a letter yesterday." Several days later, I arrived in Corning.

Essentially, I had one function, but it was not to do direct treatment of people who were psychologically ill. They were not psychologically ill; they were victims—direct, indirect, and hidden. My job was to be a facilitator. I helped to resensitize, reorganize, and reeducate people to normal, healthy, adaptable reactions to loss—whether it was of a loved (or hated) human being, a home, a job, a history, or self-esteem. A community that has been stricken by a disaster is severely and sometimes shockingly demolished. This does not mean that individuals and groups within that community cannot function. Perhaps one of the most distinctive reactions of community caregivers, no matter what their discipline or their orientation, is to take over the functioning of people suffering from loss—of a human being, an object, or a part of their lives. It is seductive to arrive and do good: to take over, to protect, to nurture, to make decisions for people, and to feed pap. Yet there is no more disruptive way to revictimize victims than to give them the message that they are helpless, that they cannot cope, or that the situation is too terrible for them to face.

One of my harder jobs in both Xenia and Corning was to help the adult community function responsibly. It was important to return the children and the elderly to their communities even if their homes were gone and they had to live in a trailer, a park, or a friend's apartment. Is there ever a time in human experience in which families need so desperately to be together than when their lives and their environments are disrupted catastrophically? What kind of help do we often give to the most vulnerable—not necessarily the weakest—in our population? When we isolate them emotionally and geographically, when we do not allow them to cope and function, to do work, and to turn from a passive, victimized position into an active, coping and growth-promoting one, we are not helping.

We see this on every level. A member from the Department of Housing and Urban Development, from the Red Cross, from the police department, from the clergy, from the hospital, from the Visiting Nurses Association will come in and say, "Now, my dear, don't worry; we'll take care of things for you." Physicians also get trapped, not out of malice or stupidity, but out of the intensity of their own pain. Like widows or widowers, the members of a demolished community are suddenly put on a regimen of amphetamines, barbiturates, and tranquilizers to ease the emotional pain. You can't sleep? Take a pill. You have a hangover from the pill you took the night before? Take an upper. You start shaking when you look where your house used to be? Take a tranquilizer. In investigating with the pharmacists in both communities, I found that the prescribed use of all amphetamines, barbiturates, and tranquilizers increased more than 600 percent after a disaster. To my knowledge there has been no systematic study of the gentle drugging of the bereaved, but my experience tells me this is done in a similar fashion.

Professionals and researchers have questioned whether or not it is advisable to intervene at the time of acute loss, whether or not those who are acutely and suddenly and horrifyingly bereaved are in a state of shock, essentially in a stage of denial. Too many have concluded that there is no way we can intervene. I suggest that their conclusions are untrue and their attitude disruptive. When I talk about intervention or facilitation, I am not talking about bringing a patient or client into the office and saying, "Well, now I know you have lost your son, your grandmother, your home, your job. You must be severely upset, so let's deal with the problems of avoidance, denial and repression." This is an unrealistic approach. We do not know what any individual mourner or grief-stricken person is feeling. No matter how experienced or how educated we are, we know only overviews and generalities. We presume that there are intertwining stages of mourning and grief. People move back and forth among them, but we do not know what any one individual is feeling at any given time. Nor can we afford to assume that we do know. A very harsh and embarrassing lesson was taught me by an 11-year-old child with whom I was working following the sudden and mutilating death of his father. I was trying to connect for him what he had been telling me about his rage, which had been displaced onto his sister. I said, "You know, Jimmy, I think that Jane isn't the person you're really angry at. Do you really believe your sister deserves this kind of anger?" This was a two-pronged error, for one never tells somebody what he should or shouldn't think. This was a pretty tough little kid, and he said, "Kliman, you're assuming." He wrote the word "assume" on a piece of paper, drew a slash after the second "s" and then another slash after the "u." Then he underlined this by saying, "When you assume, you make an ass outa you, and you make an ass outa me." He was right. But how often do professionals assume that they know the quality, the specificity, the depth of the mourning, the grief, the rage, the sadness, or the loneliness?

There is only one way to know: not by being active, but by being able to listen and by listening and occasionally asking an open-ended question that carries no judgmental value. Then we can hear where that person is. We can hear where that community is. This is true not only in terms of one-to-one work. Often I work long days. Like anybody else, I get tired, frustrated, irritated. I have learned that, to do the work I do, dealing primarily with the horrors of life, I must be able to acknowledge how I feel about what I do and be able to share those feelings with other people. I meet for an hour and a half every week with my staff, not only to supervise, not only to discuss techniques, not only to discuss individual cases, but also to share our feelings about the work we do—we who work daily with dying people, mutilated people, raped people, fire victims, tornado victims, battered wives, and even battered husbands. Often we are not proud of our feelings. But we accept them.

Before I went to Xenia, I tried to learn a bit about the place—as I generally do when I am going to a new community. I like to know where I am going and what the people are like: How do they think? What are their orientations? What are their ideals? What are their prejudices? How does the community function? What is the power system? Who are the people who feel disenfranchised? I learned a great deal about Xenia: that it is in Green County, that Green County is a bastion of Republicanism (more than 90 percent of the county normally votes Republican). I think that only the Antioch community does not.

Tornadoes and floods do terrible things, not only to the living, but also to the dead. Because in both communities cemeteries were disrupted and torn apart, the work of the funeral directors and the Public Health Service and the volunteers was overwhelming, as they tended to and buried the dead while caring for the living and the dying. At 11:30 one night, after I had been going from group to group in Xenia, working with the school system, working with the funeral directors, during a long, hard, irritating day, I was not sure that I was going to be able to do much. My self-esteem was low, and I fear my judgment was not very good either. I had been discussing with the groups the fact that, as dreadful as this tornado had been, it did offer them an opportunity. This was a community in transition, a community planning a huge renewal project within the inner city and the extended city. Their options were now wide open. It was no longer a matter of "shall we rebuild?" "we *must* rebuild." Someone stood up and said, "President Nixon was here yesterday [April 9, 1974]; he got into his car in front of the airport and said that this was the worst disaster he had ever seen." Unthinkingly (and this was during the height of the Watergate scandal) I responded, "He's right; it's the worse disaster he's ever seen for which he has not been personally responsible." I felt that I had destroyed the entire project right there. Interestingly, I had not. What I heard from the group—and I am sure that I would not have heard this before their community had been virtually wiped out—was one voice saying, "He raped us." Someone else said, "We trusted him, and he betrayed us." People were angry and were able to express anger, sometimes quietly, sometimes very sadly. Indeed, that was an option for them—not only to have the feelings of anger that are inevitable when things we care about are taken away from us but also to take that anger and direct it and use it in a productive manner so that something better than had existed before can be gained. The anger directed thinking toward new options and opportunities.

The ancient Chinese knew this. The word for "crisis" in ancient Chinese is made up of two ideograms—one for danger, the other for opportunity. As hurt or frightened or lonely or wary or angry as we may be at any time of acute loss, we do have the opportunity to rebuild, constructively and productively. Although we can never replace a lost human being—or even a lost photograph album—we can use what we have left. This is true if we have cancer or if we have a simple hangnail. We all have a life to lead. How we lead it is up to us generally.

It is our job as caregivers to let people know what opportunities still exist. It is not our job to direct them into opportunity A, B, or C, to tell them what they should think or should not think. It is our job to facilitate and to be able to bear with the frustration and the pain when we cannot do anything—and to enjoy the pleasure and the gratification when we can.

References

Lindemann, E. 1944. "Symptomatology and Management of Acute Grief." *American Journal of Psychiatry* 101 (September): 141–48.

Toffler, A. 1970 *Future Shock*. New York: Random House; paperback ed., New York: Bantam, 1971.

9

Grief and Bereavement in the Military

Carl T. Noll

I am not a psychiatrist, a psychologist, a clergymen or a medical doctor. Yet, for the past 30 years, a common denominator has existed in our respective careers or professions. That common denominator is death. I am not involved with the dying and I do not counsel the bereaved; I am involved with the dead. Because of this, I am intimately identified with the bereaved and with grief.

I present no scholarly treatise or learned dissertation. I have really not had to do any particular research other than to check the accuracy of some figures or statistics. Rather, I describe some of my experiences with respect to the death and burial of military personnel and veterans. Some of the factors that aggravate grief and, in a sense, add a different dimension to grief and bereavement should be apparent. These causative factors have a uniqueness that can derive only from the military circumstances related to death, grief, and bereavement. They add distinguishing features to the grief of survivors of young men killed in warfare and of veterans of past wars. Grief can be rekindled or prolonged by those events that precede or follow the funeral.

During World War II when soldiers, sailors, and airmen met their death overseas in action against the enemy, their bodies were buried in temporary military cemeteries. The number of Americans killed in that global conflict was about 358,000. Many servicemen were lost at sea, and their bodies were never recovered. About 280,000 were found and buried overseas. Of these, at least 10,000 could not be identified. After the war, our government undertook an enormous project called the "World War II Dead Repatriation Program." The next of kin of men killed abroad were given the opportunity of leaving their loved ones permanently interred in an American cemetery overseas or having them brought back home for burial. The majority wanted them home, and so the enormous task confronting our government called for the disinterment and return to the United States of 171,000 remains.

My first exposure to real grief and bereavement occurred at this time. In 1946, I had just returned from service in China as an infantry officer and was ready for release from active duty. Someone in the Pentagon discovered from my records that before the war I had studied mortuary science. I was asked if I would help initiate this tremendous repatriation program. I agreed to accept this assignment and become a senior participant in all planning phases, playing a key role in the execution of the program.

In regard to the World War II dead, it is important to remember that the fathers and mothers, the families of these young men, had already experienced the acute grief attendant on their first hearing the shocking news of the death of their loved one. Many men had been killed in the early years of the war, 1942 or 1943. For the parents and spouses of these men, a number of years had elapsed by the time the first remains were returned home, beginning in the fall of 1947. It is not my intention to imply that their grief had not continued in these intervening years. Grief varies from person to person in terms of its duration and intensity. Therefore, for many, grief had abated or diminished considerably.

What occurred was the following in many instances: a son had been killed, for example, in 1942; his parents were notified almost immediately and informed later about the place of his burial overseas; then six years later his body was brought back home. All sorts of official contacts or communications had to be made with the family, of necessity. But the process caused a rekindling of grief that had subsided over the years. That moment of greatest anguish struck on the day the body arrived home. Then the grief was renewed fully. There was often a wake at the funeral home, a church service with an emotional eulogy, and organ renditions of traditional hymns. Then, the scene changed to the cemetery and the gravesite. The flag-draped casket was placed in position. The committal service began, and prayers were said. Three rifle volleys fired by a veterans group or some servicemen from a nearby camp or base broke the solemn stillness in the cemetery. A lone bugler played "Taps" a short distance away. The flag was folded with precision and presented to the grieving mother or father. And now the grief that we knowingly, but unavoidably, had caused to be renewed reached the same intensity that prevailed when that first telegram had been received back in 1942, the telegram that started off: "The Secretary of War desires me to express his deep regret that your son. . . ."

This program, which ended on December 31, 1951, affected millions of Americans. For each dead serviceman brought back there were probably 15 or more family members who felt acutely the sorrow and heartaches of grief. For each surviving family member the grief was renewed, certain to endure for many more months before it would begin to wane. Extended to the friends of the deceased and repeated in all the various communities in every state in the Union, the program initiated collectively what could be called the bereavement of a nation.

In my position with the Memorial Division of the Department of the Army, I could not help but be aware of the fact that this program had rekindled the dormant grief of these families. The fact that almost 5,700 of these reburials were made at Arlington National Cemetery near Washington increased my awareness of what was happening. That cemetery is very close to where my office was at that time, and I had many discussions with the cemetery superintendent and with the chaplains serving there while this repatriation program was taking place. I also attended a number of the interments at Arlington.

In most instances we had a situation that almost never exists with civilian deaths and burials. Many of the families had agonizing doubts that the remains in the casket before them were, in fact, the remains of their son, or their father, or their husband. We were dealing with skeletal remains, and so there was no such thing as an open casket or even a private viewing. They could trust only in the government's assurance that it was their loved one. We received many letters demanding to know how we had established the identity, what our proof was.

Adding further to their grief and creating problems for us in dealing with it was the matter of the personal effects of the deceased. In the military, when a man dies, his personal belongings are recovered as quickly as possible, inventoried, recorded, and safeguarded for ultimate return to the next of kin. When the mother or father or wife received this package, the grief was renewed. Just the sight of these belongings would often bring about the collapse of grieving parents. When they had regained their composure and had time to think about it more calmly, they would start recalling possessions that had not been returned to them. Where was the wrist watch his grandmother gave him when he graduated from high school? Where was the black onyx ring he had bought with his own money, earned by working in the grocery store on Saturdays? Under these conditions their grief worsened, and frequently it turned to bitterness. The least the government could do, they said, was see to it that everything that their son had was returned to them. Our involvement in this phase of their grief took the form of responding to the letters asking why some treasured item was missing. This was difficult to do, for we could not suggest to them, for instance, that their son might have pawned his watch while on a weekend pass or that he might have taken off his ring for some reason and lost it. We had a small claims procedure established to provide for reimbursement, but a monetary payment could never alleviate grief or remove rancor or bitterness. Nor did we expect that it would. Quite often the exchange of correspondence would go on for months.

Dr. Edward Steere, a historian in my office, recorded the following case for inclusion in one of the Army's Historical Publications:

One of the most celebrated and moving operations in the repatriation program involved the return of the four Borgstrom brothers of Tremonton, Utah, to their native soil. The plans for the silent reunion of these four servicemen, who, within a period of six months in 1944, had lost their lives at scattered points throughout the world, attracted nationwide attention.

The first of the four sons of Mr. and Mrs. Albert Borgstrom to give his life in World War II was Clyde Borgstrom, Pfc. U.S. Marine Corps, who died in the Solomon Islands on 17 March 1944. On 22 June 1944, Elmer LeRoy Borgstrom, Pfc. 91st Infantry Division, was killed in Italy. The third brother to perish in World War II, Rolon D. Borgstrom, died on 8 August 1944 in a bombing mission over in Germany. The final tragic blow to strike one American family came with the death of Rulon, twin of Rolon, who succumbed to wounds in France on 25 August 1944. Shortly after word was received of the fourth death, the last surviving son of military age was released from the Marine Corps to prevent further tragedy to a family which had already borne far more than its share of grief.

Elaborate plans were made for a two-day tribute to the four brothers and their family. The reasons for the two-day-rites, according to Col. Leonard R. Crews, who commanded the Sixth Army Escort Detachment, was that "This is the only four Gold Star family on record in World War II. Only the five Sullivan brothers, who were in the Navy and were serving on the same ship when it was sunk, constituted a greater loss to any family.

The Borgstrom boys were in separate branches of the service and in separate theaters of action, making it important that we give them all possible honor."

The two-day event began on 25 June 1948 with the arrival from the Utah Distribution Center of the caskets bearing the four brothers at the Shaw and Rogers Funeral Home in Tremonton, Utah. During the afternoon, the bodies "lay in state." Sentries stood at each casket, representing each of the services—Army, Navy, Marine Corps, and Air Force. One sentry kept vigil throughout the night.

On the morning of 26 June, the solemn funeral service took place in the Mormon church at Garland, Utah. Speaking on this occasion were Gen. Mark W. Clark, Commanding General, Sixth Army; Gov. Herbert B. Maw of Utah; Pres. George Albert Smith of the Church of Jesus Christ of Latter Day Saints; and Clarence E. Smith, principal of the high school attended by the Borgstrom boys. Other high-ranking officers of the four services and dignitaries of the State of Utah attended the event as well as thousands of private citizens. The parents of the deceased brothers received posthumous decorations from the three generals and the admiral present at the rites, including three bronze stars, an air medal, and a good conduct medal.

Following the morning service at the church, the Sixth Army Escort Detachment furnished a luncheon for more than 700 persons at the Garland National Armory. A private dining room was provided for the Borgstrom family and distinguished guests. Following the luncheon, the funeral cortege formed and moved slowly southward to the cemetery. Traffic was diverted all along the route to give the right of way to the long, solemn procession. When the band finally passed through the cemetery gate, the hundreds of on-lookers watched in respectful silence. As the procession approached the canopied gravesite, tears could be seen in the eyes of men and women alike. Behind the band came the four dark olive drab hearses, each bearing the flag-draped casket of one of the brothers. After each hearse were Army, Navy, Air Force, and Marine pallbearers. The rites at the gravesite were brief but impressive. After the caskets had been lowered to their final resting place, the military band marched silently through the cemetery gate. The family and high officials began to leave the rostrum. For the Borgstroms and all of Bear River Valley, a tragic occasion had ended.

While the case of the Borgstrom brothers was atypical, it reflects, nevertheless, the thousands of other reburials where griefing families sat, huddled together, at the gravesite with much of an entire community gathered around them sharing their sorrow and, in a small but meaningful way, reflecting the grief of the nation.

In June of 1950 the Korean War started and again American lives were sacrificed. During this war, however, we achieved something never accomplished before in the history of warfare. When soldiers, sailors, and airmen died, we evacuated their bodies to field mortuaries we had established in combat zones. For those who could not be identified immediately, there were several Central Identification Laboratories in Japan where identity could be established scientifically. After preparation of the bodies, we returned them home— some by air, some by water—to military mortuaries in this country. There they received further preparation, were clothed in a new uniform, casketed, and transported with a military escort to the funeral home or cemetery designated by the next of kin. We did not bury these men overseas. Thus, we precluded the need for another repatriation program. In reality, we had a Current Death Return Program.

During the Korean War, the Army, Navy, and Air Force each had their own mortuaries and took care of their own deceased. However, the Army had the bulk of the work, for of the 33,629 American fatalities in that war, 27,704 or 82 percent were Army personnel. Once again my office had to face the problems of bereavement and grief, but under different circumstances. For the most part we were sending home bodies rather then skeletons. Many of these bodies were in good condition and were considered viewable, although some had to be tagged "nonviewable" because the body had been badly disfigured by an exploding land mine or 20 to 30 days had elapsed since the date of death. There was a recommendation made to the family's funeral director that there would be no open casket in the funeral home. Here is where grief took a new dimension in our program. Often, some member of the family wanted to see that the body in the casket was, in fact, their loved one. Obviously, this had to be avoided, and parents became infuriated. The numbing grief that had come to them less than a month ago with the shattering news of their son's death was now exacerbated by their belief that the Army had sent home to them as the body of their son the body of someone else. Their grief would manifest itself in indignation. They would call our office on the phone or send a telegram. Often, we would have to send someone out to visit with them to explain our identification procedures and attempt to assuage and assure them. Sometimes the family postponed the funeral until the matter could be cleared up and this, of course, added to their grief. As in World War II, we also had the problem of the personal effects—something was missing, where was it, someone had stolen his watch, and so forth.

During the Vietnam conflict, which actually lasted longer than World War II, we lost 57,000 lives. The highest percentage again was in the Army, although the Marines suffered many fatalities. We had several mortuaries in the Far East during that war. By this time we had been able to refine the current death return procedures used for the first time in Korea. As a result, we were able to reduce the time frame between date of death and date of return to the family to 10 days. Two military mortuaries were established in this country to receive these bodies, and all came by air. One, at Oakland, California, took care of those whose homes were west of the Mississippi, and one at Dover Air Force Base in Delaware took care of those from the East.

The grief of Vietnam war bereaved was bitter. There was bitterness toward the United States Government, bitterness against the Army or the Marine Corps or the Air Force or the Navy. Many of the families of these young men who were killed resented their loss because, in their opinion, there was no justifiable basis for this war. They could not say proudly that their sons died gloriously in defense of their country because they did not believe this to be true. Their resentment could be felt in our office. We were identified with the "War Lords," guilty by association. Their grief was characterized by irrationality, and this compounded our problem in dealing with them.

Other situations involving our office caused sorrow over and above that normally experienced. One such involved group burial. This usually found its origin with a multiple-fatality air crash where those on board the craft were either burned beyond recognition or so badly disfigured, dismembered, and comingled that identification of all or most was impossible, even though we knew, by name, who was on the craft. Under such circumstances, all whom we could not identify were returned as a group to this country. We would take the addresses of the next of kin, select a national cemetery as near or as centrally located to the majority of the families, and then hold a group burial service in that cemetery. Many of these took place at our Jefferson Barracks National Cemetery in St. Louis because of its central location. Travel costs would be paid for the next of kin and one other to attend the funeral. Later, a single monument would be erected over the grave and inscribed with the names of all interred at that site. Subsequently, each family would be sent a large photograph of the monument. Under these conditions, the family had a new cause for grief. Their son could not have a normal funeral; he could not be buried close to home; many relatives and friends could not attend the funeral, because of the distance and expense; he could not be buried from his own church; and so on. Unfortunately, little could be done about any of these painful events.

Grief entered my official life in other ways. One of the problems faced was that which would arise when a young man married just before he went overseas. Perhaps after four months he would be killed. He was still his mother's "baby" and had lived with his parents until he went into the service. He was born and raised, for example, in Pittsburgh. But he was stationed at an Army camp in El Paso, Texas, when he met and married this girl. She was from Texas. When he was killed, she was the next of kin and and the one authorized to tell us where the body should be sent. She wanted him sent to El Paso for burial in the national cemetery at Fort Bliss. As noted, she had been married to him for only four months and probably had never met his parents. His mother and father who had raised him and with whom he had lived for 22 years could not have him buried in a cemetery near home where they could visit his grave. They were poor and could not afford the transportation expense to go to El Paso for the funeral. But there was nothing we could do about it. Legally, the young bride was the next of kin, and her wishes prevailed.

When parents were divorced, a fight would arise between the two over the custody of the body and the right to decide where it would be buried and the right to the son's personal effects. It can readily be seen how grief was compounded. As a result of this background, my career became involved finally with the operation of the National Cemetery System. This system of cemeteries, established during and because of the Civil War, had been under the jurisdiction of the Department of the Army until 1973, when it was transferred to the Veterans Administration. At this time I transferred to the Veterans Administration and became the Director of the National Cemetery System. Interments in the national cemeteries involved principally veterans of past wars and their spouses and minor children. Approximately 40,000 burials a year take place.

Here grief is observed in a different light. The veterans are generally older persons, often retired, who die from various causes and who have lived a normal life span, sharply in contrast to the young men in their twenties killed in military action. The deaths of these veterans and their spouses are more readily accepted, for they have lived out their lives. Many have been living with a physical ailment, in a state of failing health. A degree of resignation prevails, and death is more likely to be accepted. Although there are many veterans who are not old, and who die or are killed suddenly, as a group, veterans are older people. With age, death expectancy is greater.

The grief I have observed in the widows of veterans who are buried in our national cemeteries takes the form of what can be called "aggravation grief." These bereaved are easily upset by imperfect conditions relating to a grave's appearance or a headstone; or they are irritated by some cemetery regulations that are contrary to their wishes. Examples of this kind of grief reaction are numerous, but a few are cited here:

After an interment, a grave will sink, possibly as many as 11 times in a span of 20 years. Initially, the sinking is caused by the settling of the soil. Later, the sinkings are caused by decay, the collapse of the outer case and, finally, of the casket itself. Of course, these graves are filled in and leveled as the sinkings occur. But in a large cemetery with thousands of graves, there is no way of knowing when a grave will sink, or where it is when it does. The widow visiting her husband's grave will know. She will be quick to advise us, usually in a letter of complaint, or sometimes in a letter to her Congressman. Similarly, when the grave is filled in after the burial, it is leveled and later seeded or covered with sod. Often there is a period of time when there is no grass on the grave. The widow complains. On Easter Sunday, she places a potted lily plant on the grave. Sooner or later its bloom falls off and the plant dies. Dead flowers or plants are not left on the graves very long, and a month later when she comes to the cemetery and finds the plant gone, she lets us know about it—with indignation.

Widows have asked permission to plant a dogwood tree or some species of bush at their husband's grave. Usually, it is accepted for placement in the cemetery where it fits in with the landscaping plan, but not right at the foot of the grave. These requests are denied and Congressmen receive the complaints.

Situations arise with respect to the government headstones, or gravemarkers that are furnished for the graves of veterans in national cemeteries and in private cemeteries if the widows request them. When a grave sinks, usually the upright headstone sinks or tilts also. The widow sees this before routine cemetery maintenance work can be done, and she is greatly disturbed. Sometimes mistakes are made. Occasionally, the name inscribed on the headstone is misspelled or the date of birth is wrong, or a Christian cross is incised on the headstone of a Jewish veteran. Of course, the widow is furious until the mistake is corrected.

All of these represent valid complaints, but they illustrate the manifestations of grief referred to as aggravation grief. Most of these episodes occur many months—even years—after the interment has taken place. The widow has usually resumed a normal life, with grief abated. However, subliminal grief reveals itself time and time again. Visiting her husband's grave is certain to revive her anguish and grief.

There is no doubt that the loss of a young life as a result of military action invests survivors' grieving with dimensions that differ, if not in their depth, then in their kind. Grief is prolonged or rekindled and expressed in ways that rarely occur when a civilian dies. Those in Government service can relate to these bereaved individuals by demonstrating an understanding of their deep distress and by trying to honor their loved ones in ways that give solace to the survivors.

🌿 10

A Man Came
and Killed Our Teacher

Bruce L. Danto

November 10, 1976, was a cold and snowy day. Early that morning, children rushed to the C School to escape the bitter cold. Once there, they warmed to the heat and excitement of seeing friends and teachers who had prepared to spend the day with them. As was the case with most other days, the 30 children in Mrs. A's room listened to her stories, danced to music, and took in her lesson plan for the day. Then it was lunch time.

As lunch bags were about to be opened, an angry-looking stranger entered the room. He began talking to Mrs. A. She looked frightened, screamed, and shrank away from the man. Suddenly, he pulled out a dark blue revolver and began shooting at her. Room 213 was filled with terrible sounds. Bright red blood spurted everywhere and the teacher slumped forward over her desk. Without a word, the man fled.

In the tumult following the first shot, some children sat stunned and motionless in their seats. Others were catapulted into action. Some ran out of the room. Seven-year-old William dashed two blocks to his home without a coat. Speechless, he sat there on the floor, shaking violently. In the nights that followed, he spoke through his nightmares of that event in Room 213.

Back in Mrs. A's room, the English papers she was about to correct during the lunch hour lay on the desk under her body. In the ears and minds of her 30 pupils, her screams continued to echo off the walls of that room.

This tragic scene was interrupted by Mr. B, the school's principal. Soon after his arrival into Room 213, snow-splashed police cars with their flashing lights and shrieking sirens appeared at the C School. The school filled with police, neighbors who had seen the commotion, and parents of children from all classes who rushed there after receiving notice of trouble. Among those present was Mr. D, Regional Superintendent of the city's public schools. The police immediately established an interrogation room, and frightened children were questioned by a battery of homicide detectives. (Detroit *News*, 1976).

What happened to those children? Had any school staff ever anticipated such a tragedy? What can be done to deal with the nightmarish psychic trauma that such an event can produce for anyone, especially for children?

I believe there is a need to present the facts as they occurred. This is in keeping with the method of process recording familiar to social workers. Process recording reports details of events in the order of their occurrence. The interactions among those persons present are also recorded.

To serve as an aid for any future similar happening, I have written in detail the steps taken to deal with the traumatic effects of an overwhelming horror story.

This is what happened.

In the afternoon, about an hour following the shooting of Mrs. A by her estranged husband, I was returning from Monroe, Michigan, where I had lectured on the management of the violent person. I tuned in the news and heard the story. It left me as shocked as any other listener. For the next two days I followed the news with concern.

On the second day following the shooting, the teacher's estranged husband was accused of the killing and placed in custody.

It was learned that the teacher had just recently transferred to the C School and had changed her name to A in order to hide from her husband because she feared for her life.

Witnesses are vital to convictions. The only witnesses to this particular event were six- and seven-year-old children. These same youngsters, who had been traumatized by the horror of the killing and the death of their teacher, were now facing the fears of testifying in court.

Early in the afternoon on November 11 I received a call from Superintendent D. He asked if I would be willing to meet with his staff as soon as possible to map out a program to deal with the psychological problems that were appearing among the children and their families. I agreed to meet with the staff of the region early the next morning.

At the meeting, Superintendent D, a psychologist, a social worker, and a supervising educational psychologist shared with me some of the problems that had already appeared, for example, the tremendous anxiety of the parents and their children who had witnessed the event, the need for a new teacher to replace Mrs. A, the new room to which the students would be assigned (while the death room was being cleaned and repainted by volunteer parents), and finally, the approach to be used to help the children handle their anxiety and mourning.

I was opposed to advice, given by a social worker present at the meeting, that parents keep their children from talking about the event, watching television, and discussing and hearing news accounts. I believed they needed to talk about it and follow the story so that they could master the event psychologically and maintain the memory within a proper framework of reality. The children needed to straighten out the facts and learn what the police were doing, what the school was doing, and what was happening to the families of the children who had shared the fatal event.

I reviewed what is involved in mourning, for example, memories of the deceased, guilt feelings about not being able to say goodbye, fear of black people in this particular situation, possible fear of men, apprehension that grownups could not protect children from such danger, and the children's fear that a new teacher might suffer the same fate.

I talked with the staff about the need to teach children about death and ways to handle the various stories they would hear about what happened to dead people. Ghost stories and the like usually arise when children are confronted with a death experience.

Because some children had already contacted the social workers and social psychologists through their parents, I felt that I could best be used if I met with the parents, the prosecuting attorney, the police, and the school staff. A meeting was scheduled for the evening of November 17 at the C School. The material that follows represents some detailed notes I made of that meeting.

Meeting at C School, November 17, 1976
There was much anxiety present during this first meeting, both on the part of school personnel and parents. Mr. D opened the meeting and introduced various staff members who would be involved. He then stressed that these

people would be there to help the children; he assured everyone that the children would not be used as "guinea pigs." He introduced me and explained why I had been called in. Because nothing like this had happened before, there were no precedents to follow; therefore, it was felt that my expertise in this area would be extremely valuable. Mr. D also answered questions that parents had regarding the facts of the incident.

Mr. B, the principal of C School, then spoke and tried to clear up any misinformation parents had acquired as a result of newspaper accounts. Mrs. E, the new teacher for this class, was introduced to the group.

The precinct chief greeted us. He had little to add to what had already been said, but he did assure the parents that the police were trying to work cooperatively with them in order to minimize any anxiety the children might have when dealing with the police. The homicide detective, Mrs. F, spoke next and explained step-by-step to the parents what would happen in terms of court proceedings, as well as what would be expected of the children at the pretrial hearing.

Some parents were concerned about the lack of evidence (for example, the missing gun) and the fact that the children had been asked to testify. The parents were mainly concerned about the effects of the court experience on their children, as well as the inadmissibility or inaccuracy of the testimony of the children. In general, the majority of the parents worried that the killer would go free or not be prosecuted to the fullest extent. Some parents also expressed a fear that if the man were released, he would then seek out the children for revenge. Mrs. F reassured the parents that there was substantial evidence against Mr. A and that there were some adults who could positively identify him.

Then I spoke regarding some of the natural and most likely short-lived reactions the children might experience. These reactions could be considered natural for their ages (six and seven) and might have nothing to do with this particular trauma alone: sleep disturbances, clinging and dependent behavior, the need to be alone, bed-wetting, academic problems, reactions to violence on television. In general, these symptoms consisted of regressive behaviors or reactions that directly related to violence and were part of the natural experience of six- and seven-year-old children.

Then I talked about four basic learning needs underlying the management of these children:

1. Learning about death.
2. Learning about how totally unacceptable violence is.
3. Learning about one's responsibilities as a citizen to ensure that wrongdoers are brought to trial.
4. And learning, through the experience of the judicial process, that punishment is a consequence of violent action.

I told the group that these children could benefit from this experience if they were taught to understand it and to integrate it into the broader aspects of living. I explained that participation in the judicial process would also provide them with closure. I stressed the importance of explaining the events logically and rationally in order to serve the needs of the children.

While not emphasizing the trauma of the experience, I pointed out that the children needed to explore and understand why some persons became violent, what death entails, and that they needed to look at both the positive and the negative traits of their teacher so that she would not become deified.

I stated that if the children were to "work through" and integrate this experience, they needed to play a substantial role in the process of mourning. I suggested that the children should have a memorial service that would provide ideas other than a "trip to heaven." This would begin to provide them with closure. This was not done, however, because some parents objected to it.

I then asked the parents how their children were reacting. One parent said that her child (who had not exhibited this behavior before the shooting) was now pretending to shoot other children, using his fingers as a gun. He was one of the children who had been highly anxious after the shooting. I interpreted this behavior to the mother, saying that her child was trying to reverse the nature of the trauma by seeing that when he "shot" people, they did not die.

Another child was reported to be playing policeman almost constantly since the killing. I explained that this child may benefit from acting out the role of a policeman because he was identifying with that part of society that is helpful to others and brings wrongdoers to justice.

Another child had developed a fear of returning to school, began clinging to her mother, and complained of nausea.

Another child, who denied any shooting had occurred, also was clinging, nervous, and had become shy. Other children, like their parents, had fears because the man had not yet been convicted. They too worried that he would return to get them. Some parents thought that the children should not be treated as adults and, thus, should not have to go to court and be required to testify.

There was anxiety that some of the children could not identify the man in the lineup and that, therefore, he might not be found guilty. According to the police, only three out of eleven children positively identified the killer. Again the parents were reassured that three identifications would be sufficient for conviction.

Another group of parents who had fully explained the event to their children said their children were having no problems.

Some parents felt there was an overemphasis on the situation and that the children should forget what had happened. One parent was somewhat hostile about the intervention of the school social work service and the psychological service. He wanted the classroom situation to return to normal so that his child would begin to forget.

I explained that even if a child is *taught* to forget, he in fact does *not* forget; the knowledge is repressed. Thus he keeps the trauma intact, never learning to cope with it. Only by facing the situation directly and dealing with it openly, can he learn to cope with it. And if he doesn't talk about it, he also gets the message that talking itself is dangerous and he never learns to verbalize what he feels.

The purposes of this meeting were to alleviate parental concerns about misinformation gained from newspaper accounts, to familiarize the group with police and court procedures, and to deal realistically with the overall effect on future emotional development of the children. By the end of the meeting, most parents appeared more relaxed and knew better how to respond to their children. Both the parents and the school staff learned about the legal work needed to bring the killer to court and to justice.

Finally, the meeting created an opportunity for me to insert myself as a spokesman and an interpreter who could see both the view of the parents and the view of the police. It allowed me to play a supportive role with the children, as well as with their parents, moving in the direction of aiding the police and the school in their work.

This first meeting was terribly important; it provided an opportunity to accomplish several things. The parents were able to share their concerns with school personnel and the police; in turn, school personnel and the police gained some valuable insights and awareness about how the parents were reacting to the shooting.

These goals were established; we were moving in a positive direction by the end of the first meeting. I was able to help the parents see that specific work and therapeutic tasks were necessary; their response was positive when they were assured that they would be consulted every step along the way. They were told that justice requires community participation, even for children, and that this experience could teach the children a valuable lesson in responsibility.

The reduction of anxiety in the group of parents, teachers, and region staff was obvious; everyone had agreed that working for the children was a possible and important goal.

The police were especially relieved because they did not know how to handle either the anger of the parents or their questions concerning what could be done for their children. The initial hostility felt by the parents toward the police and court was diminished by patient explanations and reassurance.

When I said there would be no fee for my work, all other parties felt more motivated to offer their assistance to these kids. There were fewer complaints about attending evening meetings and extra time involvement for the counseling staff, teachers, and the police officers.

After that most important first meeting, additional contact involved my receipt of notes from the new teacher, Mrs. E, who shared observations of the children. I also received calls from school social workers and psychologists who had problems and questions regarding particular children who had entered supportive psychotherapy with them.

The next meeting with the parents took place on December 15.

Meeting at C School, December 15, 1976, 7:30 P.M.
Superintendent D offered a brief review of the previous meeting and then reintroduced the homicide detective, Mrs. F. She discussed the preliminary hearing, at which time the children had appeared in court and identified the defendant as the killer of Mrs. A. Mrs. F reported on how well the children behaved in court. Some of the parents of those children gave a different version of what happened. They felt that the children were brought into court cold, unprepared for what would take place. They thought the judge talked too rapidly to them, despite the fact that ordinarily he is a low-key and slow-talking man. Those who witnessed the event agreed that the judge and attorneys were kind to the children.

Mrs. F described how the killer was offered a plea of second-degree murder so that it would be unnecessary to have the children appear as witnesses; he would still face a life sentence for the murder of his wife. However, the defendant refused that plea. Mrs. F explained that, consequently, it would be necessary for the children to appear as witnesses. On hearing this, many of the parents were upset about having their children go through the court experience. One parent recounted how she had read that court officers had forced the children to touch the defendant as a way of identifying him. Mrs. F and other parents who had been present in the courtroom stated that the newspaper account was not true. All parties agreed to my urging that the children should be conducted through the court chambers and be introduced to the judge and the attorneys. Also they should be given some explanation of what was ahead for them. From what had been said, it was apparent that some of the children were most anxious about their court experience. One boy was not able to identify the defendant even though earlier he had clearly identified his picture from a newspaper and was able to accurately describe the clothing worn by the defendant on the day of the shooting.

Mr. B, the school principal, called upon the children's new teacher, Mrs. E. He said he wanted us all to see how she had decorated her new room for Christmas. He told us that Mrs. E's car, which had been laden with Christmas decorations for the class, was stolen right in front of the school and was still missing. Mrs. E, a plump, middle-aged black woman, exuded warmth. When she smiled, her face lit up. She described the adjustment of the children to her in terms of seeing how withdrawn they were in the beginning when she took over the class and how their quiet demeanor changed to a more affectionate relationship with her. At the time of this meeting, she felt the children were becoming more outgoing and verbal.

When she ended her presentation, one of the parents commented on how her child had identified the gray suit of the defendant rather than the man himself.

Another parent said that, because some of the children are now afraid of black men, he felt that racism would be used as an issue in the killer's trial; he said the defense would try to show the children were racially biased. Most of the other parents were indignant about this possibility; among those who were indignant were black parents. One black father expressed his resentment toward police officers based on his earlier contact with them and said that racism was a fact of life in the judicial and criminal justice system. His wife cringed as he said that, if his son were to be subpoenaed to appear in court, he would literally ''head for the hills'' rather than have his son face such racism and police abuse.

I said that I could understand his feelings but that he was offering the wrong model for his son and that respecting and trusting the police and the court were important; no parent should use his own bitter feelings as a model for his child. Otherwise, his child would never be free to develop an attitude of trust for any person of whom the parents did not approve. I said further that white parents would have to ensure that their children were not taught racist fears about black people for the same reasons. Most of the parents and school staff agreed with my statement. The black father fell into silence. It was my impression that he too agreed.

Mrs. E responded to my question about reports of the children's talking about ghosts in the school by describing how older children had reached the younger children of this particular class in which the shooting had occurred. She narrated how, at playtime in the school yard, the older ones had told the younger ones all kinds of tales about ghosts. The children returned to class from the playground and discussed how many ghosts must be in their old room where their teacher was killed. Mrs. E had tried to reassure them that there were no ghosts.

I asked her how she felt about leading the children on a tour of the old room so that they could be reassured about ghosts' not being present, see how fearless their teacher was about being in the room, and achieve a memory picture rather different from the blood-filled one they associated with the last scene of their former teacher.

One of the white parents immediately reacted with hysteria. She shouted she wouldn't permit her daughter to go to that room. Another mother indicated that her daughter would certainly not go there, since she did not even want to return to school.

I argued intensely for my plan. I discussed the mechanism of developing an action counter to the phobia as a means of helping the children not feel that contact with a room held magical properties such as a haunted house. I argued how necessary it was for them to have a different memory of the room, one that reflected how life had been brought back into a state of order. Others supported my argument and we were able to sway the reluctant parents. Another person suggested that the basement be included in the tour because the children believed ghosts were there too.

I asked for any observations made by parents concerning dreams and somatic symptoms in their children. All the parents eagerly shared experiences concerning their children who had developed sleep disturbances since the shooting. Some dreamed of ghosts, others had nightmares of being chased by large monsters. Because of the talk about ghosts when the children were playing, some of them remained close to home with a dependent clinging. Some feared loud noises. They were seen covering their ears with their hands when a popping noise was made while they played the game known as "perfection." Some of these children could no longer tolerate acid rock music. One of the children dreamed of his teacher smiling as he had seen her before she was shot. Two children claimed they had seen her eyeball shot out; this was clearly a distortion and not what the autopsy had shown. I was able to interpret how these children were showing signs of the traumatic anxiety and how the dreams helped them to dispel some of that anxiety. The dream of the smiling teacher was an example of denying her fate and an attempt to remember her as a living person.

Some of the children stopped watching television police programs. One of the children followed his grandfather through his house as he was cleaning his gun in preparation for a hunting expedition. Others were more upset about parents' leaving home for the night, even to attend a movie, and they became more dependent and more clinging. In class one day, a child brought in a toy gun and this startled the other children until they were assured that it was only a toy. One child suffered from stomach upset chronically after the shooting.

Another child suffered from dreams of someone breaking into his home. This was partly because the house next door to him was broken into a week after the shooting. The parents of this child spent much time discussing how they had reassured their son that it was safe to live in his home. The father had a gun and would lock up all the windows at night. He made a big production of how safe they were making it. I pointed out to them and all the other parents that, if they made such an elaborate effort to demonstrate how safe it was, they would be indirectly reinforcing the danger the child felt. After all, if it was so safe at home, why all the need to check each night to ensure safety and to have a gun around? The parents understood and agreed to check on security after the children were asleep.

This example illustrated how the general prevalence of violence in the community reinforced the traumatic event of the shooting in class. All agreed that such happenings made all of us feel a little paranoid about being out on the streets or even staying at home. Our anxiety is increased by watching violent television news and entertainment programs and we are feeling more and more apprehensive about leaving the safety of our beds.

When the problem of racial paranoia was raised, I suggested that contact between the children and black male teachers be fostered. In addition, a parent suggested that black female teachers could introduce the idea that they were married to black men who were not violent, who were fathers and cared about little children.

One incident was discussed that involved a white teacher's having lunch with a white child who became frightened when she saw a black male teacher in the gym. I suggested that the black male should have been invited to join them for lunch. Otherwise, the white teacher would be reinforcing the fear of blacks by saying, in essence, "Yes, you're right to be afraid, let's stay away from him."

Feelings of racial paranoia were strengthened by a report of another incident at the school. A black female bus driver had pulled a gun on children in the bus just about three weeks after the shooting of Mrs. A. The bus driver was arrested. The newspapers kept the fact that it had occurred at the C School out of the press account of the event because they rightly felt it would be harmful. But even so, most of the parents of this particular group were aware of the school connection and some of the children were also aware, since they were riding on the bus when this incident occurred. We responded by discussing the potential to globalize about black violence in the community and how important it was for parents to keep cool heads and assure their children that persons who were violent behaved that way because they were disturbed or had serious problems, and not because of any particular racial or ethnic identity. We instructed the parents to point out that black parents were equally concerned.

The meeting ended on a note of caution to parents not to express their anxiety about the need to attend court, if that was required, because that attitude would only make it more difficult for the children.

Following the meeting, Miss G, a school psychologist, and I went into a vacant office and discussed one of her cases involving a child in this group who had developed a school phobia following the shooting. His mother could not handle separation anxiety, because of her own anxiety, and she was unconsciously exploiting the shooting to find a way of keeping her son at home to meet her dependency needs. We discussed management of this mother in terms of bringing the parents into therapy and stimulating superego anxiety by confronting her with how destructive her behavior was for her son, for example, in his development of learning inhibitions, inability to form peer ties to his classmates, and inhibition of the ability to achieve self-sufficiency.

It struck me that the second meeting was attended by fewer parents, either because they thought they could handle their feelings and children without more help, or because we could not offer them any real assistance.

I think that the parents who did not return were those who could handle their feelings and had been assured by the first meeting. Their children were the ones who had made a good adjustment to school and were relatively free of problems in their families. From what was stated at this second meeting, it appeared to me that most of the parents who did attend generally had difficulties in rearing their children. The killing was only one more problem to cope with.

This second meeting provided an opportunity for both black and white parents to express some racist feelings (if they had them) and concerns. My role made it possible to set limits on some of the more impulsive and more hysterical means of coping. Such control of negative behavior reinforced what the school staff was trying to do with the children and made coordination between home and school more effective. This meeting also helped some of the parents understand how thinking about the consequences of decisions was important.

I was not present at the third meeting, held on January 17, 1977. School staff had forgotten to notify me of the meeting until it had already started.

This is the report of that meeting written by Ms. H, a psychologist for the region iv:

C School meeting of January 17, 1977
Most of the same parents were at this meeting as were at the previous one. Mr. D and Mrs. F were both absent because they were attending other meetings. Because of a mixup in communication, Dr. Danto was also absent.

Mr. B informed the parents that Mrs. F indicated that the trial date was scheduled for May 16, 1977. Authorities were trying to have Mr. A plead second-degree murder, but at this point, he was not willing to do so. It was also noted that all the children may have to be subpoenaed, which still concerned many parents.

Mr. B then asked parents what kinds of problems their children were having that appeared to be related to the shooting. One parent indicated that her older boy was having a reaction to the shooting while the younger child, who had been in Mrs. A's class, was adjusting well. She described her older child as "working on an ulcer," but indicated that he was a "nervous" child before this happened. She also said that the child was seeing the school social worker.

Another father described the following incident. He and his son were talking about the United States Tricentennial, and the father said that he would not be around. His son became concerned that his father was going to die now, and the father had to explain that he was not going to die at this point. This father also indicated that his son has been aware of the Gary Gilmore case and felt it was fair to kill Gilmore because he deserved it. In addition, this father said that his son was "jumpy" in his sleep and he wanted to get into bed with his parents, although they do not permit it.

This child was also questioning the concept of death and asking things such as: "Why is the body in the ground?" "Does a person come back to life?"

Mrs. E said that this child is fairly well adjusted within the classroom setting. She said he was fearful about going to the Christmas play because the last one had been based on "A Christmas Carol," and he remembered the ghosts of Christmas past, present, and future. He did, however, attend the play.

Another parent, who along with her child is seeing a psychologist, said that her child had developed a fear of open, crowded places such as parking lots and grocery stores because he was afraid of the killer. Also, this parent said that, for the past several weeks, her child had been wetting his pants at noontime. The pants-wetting was news to both Mrs. E and the psychologist; the mother had not previously mentioned it. But Mrs. E said that this child does not change clothes at noon. Therefore, the mother's reporting seems somewhat suspect.

Mrs. E said that the children have settled down and are doing better. She also related that one boy brought a 22-caliber bullet to school and showed it around. Some children told her about it and she sent the child to the assistant principal. Mrs. E thought the child did this to produce a reaction in the other children. Some children had told their parents about this incident and others had not. Mrs. E also said that while the boys were helping the janitor distribute paper towels to various rooms during the Christmas party, they passed by their old room. Most of the children showed no reaction, while some said, "That's our old room." None showed an adverse reaction.

Another child told his parents that two policemen came in the room and sat down. He said that they were nice policemen. Having the policemen visit was part of the plan to prepare the children for the courtroom setting. This child's response was indicative of the benefits gained from this preparation.

This meeting, in general, seemed to revolve around the same issues as the last one and many of the incidents discussed were similar to the ones discussed at the December meeting. This meeting provided a small group of parents an opportunity to ventilate some of their concerns. They also decided to schedule another meeting closer to the trial date.

It was obvious that the parents of these children were still displaying considerable anxiety about the effect of the shooting on their children and themselves. Furthermore, the children were expressing anxiety about death in general and about separation anxiety concerning the deaths of their parents. This is psychological material that should have been dealt with at this third meeting and that should have been handled in general by discussion in the classroom. Any opportunity to handle it at home or in the school was lost because of the lack of understanding on the part of the teachers and because of my inadvertent absence from this meeting.

One thing became very clear to me: children need an opportunity at home and in school to discuss death, what it means, and its effect on survivors. This is important for all children, especially when they have witnessed a death or when someone they know dies.

The fourth meeting was held at the school on March 16.

Meeting at the C School, March 16, 1977
We did not need a meeting until tonight. Three sets of parents and five single parents were present. Three parents complained about a play Mrs. E

wanted to put on. White parents defended her play, *Children of the World Say Good Morning,* in which greetings were given in different languages. The play was dropped because these three parents did not want their children to see an ethnic image different from their own. Some parents expressed their anger. The objecting parents were the same ones who have been negative to other suggestions, for example, having children watch television reports, talk about the shooting, the death room tour, and the like. Because of the negative response, Mrs. E dropped the play.

I urged that they go ahead with the play and encouraged a discussion that might possibly reverse this decision. I pointed out that, because a majority favored the play, giving in to a negative minority would not serve the democratic process.

A social worker was quick to point out that the democratic process was not an issue here. Rather, it is the responsibility of the teacher to make decisions about programs, since this is the power invested in her by the Board of Education.

A decision was made to continue the play.

Some teachers were upset when the custodian took some boys to bring chairs up to the death room. One teacher worried that parents would complain. However, it was reported that the children were not upset.

A parent asked how to discuss death with a child. I advised a casual approach to reassure the child that death is not magical or necessarily filled with horror. The death of a pet can serve as an example of death as a natural process.

Some of the parents shared concern about their children who are aggressive toward siblings.

Parents were unable to discuss their child's dreams. They were embarrassed at not being able to answer questions that the dreams evoked. They felt that discussing the dreams would reveal their own fears about death.

Some parents were upset by press and news media coverage, and they accused the school of giving their names to the press without permission. Mr. B said that all parents had been contacted, that they had made their own decision about granting interviews, and that those who wanted them called the newspapers themselves. The parent group decided against further news coverage and offered to support a letter to the region stating their decision.

They felt reassured that I would be at the trial with the children to ensure that nothing harmful would happen to them. Proposed was a request for a closed trial and a private trip to court for the children.

In this meeting parents expressed some conservative views about strangers. It was evident that some of the parents were anxious to maintain stability and avoid anything new and challenging. Their behavior was regressive; efforts to control change were redoubled because they did not want more responsibility. Their regressive dependence was expressed in terms of others' taking over and controlling the press and court process as far as their children were concerned. They did not want the pressure and responsibility of making important decisions.

However, there were times when they did support their children. At these times I felt that it was important to offer them my support and assistance, since it was imperative to keep them functional and capable of offering whatever support they could to the children. Obviously they needed some assertive leadership and direction to help them bind the anxiety created by the crisis of the tragedy at the C School.

Meeting at the C School, May 4, 1977
Four sets of parents and three single parents were present. The meeting was chaired by Mr. B. Mr. J of the prosecuting attorney's office attended.

The trial date was set for May 16. The authorities were uncertain about whether the trial could begin as scheduled because a new defense counsel had replaced the old one (who had withdrawn from the case). The meeting was opened for questions.

A parent asked where subpoenaed children would be kept and who would protect them from being badgered by the press. The prosecuting attorney was opposed to bringing them in for a visit to court, but the parents stood firmly for this request. He assured them that they would be with their children and he believed a jury trial would be waived. The group wanted me to be present at the trial and the prosecutor agreed. Parents were concerned about how much school would be missed. They wanted to know if the children who did not actually see the killing would have to participate in the trial. I explained that the children would have to appear when the people's case was presented and they would miss very little school. Secondly, I presumed that the defense would opt to prevent too many kids from testifying, since their reaction of fear of the defendant would adversely affect the jury.

One parent raised the question of how court personnel talk to children. There was concern that the court reporter had obscured a child's view of the defendant at the preliminary hearing. I cautioned parents to play down the protection and preparation of their children for the trial. A teacher broke the tension by saying that, while the adults were expressing so much anxiety about the upcoming trial, the primary concern of the children was how each would spend the $12 each was to receive for being a witness!

Vocabulary was discussed, and it was pointed out that blacks and whites sometimes use different terminology. It was stressed that both the court and the police should make sure that the children understand the words being used, and when colors were being used for description, it should be verified that the child actually knows colors.

Again, the parents expressed worry about whether the killer could be identified and consequently convicted because most of the children were unable to recognize him.

At the time of the shooting, some were so frightened that they immediately repressed what they had seen. Some were in a part of the room where they could only see his back. Some heard the shot and immediately closed their eyes and covered their ears. There was the one boy who ran out of the room and all the way home. In fact, there were only three children who could accurately describe Mrs. A's killer.

I reassured the parents that the three identifications would be sufficient for conviction.

I commented on how the children can have positive feelings about the act of identifying the killer if they understand that they are helping to bring a wrongdoer to justice. One parent told how her children had witnessed a holdup in a pet store. They saw this happen with other witnesses who testified against the robber. The children saw that, even though the witnesses had testified, they were not harmed. They saw that, despite their fears, the best thing did happen: the robber was convicted and the witnesses were alive and well. They learned that their being fearful did not mean that bad things would happen, and they also learned how to cope with their own fear.

Many parents were upset by stories in the press about their children. They objected to the press's taking pictures of the children.

There was some concern about the children's home addresses' being available to the defense and, therefore, to the defendant. One parent wanted assurance in writing that, if future problems were to occur because of the availability of their addresses, the Board of Education would offer their services. Mr. D reassured them.

A parent asked, "How can we say things will be okay? How can we help our kids to overcome trauma?"

I responded that we cannot tell them that disasters will not happen. We cannot always prevent them. But what we can say is that there will always be supportive persons who will help them work things out. This is what they needed to hear.

One mother revealed that her son had an asthma attack after the shooting. Another mother reported that her son urinates frequently in school and at home. Another child does not want to leave Mrs. E and is also sleeping now with seven dolls.

I explained that such behavior is normal for their age and is very possibly unrelated to the trauma. I cautioned them to guard against assuming that all such behavior is a reaction to the killing. I pointed out that these children are at an age when they are feeling tense and insecure about a number of things in their lives.

At this meeting, the parents were showing more anxiety. Although they mobilized forces to come up with some practical ideas on how best to handle their children in court, they were still very tense and looking for direction. Their need for psychological support from those of us working with them was strikingly apparent. From the questions they asked, it appeared that they were almost obsessed with the traumatic experience of their children.

Since almost all problems regarding their children were seen by these parents as being an outgrowth of the killing, it was important to point out that their children had other sources of anxiety beside the shooting of their teacher. Their request for assured counseling help was an expression of hope that they would not be abandoned. It was associated with marked feelings of dependency that had been generated by their regressive reaction to anxiety. It was of concern that the parents' problems with anxiety might spill over and reinforce the anxiety and fears in their children.

Before turning to the final aspect of this process—the trial itself—I would like to discuss some of the observations of the children made by school personnel.

I had asked staff to keep notes and observations about the children so that we could monitor what was happening on a week-to-week basis. As early as November 22, 1976, notes were kept.

Following are brief statements relative to the progress and behavior of Mrs. E's class as presented to me by Mrs. T:

Monday, November 22, 1976
Today was court day and ten children were absent. K wet his pants on the playground at lunch time. He was very upset by this. He said the aides wouldn't let him come back into the building. The class was a little restless after lunch, and so I had them rest with the lights off and played soft music. For some reason they were watching the door.

Tuesday, November 23, 1976
Five children were absent in the morning and four were absent in the afternoon. K was home ill. I do not know if this has anything to do with the wet pants or not. M, who is a hot-luncher, wanted to go home for lunch. She was crying because she saw a black male teacher in the gym. I let her eat lunch with me. She was okay then. N's mother came over after lunch. Someone knocked N down at lunch time. The mother started crying, but soon stopped after a little "t.l.c."

Wednesday, November 24, 1976
No problems today. Seven children were absent in the morning; five were absent in the afternoon.

Thursday and Friday, November 25 and November 26, 1976
Thanksgiving vacation.
I should add that I also received a Form 657, which is a request for social worker or psychological service, from one of the mothers requesting that

Miss P, school psychologist, see her son U "regarding the incident at C School." At this time I do not know the concerns of the mother, but I will contact her and obtain further information and see that her request is followed up immediately.

January 31, 1977 (Monday)
Eight children were absent. R was sent home at 11:00 A.M. because he was ill. He had told Mrs. S that he was in Mrs. A's room. He has called me Mrs. A several times. There were no other problems.

Tuesday, February 1, 1977
Five were absent. T brought in a book called *Gus and the Baby Ghost,* which he wanted me to read to the class. U became very upset and said I wasn't supposed to read stories like that. He said that some of the children might have bad dreams. T said that Mrs. A was in the ground. V said that she wasn't in a casket at all, and some people were not put in caskets. W said that they were burned in an oven through a door, but Mrs. A was on a cloud in the sky. Everyone wanted me to read the ghost story. I could tell that some were afraid, thinking the worst about the book. I didn't read it, because I didn't know how the parents would react when the children told them I had read a ghost story in class. They all joined in telling of ghost stories on television and in the movies. I let them talk it out and then read to them from the book *Chinese Fairy Tales.*

Patrick knows some sort of "dirty" poem about his mother. He was saying it to the boys during math time. I removed him from the group and told him not to repeat it.

Wednesday, February 2, 1977
R repeated the "dirty" poem he was saying yesterday at lunch time. I had Ms. S talk with him. Two children were absent. No other problems. U is working extra hard; he wants to read to me several times during a day.

Thursday, February 3, 1977
Four were absent. No problems. X kept his head down.

Friday, February 4, 1977
Three absent, no problems. X kept his head down most of the morning. He can do the work, but he does not seem interested. I talked to his mother last week about this problem. She said he was ill with a cold. He didn't make a valentine for his mother during the art period today.

From the observations made by Mrs. E, it was plain to see that some of the children were still expressing anxiety about the shooting and the loss of their teacher two months after the event. One youngster was misidentifying his new teacher as the dead teacher.

Most of the children were discussing ghost stories despite being assured that there are no such things and that, therefore, the death room had no ghosts. It was apparent that they needed to discuss their fears openly. Their new teacher, Mrs. E, wisely let them deal with these fears in the group setting. She used the techniques of management that we had discussed in the evening parent meetings, as well as during interim meetings and phone consultations. The school, the parents, and the children were indeed fortunate in having such a sensitive teacher and staff.

From Mrs. E's notes of February 1, when she repeated the imaginings of the children about what becomes of a person who has died, it can be seen that fear of death and cremation was present independent of the death of Mrs. A.

Out of Mrs. E's experience using the C School trauma as an opportunity to ventilate feelings and learn about death, we see that the subject of death can be aired safely and openly.

The unfortunate aspect is that there has been no sensitivity on the part of the Board of Education in recognizing the need to institute a policy regarding death.

Before the trial, an unfortunate conflict occurred. I had been planning to be available for the trial. Arrangements had been made and approval received for me to be with the children during their court appearance. The children had expressed a wish to meet me, for there had been much publicity about my work with a task force to capture a child killer who had been at large.

It was planned that my meeting with the children was to take place on the morning preceding the trial. But there always seemed to be a postponement of the trial. Finally, when the day came for the trial to get under way, I was leaving for meetings in Helsinki and Moscow. I never did make it to the trial.

However, I had talked with Ms. H, one of the psychologists from the region, and we went over procedures for helping the children through the trial. I had advised protecting them from the press and television media, which had been so uncooperative. They had persisted in following the children to and from school, asking them questions concerning their feelings about the "killer," reminding them of their terror, and then taking pictures of them in a frightened state.

We decided to have the psychologist refuse to permit interviews or pictures of the children. They were to be kept in a room to which the media could not gain entry.

The parents were permitted to remain in the court, separate from their children but within their view, so that each could reassure the other. It was agreed by the judge and attorneys that care would be exercised in how the children would be questioned and that Ms. H would be able to caution them openly if she felt there were psychologically harmful or stressful questions or comments being made. The children were taken to the courtroom in advance of the trial. They met with the attorneys and the judge and saw where they would be seated. They used the microphone so that it would be familiar to them.

Here is Ms. H's report to me about this pretrial experience:

Report on the C School Incident, July 29, 1977
by Ms. H, region psychologist
Prior to the court date, most parents became anxious about how the children were going to react and the procedures that would be used for having the children testify. The anxiety the parents felt appeared to be proportionate to the anxiety they had initially experienced after the shooting. As a result, one parent spoke to the prosecuting attorney shortly before the trial date and asked that his child be excused from testifying. He felt that the court experience would produce much anxiety in the child and would be detrimental to his development. In some respects, the court date had heightened the child's anxiety and more regressive behavior was noted. In addition, some paranoid tendencies were noted; for example, the child wanted to listen to every newcast regarding the kidnapping of the children in Holland and was afraid this would happen to him.* The prosecuting attorney excused the child from testifying because his testimony was not crucial to the case.

On the trial date the parents and children were sequestered in a large room, away from the media. Here they waited until taken down in groups of five to the witnesses' waiting room. Many of the parents appeared anxious regarding procedures, the media, and how the children would react. Mrs. E, Mr. B, Mrs. Y, the counselor, and I were there. The parents and children tended to rely on the support from peers more than on our support, with the exception of that of Mrs. E.

The children brought pop and candy with them, as well as activities to do; for the first hour or so they were fairly well behaved. As the day wore on, however, the children became bored. Most of them displayed an appropriate amount of anxiety; they did not seem preoccupied with testifying. It appeared that the field trip was beneficial to them because they knew what to expect (which may have reduced their anxiety). Most of the children did not cling to their parents but interacted instead with their peers.

The children who were highly anxious appeared to have parents who were also highly anxious. I felt that much of the parents' anxiety was transmitted to the children. These children appeared preoccupied, clung to parents, or began to feel ill. Some of the older girls (eleven years) appeared the most anxious. Perhaps it was because they were aware of the event's implications. In general, the older the child or the more anxious the parent, the more anxiety the child appeared to display.

---

* Terrorists had entered a school in Holland and held the children hostage. They were eventually released unharmed.

As stated before, when the time came to testify, the children and their parents were escorted through a back passage to the witnesses' waiting room. This was done in order to avoid contact with the media. Mrs. E and Mr. B were in the waiting room in case the children needed any reassurance. Although I was not in the waiting room, from what I gathered, the atmosphere was tense, and at this point, most of the children's anxiety began increasing.

The parents and Mr. J escorted the children into the courtroom. The parents were allowed to sit at the prosecutor's table facing their children. The judge then spoke to the children, emphasizing the need for telling only what they saw. The judge explained the concept of truth to the children in concrete terms they could understand and tried to reduce any anxiety they might have. The children were then questioned by the prosecution, and at this point, many were visibly anxious. When a child positively identified Mr. A, the child was cross-examined by the defense attorneys. These children displayed a great deal of anxiety at this point, some became confused, and some began to cry because of the defense attorney's implication that they were lying. During the questioning, a few of the mothers also began to cry.

Three older children also had been subpoenaed to testify: one boy and two girls. The boy handled himself quite well, even under intense cross-examinations. The two girls (who were sisters) were highly anxious and began to cry. Although they had seen Mr. A, they had difficulty identifying him or remembering details of the event.

In general, it appeared that most of the children had difficulty remembering the details of the event. They had repressed much of what they had seen or felt. Other children appeared to have distorted the objective facts of the shooting.

When they were through testifying, the children were allowed to go home. Again, they were escorted through a back passage out of the building in order to avoid contact with the media.

In general, most of the parents and children handled the court experience well. Children and parents, however, who evidenced high anxiety levels prior to the trial appeared to have the most difficulty. It was felt from talking to these highly anxious parents that much of their anxiety was due to a misperception and distortion of the objective situation. These feelings and misperceptions, therefore, were passed on to their children. Parents who were low in anxiety appeared to have a more realistic perception of the situation and thus passed this on to their children. One overall conclusion I came to was that the parents' reaction to the shooting had a significant influence on their child's reaction—which tended to mirror their own.

From Ms. H's report, it was clear that anxiety ran high for many parents and their children; 30 children had been witness to the traumatic situation and few were scarred. Of those anxious as the time for trial approached, there was ample clinical evidence that these parents and their children had problems arising from causes other than the trauma itself.

To what extent was my absence at a critical time a factor in the failure of some of the parents to cope more effectively with their anxiety? This question is undoubtedly hard to answer, but it should be asked. An important support that had been promised was removed from them at a time when they needed it. This was unfortunate. None of us had anticipated that the trial would be postponed and then rescheduled to a time that was in conflict with the international meetings to which I had already commited myself.

What would I have done if I had been present? I know that I would have done everything possible to urge that the child who had been frightened of the hostage situation in the Netherlands be at the trial. To have permitted him to remain at home at such a crucial time was to encourage him to run from a source of anxiety and to develop a direction of flight from fear. Such a decision might well be costly to this child. Almost everyone knows that, following an auto accident, the driver of a car is urged to master the trauma by driving again. Most people would not urge him to stay at home and give up driving.

This same principle applies to children who develop school phobias. They should be handled firmly, and one should insist that they go to school. They must, if necessary, even be dragged to school because school attendance is vital to overcoming school phobias.

The child who feared going to the trial should have been treated in this same manner. He should have been forced to attend the trial. This is the only way he could have overcome his phobia.

What about the parents themselves being at the trial? Did it help or hurt? I think that it helped neither the parents nor their children. I think it would have been better not to have had the parents there. Some of them wept in court as their children cried. Such behavior did not lend support to their children at a time when they needed it. In their general living situations, these same parents failed to lend support to their children. This could be seen in the pretrauma histories of the families. Their presence would not be permitted if I were to be involved again in a similar experience. It would have been better if the parents had waited for the children in the waiting room upstairs or outside the court.

Justice triumphed. Mr. A, the estranged husband and killer of Mrs. A, was convicted of second-degree murder. The children who were witnesses made their appearance in court and were safe. Everyone connected with the case sighed with relief as summer vacation got under way. There was no more murder trial to anticipate. It was all over.

The small group of teachers, administrators, social workers, psychologists, and I had never been through such an experience. No guidelines had been laid down by either the experiences or the theories of others. Although most of us feel good about what we did, it would be fair to say that it may take many years before we get to see how successful we were in terms of the growth and development of the children who saw their teacher killed.

After the C School event occurred, *Clinical Psychiatry News* (1976) carried a story about 50 children in Elmhurst, Illinois, who witnessed a fatal stabbing of a father by his son on May 3, 1976. The killing happened as the elementary school children were on their way home for lunch.

A psychiatric social worker was called in to consult with the school counseling staff in regard to the psychological management of the children. He advised the teachers that the children should be encouraged to express their feelings about their obviously traumatic experience through art as well as through verbalization. Small group psychodramas were staged; he felt that, in this way, fantasy could be cut away and the children would be able to stick to reality.

Parents were involved, and within 36 hours, a PTA meeting was called. The social worker explained how their children's feelings should be handled and how parents could assist their children in dealing with angry feelings. Unfortunately no explanation was offered of why the social worker felt that angry feelings were involved with the homicide. Little, if anything, was mentioned about anxiety and other symptoms of trauma.

The social worker advised against separate child and parent vacations and recommended that, instead, families should be together for the summer because of the experience. He offered no rationale for this advice. Why he felt camp would not be helpful to the kids is unclear to me, since in the C School situation, it was apparent that, on the day of the trial, peer support of one another was a key factor in helping the children bind their anxiety. Peer support proved to be more supportive than anything coming from the parents at the trial.

The Elmhurst report mentioned nothing about working with the court and the police to help the children who were witnesses. Contact to help those parents with actual problems was not discussed.

In my opinion there was nothing in the reporting of the Elmhurst experience that was basically of assistance to us, even though the Elmhurst killing preceded the A killing.

As a result of my experience with the C School event, I feel the following guidelines can be suggested for future traumatic situations involving children who witness a homicide in or around a school. School staff should be used, along with any competent outside consultant skilled in the art and application of crisis intervention management techniques, thanatologic principles, or forensic psychiatry or psychology. Such a consultant should be able to work with lay or parent groups and should have had experience working both with the police and with the court. The consultant should instruct the staff with whom he works about the use of the process recording method to keep records and observations of contact with the children, as well as with their parents and teachers. This person should be available for consultation as needed and should prepare to meet with parents at their convenience. This means at night for the most part.

Parents should be in the decision-making process concerning the policy of voluntary treatment of children and concerning what will be shared with the press in terms of knowledge about what is happening to the children. It is important that the consultant establish a policy with the school staff that ensures that parents are not drawn into the traditional bureaucratic structure in which they are told what to do.

Finally, the consultant should be with the children and/or parents at the time of the trial, when they may have to testify in open court. It would have been helpful in the C School situation if the court had been more cooperative about working out a docket so that I could have been there. But fortunately, the parents and children had been capably prepared, and staff members were there to help offer support and control in an effective and meaningful manner.

Looking back, I see that this tragedy provided an opportunity for various community resources to work together toward helping these children to learn to cope with trauma. In particular, we were able to teach some psychological principles to the court and to the police for the handling of young children in a stressful situation.

In summary, we learned that not all the anxiety expressed was solely related to this one event. We found that there were recurring worries evoking recurring questions. The questions mainly involved anxiety concerning death and mourning. These concerns did not just develop at the time of the killing—they were there all along.

What occurred here points to the need for educational institutions to address themselves to the subject of death. Another important fact to remember is that the children were not the only ones traumatized; we also found that the parents were overwhelmed with anxiety generated by the killing. They felt guilty about not having fulfilled their sociological role as protectors of their offspring. They also suffered from feelings of inadequacy because they were unable to answer many of the questions that their children asked.

The parents also feared that, if the criminal justice system did not find the killer guilty, he might revengefully harm the children. Those expressing the most anxiety were the persons who experienced the most anxiety prior to the C School tragedy. It was undue anxiety expressed by the parents that created undue anxiety in the children; of great significance is the observation that the children who did not cope well had parents who did not cope well. Those children who did cope well had parents who coped well.

The most effective parents had children who were able to identify the killer. Consequently, we might conclude that an effective rearing enabled children to see reality.

We must remember that children are always imitating their adult role models, especially during a crisis. Role models affect others both positively and negatively. Adults in positions of authority are role models for children in their charge as well as the parents of those children. When sensitive parents pattern their behavior after supportive authorities, they reinforce positive role modeling for their children. Teachers, school counselors, and administrative staff must be aware of this enormous effect they have in assigning their own attitudes to others. The police and court personnel also share in the process through their own behavior role modeling.

Finally, I would suggest to the consultant who takes my coordinator position in any similar situation that he or she stress to all adults involved the importance of their behavior. The consultant must always be aware of his or her own importance as a role model, not only for the children, but also for all those adults involved who will in turn serve as role models for the children.

References

"School Fears Teacher's Killing Could Scar Her Pupils for Life." *Detroit News,* November 11, 1976.
"How School Dealt with Children's Trauma of Witnessing Murder." *Psychiatry News,* November, 1976.

11

The Biochemistry of Acute Grief with Regard to Neoplasia

Jerome F. Fredrick

More than a decade ago, Engel (1963) proposed that grief fulfills all the requirements for a disease process. The statistical study of Rees and Lutkins (1967) has underscored the pathology of bereavement as evidenced by the greatly increased mortality rate of grief-stricken individuals as compared with similar groups of nonbereaved persons. The physiologic effects of grief were examined in a preliminary study some years ago (Fredrick, 1971). Recently, the possible suppression of the immune response in the bereaved was explored by Fredrick (1976). The psychoendocrinologic studies of Hofer et al. (1972, pp. 481, 492) have shown that grief causes an increase in urinary 17-hydroxyketosteroids, the end products of corticosteroid metabolism. There seems to be little doubt that grief imposes a stress on the human organism. It seems probable, therefore, that this nonspecific, acute stress imposed by grief results in the secretion of corticosteroids far above baseline levels.

Normally, the synthesis of corticosteroids by the adrenal cortex is stimulated by the adrenocorticotropic hormone ACTH, secreted by the pituitary. The cycle is regulated by a biofeedback mechanism: when the level of corticosteroids circulating in the blood attains a certain concentration, the release of ACTH is inhibited, and hence, the biosynthesis of corticosteroids by the adrenal cortex is reduced to baseline levels. It has been found, however, that the stress of acute grief acts to bring about a rapid, reflex release of ACTH by the pituitary that is relatively independent of the corticosteroid levels in the circulating blood and that this release of ACTH can be only partly inhibited and then only by extremely high levels of corticosteroids (Schreiber, 1974).

The scenario is set for the "oversecretion" of corticosteroids as a direct result of acute grief. With increases in circulating corticosteroids, there is a resultant decrease in the overall immunity. The suppression of the immune response by corticosteroids is well documented both for short-term (Gisler et al., 1971; Folch and Waksman, 1974), and long-term (Hill et al., 1967; Yamada, 1964) periods.

The "immunity" of an organism is the complex result of the interaction of many different factors. Some of these are on the biologic level in that cellular entities are involved and participate directly in the destruction of the "invader," be it a bacterium, a fungal spore, a viral particle, or a transformed (and therefore malignant) cell. Others are strictly on the chemical level (antibody formation in response to antigen stimulation, etc.). The effects on both biologic and chemical factors have been demonstrated by the actions of the corticosteroids.

An appreciation of the dimensions of immunosuppression by these hormones can be obtained from the study of Dougherty and Schneebeli (1955). Using the number of polymorphonuclear lymphocytes as a gauge of the inflammatory reaction, they found that microgram increases in the amount of cortisone were able to nullify totally this essential first reaction of immunity. It is not unusual, of course, that the corticosteroids, being hormonal, would cause profound biologic responses in only minute concentrations. The probable effect of increased titers of corticosteroids resulting from bereavement in suppressing immunity to bacterial, fungal, and viral pathogens has been reviewed recently (Fredrick, 1976). The Rees and Lutkins study (1967) has shown that the end result of bereavement can, indeed, be deadly.

Perhaps the most direct formulation of a "principle" of preventive medicine for the bereaved is that expressed by Seligman (1975).

> Helplessness seems to make people more vulnerable to the pathogens, some deadly, that are always around us. When one of our parents dies (or when our own spouse dies), we must be particularly careful. I suggest complete bimonthly physical check-ups during the first year following the loss.

These observations apply to the so-called "infectious" disease category of human ills. From infrahuman species we have sufficient evidence that, when cortisone is administered before a challenging dose of the tuberculosis bacillus, no activity of the protective macrophages occurs (Lurie, 1960). Those phagocytic cells already in the area show no destruction of the ingested bacilli. The same effects of cortisone have been reported when fungi are used as the challenging pathogens (Merkow et al., 1968). In fact, those fungal spores that are engulfed by the phagocytic white cells tend to germinate within these cells. Likewise, the potentiation of viremia by corticosteroids is common (Hallett et al., 1951; Ormsby, 1951).

More ominous is the emerging relationship of the grief experience with the subsequent development of malignancy. In a deeper analysis of the Rees and Lutkins data, Rees (1974) indicated that the number of cancer cases appearing in the bereaved group was five times that in the control or nonbereaved group. Schmale and Iker (1966) reported on a study involving 51 women who had had regular "pap" smears. Each had shown evidence of "suspicious" cells in the cervix, but these were not diagnostic of cervical cancer. The investigators found that 18 of these women had experienced a serious loss within a six-month period preceding the pap test. The others had experienced no such event. It was predicted that the bereaved patients would be predisposed to developing cancer, even though both groups appeared to be equally healthy. Of the 18, 11 subsequently developed cervical malignancies. Of the other 33, only 8 developed malignancies. Hence, the cancer rate among the bereaved women was two and a half times greater than that of nonbereaved women.

These studies, while not conclusive, are certainly at least suggestive of a possible linkage between the stress of bereavement and the subsequent appearance of cancer. Such a relationship had been suggested earlier by many investigators (Muslin et al., 1966; Greene, 1966).

Recent research in oncogenic viruses has unearthed disturbing evidence of the persistence of these viruses in tissues. This is seen particularly in that group known as the Herpes viruses. These viruses have been associated as "passengers" in human cells for a long time. The uniqueness of their being able to cause recurrent symptoms such as fever blisters, cold sores, and the like, after periods of stress must be considered as playing a role in their possible onconogenicity.

The Epstein-Barr Virus (EBV) is a Herpes type-2 virus that has been implicated in cancer (Rafferty, 1973). It appears to be the causative agent of infectious mononucleosis, a relatively benign disease of the lymphatic system, as well as Burkitt's lymphoma, a malignant disease of the same system (Grace, 1968; Henle et al., 1968; Grace et al., 1969). Antibodies to the EBV have been detected in more than 90 percent of people before the age of 10 (Grace, 1970). Therefore, it is undoubtedly widespread and persistent. It seems to fulfill the essentials for an oncogenic passenger virus.

Wagner (1974) has described three possible types of immune responses to the EBV: none to minor (trivial symptomatology but definitive antibody production), intermediate (infectious mononucleosis), to severe and rare (leukemia and lymphoma). From a molecular level, both the intermediate response (infectious mononucleosis) and the severe response (leukemia) are so similar that the blood picture is often confused about which illness is present—so much so that infectious mononucleosis has been termed "benign leukemia" (Grace, 1964). In fact, an unusual type of enzyme called "Phosphatase-N" is found only in cases of both illnesses (Neumann, 1974) and is probably synthesized under the influence of the EBV.

Since the body's response to EBV is undoubtedly dependent on the state of immunity of the individual, and since this immunity can be impaired (suppressed) by increased levels of corticosteroids, it is not unusual to find that many leukemia patients report a "loss" experience prior to the disease's manifestation (Fredrick, 1971).

Studies of passenger viruses capable of causing tumors in infrahuman species have proved of value in elucidating a probable mechanism for impaired immunity and the time of the appearance of the tumor. The C3H mouse carries an oncogenic passenger virus from the time of birth. This virus, the mammary tumor virus (MTV), eventually causes breast cancers to develop in more than 90 percent of female mice of this strain (Riley, 1975). The median time for the cancer to appear is 400 days. If the mice are stressed, the median time can be shortened to one-half (about 276 days). If, on the other hand, stressful events are kept as low as possible, the median time for the development of mammary tumors in this species can be lengthened to 800 days or more.

It was further found by Riley (1975) that corticosteroid levels after stress in these C3H mice could be very highly elevated (up to 17.5 times the baseline titers) and that these levels were correlated with a steady decrease in the number of circulating T-cells. These lymphocytes originate in the thymus gland and are thought to be an essential part of the surveillance system for detecting and eliminating "transformed" or potentially malignant cells. A more recent study

(Monjan and Collector, 1976) has shown through assays of plasma cortisol in nontumor-carrying mice that there is an increased titer of this hormone during even moderate stress and that the increase in this corticosteroid corresponds directly to the depression of the overall immunologic response as measured by lymphocyte-mediated cytotoxicity.

There seems to be no doubt that the immunologic response, both on a biologic and a chemical level, is directly influenced by corticosteroids secreted by the adrenal cortex under stimulation by ACTH released by the pituitary. During periods of stress, the levels of corticosteroids may be elevated quite a bit above the baseline. It is precisely during these high-stress periods (such as bereavement) that immunologic suppression is greatest. Particularly in the case of passenger oncogenic viruses, the depression of the T-cell surveillance system may allow the establishment of transformed cells (caused by EBV or MTV) beyond the point where they can be kept in check. If so, then active malignancy would appear to be the apparent result.

It is known that glucose transport is blocked by cortisone and that the activity of the enzyme glycogen synthetase is stimulated (Mersmann and Segal, 1969; Van den Berghe et al., 1970). Since the formation of the storage sugar glycogen is the result of the activity of this enzyme, there seems to be the possibility of excessive glycogen deposition in cells if the corticosteroid levels are high. Arcadi (1963) has reported that malignant and transformed cells show a high glycogen content. This may be a contributory factor to the malignancy process; moreover, it may be a direct result of corticosteroid action.

In this age of chemotherapy it is not unusual to suggest the use of drugs for restoring these temporarily depressed immunologic functions. For example, the release of ACTH is thought to be brought about by neurotransmitters such as the catecholamines. It has been observed that drugs (l-dopa and clonidine) that release catecholamines inhibit stress-induced ACTH release in dogs. But, even though catecholamines seem to be involved in the biochemical process of ACTH release, it has been found that, when catecholamines were administered systemically, no inhibition of ACTH release was obtained (Ganong, 1977).

Serotonin is another chemical structure that appears to be involved in ACTH secretion. Although its exact role is unclear, it appears to be stimulatory. However, cyproheptadine, an antiserotonin agent, appears to decrease the secretion of ACTH in patients with Cushing's disease and Nelson's syndrome. This may show promise for the bereaved.

It seems logical that a relief from the stress of grief should allow corticosteroid levels to return to baseline normal values. For the bereaved individual the resolution of the grief would be expected to restore the immunologic health of the person. In so doing, it is possible that, if the transformation of normal cells via the ever-present oncogenic passenger viruses has not progressed to an irreversible degree, the natural protection against malignancy can be made to function physiologically once more. It has been found that, where the immunocompetence is good, even in the case of cancer patients, the prognosis is excellent. However, where the immunocompetence falls, the prognosis is poor.

Certainly all these argue for the rapid restoration of the immunologic health of the bereaved. The resolution of the grief, by whatever psychological, social, or physical method available, can bring this about.

Acknowledgment

This study was supported by the Dodge Institute for Advanced Mortuary Studies, Cambridge, Massachusetts 02140.

References

Arcadi, J. A. 1963. *Science* 142:592.

Dougherty, T. F. and G. L. Schneebeli. 1955. *Annals of the New York Academy of Sciences* 98:617.

Engel, G. A. 1963. In *A Unified Concept of Health and Disease,* ed., D. Ingle, pp. 339–65. New York: Basic Books.

Folch, H. and B. Y. Waksman. 1974. *Journal of Immunology* 113:127.

Fredrick, J. F. 1971. *Omega* 2:71.

Fredrick, J. F. 1976. *Omega* 7:297.

Ganong, W. F. 1977. *Annals of the New York Academy of Sciences* 297:527.

Gisler, R. H., A. E. Bussard, J. C. Mazie, and R. Hess. 1971. *Cellular Immunology* 2:634.

Grace, J. T. 1964. *Proceedings of the Fifth National Cancer Conference,* p. 637.

Grace, J. T. 1968. In *Proceedings of the International Conference on Leukemia-Lymphoma,* ed., C. J. Zarafonetis, pp. 115–26. Philadelphia: Lea & Febiger.

Grace, J. T. 1970. *Annals of the New York Academy of Sciences* 174:946.

Grace, J. T., J. Blakeslee, and R. Jones. 1969. *Proceedings of the American Association of Cancer Research* 10:20.

Greene, W. A. 1966. *Annals of the New York Academy of Sciences* 125:794.

Hallett, J. W., I. H. Leopold, and A. W. Vogel. 1951. *American Medical Association Archives of Ophthalmology* 46:33.

Henle, G., W. Henle, and V. Diehl. 1968. *Proceedings of the National Academy of Science* 59:94.

Hill, C. W., W. E. Greer, and O. Felsenfeld. 1967. *Psychosomatic Medicine* 29:279.

Hofer, M. A., C. T. Wolff, S. B. Friedman, and J. W. Mason. 1972. *Psychosomatic Medicine* 34:481.

Lurie, M. B. 1960. *Annals of the New York Academy of Sciences* 88:83.

Merkow, L., M. Prado, S. Epstein, E. Verney, and H. Sedransky. 1968. *Science* 160:79.

Mersmann, H. J. and H. L. Segal. 1969. *Journal of Biological Chemistry* 244:1701.

Monjan, A. A. and M. I. Collector. 1976. *Science* 196:307.

Muslin, H. Y., K. Gyarfas, and W. J. Pieper. 1966. *Annals of the New York Academy of Sciences* 125:802.

Neumann, H. 1974. *Science* 186:151.

Ormsby, H. L. 1951. *American Journal of Ophthalmology* 34:60.

Rees, W. D. 1974. *Personal Correspondence*.

Rees, W. D. and S. G. Lutkins. 1967. *British Medical Journal* 4:13.

Refferty, K. 1973. *Scientific American* 229:26.

Riley, V. 1975. *Science* 193:465.

Schmale, A. and H. Iker. 1966. *Annals of the New York Academy of Sciences* 125:807.

Schreiber, V. 1974. In *Biochemistry of Hormones*, ed., H. V. Rickenberg, pp. 61–100. Baltimore: University Park Press.

Seligman, M. E. P. 1975. *On Depression, Development and Death*, p. 181. San Francisco: W. H. Freeman and Company.

Van den Berghe, G., H. De Wulf, and H. G. Hers. 1970. *European Journal of Biochemistry* 16:358.

Wagner, E. K. 1974. *American Scientist* 62:584.

Yamada, A. 1964. *Proceedings of the Society of Biological Medicine* 116:677.

❧12

Sudden Infant Death Syndrome: A Medical and Psychological Crisis

Ralph A. Franciosi and Gertrude R. Friedman

Sudden Infant Death Syndrome (SIDS) is a term applied to infants who die suddenly and unexpectedly and in whom no conventionally accepted cause of death is found after a complete review of circumstances and postmortem examination. SIDS or crib death is the leading cause of infant death after the first week of life.

Any program directed to SIDS should have social and scientific goals. The social goals include identifying SIDS cases, emotionally supporting the SIDS family, and educating them and others about SIDS. The scientific goals include detection of the cause(s) of SIDS and prevention. Research efforts directed toward SIDS and the families affected by it will produce insights into the physiology of infancy and an understanding of grief and mourning in families experiencing infant death. In 1975, there were 55,581 deaths in infants less than one year of age. This accounted for 2.8 percent of the total deaths in the United States. The causes listed for these deaths were anoxia, 26 percent; anomalies, 16 percent; immaturity, 10 percent; hyaline membrane disease, 9 percent; pneumonia, 6 percent; and accidents, 2 percent. Cases of SIDS are classified in the broad category of anoxia.

Medical research is revealing causes of infant death that are not easily understood or treated. Those deaths caused by diseases that can be treated by antibiotics or prevented by vaccines are becoming fewer and even disappearing. Persisting are problems related to newborns, birth defects, and accidents. However, SIDS is the leading cause of infant death, and although the death is related to anoxia, the cause or causes are not well understood.

The epidemiologic data available show that 90 percent of SIDS cases occur before six months of age and 99 percent before one year of age. Almost every case is associated with a sleep period. Approximately two-thirds of SIDS cases have had some abnormality in the perinatal period, for example, prematurity. An upper respiratory infection is present in 40 to 50 percent of cases.

Theories that are presently tenable implicate hypoxia during sleep as the final pathway in SIDS (Beckwith, 1975; Valdes-Dapena, 1975). It is suggested that this hypoxia may have several causes, one being brain stem lesions and another obstruction of the upper airway. The former implies that lesions can compromise involuntary centers for respiration and cardiovascular control in the brain stem. The latter suggests that in young infants, the upper airway is critical to oxygen intake and may be compromised, for example, by viscid secretions.

Awareness that SIDS was not just an event but an ongoing and persistent problem for bereaved families was forcefully brought to our attention by parent groups. The concern for SIDS parents was coordinated through the formation of two national groups, the Mark Addison Roe Foundation, which eventually became the National Sudden Infant Death Syndrome Foundation, and the Guild for Infant survival, which became the International Council for Infant Survival. These parents groups were effective in providing a mutual support system for SIDS families; in educating the public about SIDS, so as to remove the harmful effects of ignorance and mismanagement associated with the disease; and in stimuling research. Their lobbying efforts were largely responsible for the enactment of the Sudden Infant Death Syndrome Act of 1974.

The federal government has two separate programs directed toward SIDS. The National Institute of Child Health and Human Development (NICHD), Pregnancy and Infancy Branch, is involved in coordinating a basic research program. In 1976 the Institute supported 28 SIDS projects. These projects are part of a comprehensive approach to maternal and infant health that includes high-risk pregnancies, fetal pathophysiology, premature labor and birth, disorders of the newborn, and congenital malformations. This approach has indicated that significant findings in one area are related to problems in other areas. The management of SIDS cases, which includes identification, family counseling, and education, is the responsibility of the Community Services Bureau of the Department of Health and Human Services. This program administers 31 SIDS centers in 28 states.

An SIDS death differs from other deaths because it occurs suddenly and unexpectedly in apparently healthy infants. The usual report is that an "apparently healthy infant is put to bed without the slightest suspicion that things are out of the ordinary." He may have mild symptoms of cold or stuffy nose. Sometime later he is found dead. This represents "trauma" in the fullest psychological meaning of the term, because the family has had no warning, no opportunity to anticipate or prepare mentally or emotionally for the tragic event. Numerous studies, beginning with Erich Lindemann's (1944) classic work on acute grief, have pointed to the devastating effects of such a sudden unexpected death. Added to the intensity of reaction is the absence of a known etiology. Unacceptable as they may be as reasons, most sudden deaths can be explained in terms of accidents, illness, or homicide, but in the case of SIDS the cause is as yet unknown. As a result, family members, lacking an adequate explanation, may hold themselves accountable; the guilt associated with SIDS is pervasive and almost universal.

The death of a young child always evokes the strongest kind of grief reaction in terms of intensity and duration because of the closeness of relationship, the complete dependence of the infant on its parents, and the interweaving of their lives in daily care. We must recognize the betrayed expectations that children will outlive their parents. Harriet Schiff, an author and bereaved mother, asks in her book *The Bereaved Parent* "how could it be that a parent outlives a child?"

SIDS families are further traumatized by the investigations and interrogations that follow. Since SIDS deaths usually occur at home without the support of a medical institution such as hospital or physician, they fall within the province of a medicolegal officer. If those first on the scene, such as emergency rescue officers, are not sensitized to SIDS and the needs of the family, the results may be mismanagement and further imprinting of guilt, fear, and suspicion. In this sense, the survivors are often referred to as "victims," and these victims outnumber those who die.

We have defined SIDS as a crisis. A crisis disturbs adaptive behaviors and interpersonal relationships and leaves the family vulnerable to further dysfunction (Rappaport, 1971). Because SIDS happens most frequently to young couples with little or no experience with death, and because the marital relationship is still too new to have weathered the test of crisis, there are frequent communication problems leading to strain, resentment, isolation, and sometimes separation or divorce. Mothers, abruptly cut off from their maternal function, experience grief and pain comparable to losing a part of their body. New fathers, acculturated to deny or repress feelings, may stay away from home to avoid confronting the emotion. Bergman (1969) reported that close to 50 percent of families who lost children to SIDS in the Seattle area in the preceding three years had moved without leaving any tracing address.

There are often conflicts in decisions about having another baby and many reported difficulties in conceiving based on emotional factors. Frequently, there are problems in rearing a subsequent child. The couple loses confidence in their parenting ability and may become overprotective or fearful about investing love in another child.

An SIDS death is an equally traumatic event for the siblings of the deceased child, but parents are often not aware of the children's feelings at this critical time. It is difficult for frightened parents to convince frightened children that they should relax and feel safe. In almost all cases we found that parents' emotions interfered with their parental roles. The children struggle to understand the intensity of emotional reactions in their parents, which they may never have experienced before. In our metropolitan population, over a one-year period, we have had at least three suicidal parents with young children. The child who is poorly equipped either intellectually or emotionally to understand loss must now deal with a second kind of loss, the change in relationship to the parents.

Cain et al. (1964), studying the impact of death on children following the death of a brother or sister, found that guilt was the most frequent reaction. Guilt remained active for five or more years after the sibling's death.

Parents often lull themselves into thinking that their surviving children are all right because they are not openly grieving in adult terms. In a desire to protect these children from the pain of death, or because of the weight and conflict of their own feelings, adults opt in the direction of silence, avoidance, or partial explanations, which can further confuse, frighten, and frustrate the children. One three-year-old girl was very excited about going to church but felt betrayed and threw a temper tantrum when she did not find her baby brother there. She had been told that baby was with God, and since she knew God was in church, she expected to find baby there.

Children under five do not comprehend the finality of death, but they have a rich fantasy life and are very literal in their interpretation of what is told them. In addition to fear and anger, we know that young children feel guilty and responsible (Nagy, 1959). They equate their rivalrous feelings and sometimes bad wishes toward the baby with causing the disappearance and death. They need to know that nothing they thought, said, or wished caused the death.

Sometimes children act out their bad feelings about themselves in misbehavior. One little girl was described as very angry, hostile, and provocative. Suddenly she had attempted to drown one of her pet kittens in the toilet and to choke another with a scarf. She was reflecting, not only the badness she felt about herself, but also some of the erratic behavior she had witnessed in her mother.

One boy became a behavior problem in nursery school, reportedly stealing and lying. His behavior was connected directly with the death of his sister and the lack of communication around all the events that followed. He was angered that the family had moved because baby sister could "never find them now." He saw the police take the baby away, and he was later given an incomplete religious explanation of the baby's being with Jesus. He concluded that baby and Jesus were in jail.

Other children in our SIDS families have developed functional learning problems and psychosomatic symptoms associated with the secrecy, fear, and prohibitions around the death. One eight-year-old child could not remember which twin brother had died. She kept exclaiming that she thought it was the other one and continued to get the names of the two infants confused. In like manner, she could not remember simple facts taught at school that used to come to her readily.

One adolescent child entered the room while her mother was attempting to baptize the infant after death. She returned to boarding school depressed, withdrawn, and unable to do her work. We learned that she interpreted her mother's efforts as a deliberate attempt to kill the baby.

These, from among the many clinical examples drawn from our Minnesota SIDS families, add to the growing evidence that children of all ages are very much aware and affected by death in the family— even that of a young infant. Grief reactions are appropriate to children's ages and stages of concept development and experience. We find that we can help children in the management of grief in several areas. For the child under three, parental constancy and physical closeness are most important. For the older child we can prevent distorted grief responses by helping parents to elicit fantasies and to correct misconceptions. A third area of preventive effort is through facilitating the processes of normal grieving. For the child "normal" means dealing with grief in terms of his own life experiences. The child, like the parent, must be given the opportunity to master the experience of loss through actively working through the grief process. This can then lead to feelings of growth and self-esteem.

Following the crisis model of intervention, the Minnesota SIDS Center stresses the immediacy of help in reaching out to offer services when people cannot mobilize their energy to seek such aid or comfort. Effective management is based on knowledge about SIDS and true compassion for the family. People are more open to suggestions at the time of crisis. They need help and support in reaching decisions. We can help parents express, understand, and accept grief reactions—their own and each other's. At present there is no proven way to prevent crib death. However, it is possible to deal effectively with families to prevent further pathology. We can facilitate communication and reinforce the strengths and assets of the family unit. In preventive terms we can help parents recognize the needs of the surviving children.

Our program includes identification of a bereaved family as soon as possible within a 24- to 48-hour period through autopsy and certification. The importance of defining and using the term SIDS has proved to be of immense value in the acceptance of death and the mental health status of the surviving family. Notification is provided immediately through the medical examiner or coroner with followup discussion of any questions about the autopsy. Along with the diagnosis, parents are given basic facts about SIDS with emphasis on the fact that this is a specific disease entity, common only to infants, and that it cannot be predicted or prevented. Professional and community support is reinforced through our educational program for emergency rescue personnel, police, emergency medical personnel, clergy, funeral directors, social workers, public health nurses, and mental health staff.

The Minnesota State Department of Health, Maternal and Child Health Section, is responsible by agreement with the SIDS Center for the educational program. Since the public health nurse plays a primary role in reaching out to the bereaved family, we feel that educational input relating to SIDS, grief, and its impact on the family is of crucial importance. Extensive use is made of the media to provide information to health care professionals and to the public. We have organized workshops throughout the state for professionals emphasizing both the medical and psychological aspects of SIDS.

There are areas of education involving the University of Minnesota. The Mortuary Science Division offers a course on SIDS and infant death, as does the Department of Maternal and Child Health in the School of Public Health and the School of Nursing. Postgraduate seminars have been developed to cover the needs of SIDS families.

Community educational efforts include 11 district workshops throughout the state conducted by the Minnesota Funeral Directors Association. In Minnesota the Mrs. Jaycees selected SIDS as a priority project for 1976–78. This formed the core of their community education efforts for their 215 chapters during this time period.

Thus, reinforced by education and interdisciplinary support, a counseling visit is provided by the public health nurse within seven to ten days following the death of the child. The nurse provides additional information about SIDS, and on the basis of a mutual assessment of needs and support, she plans for followup contacts as needed. We always recommend followup contacts at the end of three months, six months, and a year to provide for time changes and anniversary reactions. We have found that the family is usually grateful for someone who will listen, who understands, who can give and receive information without being judgmental, and who facilitates communications among family members. The nurse counselor's value is enhanced by her knowledge of the grieving process and the extent to which she can allow for cultural and individual differences without imposing expectations. If unusual problems arise, she can discuss additional assessment and/or referral with the family and the mental health consultant at the center.

In addition to the individual contact, the family is informed about our Parent Support Group, which meets monthly and welcomes not only parents but also children or extended-family members. Such group discussion, led by the mental health consultant, can be useful in penetrating the isolation of grief. Families derive great comfort in learning that their adjustment problems are not unique.

It is our belief that this design for serving SIDS families could well be used as a model for service to all families who suffer a baby's death or the death of a child regardless of age. The emphasis is preventing further disease or disability within the family and community by offering a more humane system of care following death. The ultimate prevention is, of course, eliminating the disease. Lacking this capacity, we must continue our efforts to educate, to inform, to improve emergency and death-related services, as well as our capacity to reach out to the living with compassion, empathy, and hope!

Crisis implies a decisive moment. In summarizing crisis theory, an important observation for health providers is that the person or family in crisis becomes more susceptible to the influence of significant others in the environment. The degree of activity of the helping person does not have to be high. A little help, sensitively given at a strategic time, is more effective than more extensive help given at a later period. The helping person should view himself as part of a network of interventive services and not just as a single resource.

References

Beckwith, J. B. 1975. "The Sudden Infant Syndrome." Department of Health, Education, and Welfare. (HSA)75-5137.

Bergman, A. B. et al. 1969. "The Psychiatric Toll of Sudden Infant Death Syndrome." *American Academy of General Practice* 40 (6).

Cain, A. C., I. Fast, and M. E. Erikson. 1964. "Children's Disturbed Reactions to the Death of a Sibling." *American Journal of Orthopsychiatry* 34 (4).

Lindemann, E. 1944. "Symptomatology and Management of Acute Grief." *American Journal of Psychiatry* 101:141–48.

Nagy, M. 1959. "The Child's View of Death." In *The Meaning of Death,* ed., H. Feifel. New York: McGraw-Hill.

Schiff, H. S. 1977. *The Bereaved Parent.* Boston: G. K. Hall. Paperback ed., 1978. Baltimore: Penguin Books.

Valdes-Dapena, M. A. 1975. "Sudden Death in Infancy: A Report for Pathologists." *Perspectives in Pediatric Pathology* 2.

The Bereaved Parent

James P. Zimmerman

My brother and his wife have become members of what is known as the "world's most unlucky club": they experienced the death of a child. Perhaps their bereavement was tempered by the fact that their child lived only a few hours following her birth, but that experience has raised some questions:

Cannot hospital policies be changed so that a woman, suffering from the grief of a newborn child's death, is not returned to the maternity ward, where she is surrounded by the cries of babies and the happy sounds of new parents?

Cannot a system of information sharing be devised so that some unknowing nurse does not walk into the bereaved parent's room with a cheery, "Well, how is the new mother today?"

Cannot a special room be set aside within the hospital, staffed with trained personnel, so that parents who so desire would have the opportunity to hold that child, who, even though now dead, had been a part of their life for many months?

Cannot pictures of children be taken following birth and preserved as a part of their permanent birth records so that in later months a bereaved parent would have access to some visible remembrance?

Should not any person who touches the life of a bereaved parent—whether as doctor, clergyperson, nurse, hospital administrator, social worker, psychiatrist, funeral director, or lawyer—become more informed and be made more sensitive to the needs, hurts, and problems of bereaved parents?

My brother's experience and a growing acquaintance with a number of bereaved parents who have organized themselves into a group called "Compassionate Friends" have made me aware of a host of theological questions, emotional dynamics, psychological wounds, and personal needs of these people, which I had never understood before.

Therefore, to guide me personally and to provide "original resources" and documentation for this paper, I spent several evenings in long dialogue with three couples, all of whom were bereaved parents and all of whom opened up their hearts, souls, and emotions, because they wanted people to know their story. None of these people were from my congregation, and I had not ministered to them in their grief. Their theological backgrounds were varied, and although those backgrounds were not as broadly representative as I would have desired for theological reasons, many of their comments and thoughts are typical for all bereaved parents as they continued to tell me, "You really cannot understand what you have not experienced yourself."

When I asked the personal, professional question, "What can your pastor or priest or rabbi do best for you, and where did they fail you?" the answer given applies to any person who deals with the bereaved parent, and it is summed up in the word "caring." Personal presence, touch, and concern are most important, for as one parent responded, "Nothing you say can help. In fact, it is better to say nothing than to say the wrong thing."

The specific message to the clergy was not to use pious platitudes, not to hit the parents with religion, not to preach to them, but just to be there! The word to relatives and friends was not to use such inane clichés as: "It was God's will," or "You can be happy that your child is in heaven," or "God wanted a child in heaven so that he chose yours." Indeed the theological implications of these statements are horrendous.

"It is better to say nothing than to say the wrong thing." In fact, the people who need to do the talking are the bereaved parents. They need to speak, not so much about the details of the death itself, but about their child; they need to hear his name mentioned, to recall former events in his life. The best way for parents to face the reality of a child's death is to speak of that child and his death. The best way for family and friends to speak of that child is to do so with honesty, not making him out as the perfect child, but speaking his name within the element of truth.

At this early stage of their grief, bereaved parents need the presence of other people. But the need is not for people who easily throw out the comment, "If there is anything I can do, please call," for the last thing a bereaved parent can do is to call someone for help. Rather, they need people who are specific with their offers of help, "Can I make a cup of coffee for you?" "Let me do your washing and ironing," "I will pick up the children from school today."

One man became extremely angry at his relatives when they left his home on the night of the child's funeral and burial. The relatives left because they reasoned that the family would wish to be alone; that was exactly what they did not want or need. The bereaved father packed up his wife and children, drove a few miles down the road to the home of his parents, and spent the night there.

"You become road runners," said one man—running away from home, from reality, from reminders of the child, and especially so during the first year with all of its "firsts" for the bereaved parent: the first Christmas, the first birthday, the first anniversary of the death.

Although those anniversaries hurt, there is also anger on the part of bereaved parents when other family members do not remember the anniversary of the death of a child. Of special concern to one couple was that the grandparents did not or could not remember the anniversary of their grandchild's death. Perhaps this was their way of avoiding something they found difficult and painful.

During the early stages of grief some bereaved parents develop homicidal thoughts. One father expressed the desire to kill the driver of the car who killed his son. A mother wondered what it might be like to know that the doctor who had cared for her son during his long coma had died. She thought this, even though she knew the physician had done everything possible medically for her son.

Common to many of the parents was the thought of suicide, especially during the initial stage of overwhelming grief when the feelings of personal loss and agony were so severe. At this time come the questions of "why?": Why has this happened to us and not to some family down the street? Why has this happened to my child and not to some kid on drugs? Why is God punishing me? What have I done wrong to deserve this? Why did God allow this to happen, especially if He is a loving God?

Within this particular context, how interesting it was to discover that those people who claimed to be atheists or agnostics or who believed in God in only a vague and nebulous way suddenly saw God as a living force and also as the guilty party. God usually ends up as the "bad guy," as the comment is made, "'If He did not cause it, then He certainly could have stopped it.'' How interesting it was to hear one person, out of anger and frustration, call God a vulgar name and then a few minutes later hear him tell how he prays to God to take care of his son. There was a woman, too, a confessed atheist, who appreciated the prayers of the priest who ministered to her son's roommate and always included her son in his prayers.

But within this whole framework are those thoughts of suicide because bereaved parents have the feeling that they will never again know happiness, never again know peace. Later, the suicidal concepts, born of overwhelming grief and agony, change to thoughts of suicide as a positive death wish with the belief that their personal death would enable them to be reunited with their child. One couple discussed which one of them might commit suicide in order that one of them would be with their son. Another man contemplated taking his life for the same reason, but the teachings of his church prevented him from doing so. He believed that the taking of his life would mean condemnation and, therefore, would prevent him from being with his son. Such attitudes toward suicide indicate how bereaved parents no longer fear death for themselves. Many tend to live more dangerously and take more chances with their own lives. On the part of some, there even seems to be a death wish, hoping that some accident will take their lives. Thus, they reason, they can be with their child without actually taking their own lives. Regarding death, the only fear they have from that point on is the death of another one of their children.

I once assumed that the death of a child was more difficult for a young married couple to deal with than for older people who had lost an older child. I have learned that this is not so, for with parents of all ages there is that sense of life being out of order when a child precedes a parent in death. "Children are your responsibility," said one man. "The natural order is that parents should die first. When your child dies, a part of you dies, for they never will be able to fulfill the dreams you had for them." Within this context came the almost unanimous thought that it is easier emotionally to lose your marriage partner in death than it is to lose your child. One man commented, although I think not indicating the thinking of all bereaved parents, "A mate is a replaceable commodity, but a child is not."

There is great need for research and study into marriage and family life situations as they existed prior to the death of a child to determine how they may affect the attitudes of parents following such a loss. This is of particular importance, for it seems almost universal that the death of a child brings on problems within the marriage and the family. Harriet Sarnoff Schiff, in *The Bereaved Parent,* has written:

> Unfortunately, as a number of parents whose child died have discovered, it is impossible to give comfort when you feel equal grief (p. 6).

> Too much was expected of the mate and too little was received (p. 6).

> Grief cannot be shared. Everyone carries it alone, his own burden, his own way. But for a couple to discover this after burying their child can be shattering. Each thought they could lean on the other as they mourned. But you cannot lean on something bent double from its own burden (p. 58).

> Cruelly enough, in the vast majority of cases, not only do we parents have to endure the grief of having a dead child, more often than not we also undergo severe family crisis—drunkenness, separation, divorce, alienation, are frequently the aftermath of losing a daughter or son. In addition, a couple all too often is jolted by a further loss, the loss of illusion about each other (p. 5).

A prayer in our funeral liturgy states that we are drawn closer to one another by our common sorrow, but this is not true for bereaved parents. For how can you fill one empty glass from another empty glass, which also needs to be filled?

Within this context there are other emotional and psychological forces at work. There is the guilt of the parents who may feel that, in some way, they were responsible for the death of their child. There is much anger on the part of most parents as they become defiant and defensive, striking out at anyone, whether it be God, a neighbor, a store clerk, or the family, and, sadly, the family is usually the most convenient target. Criticism becomes difficult to handle and tolerance disappears. It is a chore for a wife to clean the house and for a husband to finish his projects around the house. He becomes angry at her for not keeping a clean house, and she becomes angry at him because of the mess of his unfinished projects. Mates sometimes come to the point where they do not care how the other spouse feels. If the wife had a good day (when she was not depressed or crying at the thought of the child or the mention of his name), and the husband came home feeling down and depressed, they would become angry with each other because of their opposing feelings. They could neither meet the needs nor share the joys of the other.

It is important at this point in the grief of bereaved parents to have an ongoing visitation by someone who understands their needs and who can help them verbalize and identify these normal feelings. It is necessary for the parents to be informed that they are not different and that others have experienced the same emotions.

Equally important is the need for an outsider to help the parents understand what harm they may be doing unknowingly to their other children. Often the child who has died becomes larger than life to the exclusion of the living children. Consider the father who purchased a used car following the death of his son. He did so only because his son had once admired it. He painted the car, stenciled the son's initials on both doors, ordered special license plates with the boy's first name, and then realized what he was doing when his daughter asked why he had not put her name on the car also.

Generally, bereaved parents appear to react toward surviving children in one of two ways. Either they are overly protective, especially with younger children, because of the fear that they too might die, or else they become overly permissive, especially toward the older children, because life seems to be so uncertain anyway. "When your child dies," explained one father, "all of your dreams for him remain unfulfilled. His life seems so incomplete. How sad that he never had the opportunity of sleeping with a woman. Had he done it and told me, I would have been angry. But now I feel badly that he will never have that experience."

Since the bereaved parent's mind and whole being seem to dwell constantly on the child who has died, it is important for someone who is not a family member to speak with the surviving children and give them an opportunity to vent their feelings. It is very common for children to have jealous thoughts toward the sibling who has died because of the way he has been made so important but at the same time to experience guilt for feeling jealous.

As time progresses, as healing begins, and as a parent is able to speak of the child without tears, there comes a new guilt, which evolves from enjoying life again. "You feel that you are being unfair to the memory of your child to be happy again," said one parent. "You feel guilty because you are afraid that you are beginning to forget about him."

From this reaction comes a refusal of joy, of happiness, of allowing oneself to have a good time, of letting someone help. Especially critical at this point within the marital relationship is the hesitancy to have sexual relations because these are enjoyable and good. "How can I enjoy myself and have sex with my husband," asked a mother, "when I know that my child is alone in the grave?" That comment also brought into focus the great concern in the minds of parents regarding their child's state of being within the grave. One father shudders each time it rains and thunders as he says to himself, "My son is all alone." A mother cringes when it snows because she believes her son will be cold. One couple felt a sense of relief when a grandparent died and was buried in the same plot as their son, feeling that now a member of the family was with him and he was no longer alone.

Added to these fears and agonies are the ongoing legal and institutional problems and insensitivities. From the legal world comes the realization that the child has no "economic value" or "economic potential." Therefore, if a lawsuit is involved, one would likely receive greater compensation if one's cow had been killed rather than one's child. There are the crushing financial burdens on those whose children were in hospitals for weeks and months before death, and the insensitivity of many who make contact for payment. There is a lack of understanding on the part of people who must communicate with bereaved parents, such as the policeman who comes to the door with the mangled tricycle of the child who had been hit by the truck with the comment, "Here is your property, lady."

"The pain never goes away," said one mother, "but healing comes when you begin to understand that and when you learn to live with it." How necessary for all of us to understand that pain as best we can, to walk with them through that pain, and to rejoice with them when they come to the point of being able to reach out with love and compassion to give the gift of caring to another bereaved parent.

Reference

Schiff, H. S. 1977. *The Bereaved Parent*. New York: Crown Publishers.

🏵 14

The Unidentified Bereaved

Carole E. Fudin and Wynetta Devore

Generally, the nuclear family is the conceptual framework within which bereavement is viewed. An expanding body of literature and research discusses and investigates how families attempt to cope with the loss of a significant member. These writings tend to view the family as a "closed corporation" consisting of a father, mother, and children, although it may extend to include grandparents, uncles or aunts, or cousins.

Differing emotional and cultural "climates" within families determine whether or not nuclear- and extended-family members will interact as a tightly woven unit. However, it is assumed that the group will solidify when the family deals with adversity. This assumption of family unity under stressful circumstances stems from acceptance of the basic view of the family as a social system. Hill (1974) suggests the following characteristics as descriptive of a social system:

1. Family members occupy various positions which are in a state of interdependence; that is, a change in the behavior of one member leads to a change in the behavior of other members.
2. The family is a relatively closed, boundary-maintaining unit.
3. The family is an equilibrium-seeking and adaptive organization.
4. The family is a task-performing unit that meets both the requirement of external agencies in the society and the internal needs and demands of its members.

Despite this unity, some non-family members may be permitted entry by virtue of association. The relationship of such "courtesy" members may be so close that they assume kinship roles and are addressed as "uncle" or "aunt" by the children or are referred to as "just like a sister or brother," or "like a daughter to me." Billingsley (1970) discussed how black families frequently include nonrelated individuals as family members or legitimate parts of the system. These associations are the primary concern of this paper.

Courtesy family relationships can exist within the traditional nuclear network; sometimes they make up for the lack of a member in a "deficient unit"—a childless couple, a one-child or one-parent family, or one with only boys or only girls (Hill, 1974). Lacking sufficient inner resources, such families maintain a more permeable boundary that allows nonfamily members to assume roles traditionally assigned to members of the immediate family. With the loss or absence of the husband-father, a mother-son unit will open boundaries to admit a male who assumes tasks of the missing member without legal formalization of the relationship. This kind of relationship gains approval from our family-oriented society because it contains characteristics of the traditional family system. In this example the male is usually a cousin, brother, or uncle. Even if he is not a relative, however, the relationship is still sanctioned for the sake of the family unit.

Another illustration of a societally sanctioned "pseudofamily" relationship is that of a young married couple who have moved away from the security of a family network and are "adopted" by an older couple in a new community to satisfy mutual needs for familial sharing. This relationship is described in terms such as "just like our own children" or "just like a mother and father to us."

Not all functional relationships receive societal sanction. Minimal support is given the long-term, extramarital relationship entered into by a husband who remains with his wife and family. Perhaps the external relationship satisfies unmet needs of the husband and wife and helps to maintain the marriage. If so, the extramarital relationship may be functional, although it receives no sanction.

The death of a family member is of course extremely stressful and disruptive. Family responses to stress are varied. For some, the immediate solution is to fling open the invisible boundaries that encircle family groups. Such expansion allows families to receive support and nurturance from individuals or organizations. Other families close their boundaries even more tightly and provide internal support only for each other. They deny the possibility of obtaining relief from others, including associates of the deceased member. Since bereavement is usually reserved for the immediate family, external persons are prevented from adequately expressing and sharing their grief. If they are incorporated into the system at this time, it is usually to give support to the immediate family.

Cutter (1974) points out that the intensity of bereavement is a function of closeness, which suggests frequent, long-lasting, and intimate sharing of "mutual need satisfaction." Closeness is usually attributed to blood relations rather than to functional ones. But in today's mobile society, blood relations may have only infrequent contacts with each other: a brother seen once or twice a year is functionally more removed than the intimate friend who is seen weekly or daily. In this example, grief work will be more intense when the friend dies. However, there is a social expectation that the brother's death warrants greater public expression of mourning. Grieving for the close friend is rarely regarded as proper public behavior. Given our example of the adoptive relationship between the young and older couple, at the death of the "adopted" mother, the younger couple would be expected to provide consolation and support to her immediate family. Since this death is regarded as a family affair, some family members may deny the young friends' right to feel real bereavement. Lacking bona fide status as immediate family, the couple may express their loss in the simplistic statement "a very close friend of ours died," when, in fact, an integral part of their family system has been lost. No support enters their system. They are givers and have no rights as recipients of condolences. With consideration given to the family relationship between the two couples, it is possible to view the young husband and wife as unidentified bereaved.

Society offers no alternative for the unidentified bereaved. One gains entitlement to bereavement by the use of the possessive pronoun "my," but this term is of little use unless it carries an explanation, for example, "my best friend at the office died." This phrase suggests concern for the friend's family, but not for the co-worker who has lost a friend and confidant, an integral part of his daily life.

Sudnow (1967) explains that descriptive phrases such as "she was like a mother to me" or "we were like brothers" are "category-linked" disruptions that claim at least quasi-bereaved status. While these expressions may be seen as attempts to add depth to expressions of grief, they cannot be disposed of as mere courteous pronouncements, since they may, in fact, be truthful reflections of a relationship.

Attempts to deny death consume varying amounts of effort in

any family system. Most disturbing to that balance are decisions made in relation to children and death. What should children be told about the death of a family member? The reality that death is not reserved for old age is a perplexing one. Children and young adults do die, and they do have playmates and friends who are among the unidentified bereaved.

Children's literature of recent years has confronted the reality of death for the very young. Emphasis has been placed on the experience of losing parents, grandparents, sibling, and pets. In *A Taste of Blackberries* (1973), Doris Buchanan Smith has ventured beyond that narrow network and relates the stress felt by a young child who suddenly is faced with the death of his best friend, Jamie. Instantly, he is cut off from Jamie's family, a system in which he was always welcomed "like Jamie's brother." Now there is guilt about being alive while Jamie is dead. Recognition of the legitimacy of his grief comes in the following exchange in a neighbor's garden:

> You know about Jamie?
> Yes, I am sorry about Jamie, and I am sorry about you, too, because you were his best friend.

"Mrs. Mullins was as gentle as the butterflies," and in her gentle way, she affirms the specialness of the relationship with Jamie. Peace begins. The blackberry patch inspected on the day of Jamie's death is revisited, and the best friend picks berries for Jamie's mother, hoping to assume the role of substitute son. Joyfully, he is readmitted to the system with a kiss and the role of "door slammer" previously held jointly with Jamie.

The mourning of unrelated people is often labeled as "morbid." A nursing staff devoted to long-term care is also vulnerable to grief reactions. The death of a patient with whom there has been regular contact over several years can leave a nurse bereft. Emotional displays are viewed as unprofessional, and there are almost no formal provisions made for mourning. Bereavement may be acknowledged by whispered condolences or sick leave.

Poslusny and Arroyo (1975) have indicated that a professional's grief reactions in response to the loss of a patient will be affected by how well the nurse knew the patient over a period of time and whether there was some cathexis to the patient. These authors recommend that formal provisions be made to help nurses accomplish their grief work when a patient dies.

In the examples cited, the neglected bereaved are sometimes able to find individuals capable of giving support. The lost relationship receives social approval and recognition that something meaningful has been lost.

Consider, then, the grief of persons who have lost relationships that did not receive societal sanction. Such loss may have long-term effects, impinging on other intimate relationships. Significant studies illustrate the consequences of loss for widows and widowers (Parkes, 1972). There do not seem to be any studies documenting the loss experiences of lovers. These unsanctioned relationships are hidden as well as neglected, suggesting a double burden inhibiting grief work. Bertha G. Sims (1977), a social work therapist, discovered among her patients a middle-aged woman with obsessive worries about her husband's health. Four months of treatment enabled the patient to recognize that her present behavior stemmed from a fear of punishment for an extramarital affair 10 years earlier that had ended with the lover's death. Depression stemming from guilt and unresolved grief work had plagued the intervening years. Partners in illicit relationships hold no status as mourners. In this instance the result was lasting grief and shame for what had been an important relationship.

If caregivers begin to recognize that a group of unidentified, neglected bereaved exist outside the immediate family system, then it is incumbent on them to respond appropriately to this knowledge. This expanded awareness is particularly important for hospital social workers who work with bereaved families and funeral service directors who plan services that facilitate grief work.

The following are some specific recommendations for practice:

If a terminally ill patient is able to communicate, attempts should be made to find out whom, within and without the immediate family, he feels closest to.

Hospital staff should be sensitive to people who frequently visit the patient. The person most emotionally affected by an impending death could be a close friend who is left out of medical discussions and may be unaware of the extent of the patient's condition. Once identified, such an individual should be made aware of the fact that there are staff members who will communicate with him.

For hospital staff who grieve over the loss of a patient, there should be a formally organized and sanctioned provision for the expression of such grief. This might be accomplished through a brief memorial service or within weekly staff meetings in which feelings may be openly shared.

In planning a funeral service, funeral directors should find out if the deceased had close friends whom the family would like included in the arrangements and ceremony. Funeral directors should seek out these friends during and after the funeral to offer them support. If there is to be followup care, close friends should be included as well.

In this presentation we have attempted to recognize the variety of family life styles that might suggest a need for differing provisions for bereavement. Funerals and burial rituals should allow for differences in form, to reflect open or closed family systems. An open family may plan a funeral service to provide the opportunity for "just like" family members to speak and share their feelings about the deceased with all present.

Novelist Sandra Scoppettone (1976) described a teenager's funeral that included the score from *Jesus Christ Superstar* and reminiscences of contemporaries. The buzzing and clucking of older people present did not deter the young people who shared the joy of having known Penny and their feelings of loss. All families may not be able to tolerate such adaptations in ritual, but funeral directors and clergy should be encouraged to allow for these.

The custom of "dressing graves," observed in rural southern graveyards, permits families to acknowledge publicly the condolences and the specialness of certain relationships. After the graveside service, mourners leave the gravesite to allow the grave to be "dressed" by the mortuary staff. The family mingles informally with other mourners and, when summoned by the funeral director, returns to the gravesite, which has been decorated by the floral gifts of friends. The bouquets and plants are acknowledged openly. Cards are read and given to the principal mourners. Throughout the ceremony there is continual exchange between family and good friends; the grief of all is legitimized.

Cultures, races, religions, regional influences, and changing mores shape family life styles. Yet, no matter what the style, the loss of a loved one will cause stress and the potential for crisis. Professionals should be sensitive to the complexities of family systems under stress. This paper suggests a comprehensive observation of the bereaved family to determine if it is opened or closed and to learn if there are "significant others" involved with the need for support and attention.

References

Billingsley, A. 1968. *Black Families in White America*. Englewood Cliffs, N.J.: Prentice-Hall.

Cutter, F. 1974. *Coming To Terms With Death*. Chicago: Nelson-Hall Co., pp. 216–17.

Hill, R. 1974. "Modern Systems Theory and the Family: A Confrontation." In *Sourcebook in Marriage and the Family,* ed. M. B. Sussman, pp. 302–13. Boston: Houghton Mifflin.

Lund, D. 1974. *Eric*. New York: Dell, pp. 130–38.

Parkes, C. M. 1972. *Bereavement: Studies in Grief in Adult Life*. New York: International Universities Press.

Polusny, E. and M. Arroyo. 1975. "Bereavement and the Nursing Student." In *Bereavement: Its Psychosocial Aspects,* eds. B. Schoenberg et al., pp. 265–78. New York: Columbia University Press.

Scoppettone, S. 1976. "Trying Hard to Hear You." In *We Are but a Moment's Sunlight*. eds. C. Adler et al., pp. 130–39. New York: Washington Square Press.

Sims, B. 1977. "Grief Therapy to Facilitate Healthy Restitution." In *Social Casework* no. 6 (July): 337–42.

Smith, D. B. 1973. *A Taste of Blackberries*. New York: Crowell.

Sudnow, D. 1967. *Passing On: The Social Organization of Dying*. Englewood Cliffs, N.J.: Prentice-Hall, pp. 153–68.

Part III

Counseling the Bereaved

🌿15

The Future May Be Now

Howard C. Raether

Thanatology is not an exact science. Opinions differ in regard to the psychological facets of death and postdeath activities, and these differences can stem from sociological, economical, physiologic, philosophical, and religious perspectives. These differences of opinion add to the dimension of the opportunities presented for helping those in need, the bereaved survivors. Academic and professional disciplines search for models on which to base programs for offering this help. In most professional curricula these models are designed as techniques for teaching. In law school the professor tries to differentiate between what can be learned from facts and what can be learned from intuition, as well as from the reactions of individuals to the facts. In proposing curricula for thanatologic studies, similarly, there are facts to be included, but there are also the intuitive reactions and responses of individuals, trained in a variety of disciplines, to these facts.

Deductions can usually be made from major premises. It might even be said that these premises form the framework for teaching models and for subsequent actions. Yet major premises based on the circumstances surrounding a death often lead us to deductions that are not valid. For example, there is a presumption that all members of a family are present at the time a death occurs, that these individuals gather together to support one another and receive support from each other. The truth is that most members of the family are not present when death occurs. Most deaths occur within a medical institution, and many medical institutions do not allow family members in at the particular time the death is occurring or even for a while thereafter. Often children are not permitted into hospital rooms at all, whether prior to, during, or after a death. Further, it is an error to believe that the body of someone loved can always be viewed immediately after the death if the death has occurred in a hospital.

One can ask too if the viewing of a dead body immediately after death is a positive action for every person. From my personal experience I can relate the events following my own mother's death. She died of cancer after two long years of this debilitating illness. My father and I were present when she died. What had been 160 pounds weighed less than 80 pounds. What had been a full-faced individual now had high cheekbones, sunken eyes, mouth agape. This was not the way I wanted to confirm the reality of my mother's death or the way I wanted to have my last memory of her.

Funeral service has been criticized most unjustly when it has tried to cosmeticize the body in order to make it presentable. There is beauty in memory, and there is a strengthening process activated within an individual as he strives to face reality. No reality is harder to face than the death of someone whose love has molded one's life. When a survivor, bereft of a repository into which to reinvest love, must face the reality of a death, he is entitled to expect that some element of the physical beauty that has been destroyed by suffering be restored, even if only for the sake of partially erasing the harshest memories of the confrontation with death's image. Cosmetics do not restore beauty in death; I cannot forget what cancer had done to my mother. But there is some comfort for me, at least, in the memory of my final viewing of her.

These feelings are reinforced in me when I think of how a memorial service without my mother's body present would have affected my father, my sister, my wife, my daughter, and myself. Any suggestion of this kind of finality to a loving relationship would have been resented just as much if it had come from a member of the clergy, even as individuals resent the suggestion from a funeral director that a traditional funeral be held with the body present, that everything has to be done in "my way or you don't do it at all."

A memorial service can be more spiritual if, during a funeral, overemphasis is not placed on the body. The memorial service is less emotional, is not as time limited, and can be more economical to the extent that some of the services and facilities of the funeral director are not used. Yet without the presence of the body, there may be an evasion of therapeutic pain and a denial of the fact that life and death can occupy the same place at the same time. The presence of the body during the funeral ritual makes it easier for people to vent their feelings and provides a climate for mourning and emotional catharsis. Somehow or other it is easier to approach the bereaved and discreetly help them get on the road back to the life that awaits them in the future.

A basic premise of firefighting involves the careful observation of the scene when the firemen reach the site of the fire. Such observation forces a search for the exact location from which the flames are emanating; this knowledge facilitates planning the attack on the fire. To a great extent the resolution of grief can be facilitated by the observer/counselor who makes a sensitive observation of the "smoke and fire" that can "consume" bereaved survivors during the period of acute grief and then proceeds with careful attention to the means of resolving the grief that is disrupting their lives. The funeral service professional is often the only "fireman" (expert based on knowledge often experiential) on the scene when immediate decisions about the funeral plans must be made.

Many alternatives may be suggested. It is possible to hold a tribute service with or without the body present. It is possible to have someone suggest that there be no services at all. Or there may be a cremation or a body donation with no services. Often advice is offered on the assumption that people have strong religious beliefs and a belief in some form of an afterlife. In discussions of the experiences of funeral service professionals, it is apparent that we are talking about individuals who serve everybody, regardless of whether or not those they serve have a religious belief or regardless of what that religious belief might be. It is incumbent on all occasions to know the facts, to form judgments based on these facts and on what experience has taught, and to counsel appropriately when the need is evident.

Anomalous situations present challenges that force those caring for the bereaved to be knowledgeable beyond information to be derived even from the proposed models noted. Questions are raised that require a broad knowledge of relevant facts. From these facts guidance can be given to ease the severe pain of loss. For example, there is much misleading information about both body donations and body part transplant donations. Those who wish to will their body to medical science presume that the body will be acceptable. An autopsied body is not accepted in some institutions; a body that has wasted away and become emaciated is not acceptable. When an institution determines that a body is not acceptable, usually a funeral director is called, and he is the one who notifies the family that, for all the noble intentions, the ultimate in a gift has been rejected.

Who can give assurance to the survivors of a suicide? Who can tell them not to have feelings of guilt, not to wonder what they should have done or should not have done to have been able to prevent the self-destructive act of a loved one? Counseling and caring for these bereaved during acute grief and after demands a special kind of experience and expertise.

So too with those families where an infant has died of Sudden Infant Death Syndrome (SIDS). With SIDS, those in funeral service have been in constant communication with the various chapters of the National Foundation of SIDS. Information has been developed about helping the family that has lost an infant as a result of this still mysterious ailment. They too must be convinced that the death had not been caused by anything they had or had not done for the child. Among other things he can do, the funeral director in the actual practice of his profession can also possibly erase from memory the image of the child, huddled and blue in the corner of the crib.

There will be a future. Perhaps it would be advantageous to take a look into the immediate future. Fewer than 25 years ago, very few funeral directors would have gone into a hospital to see a patient, because society warned, "We don't want you to see our sick people; we think you are trying to solicit business. You are a symbol of death to remind us that someone is dying." This attitude is changing. The hospice movement in this country has had something to do with this change. In home care programs the funeral director is often introduced to the family, as well as to the patient. Everyone becomes involved in what is being done, not only after death, but also before it.

In the future, comfort for the bereaved may come from a multitude of new sources. Each teacher tries to educate specifically for his own discipline. In caring for the bereaved there is little doubt that the disciplines can be blended, almost one into the other. So it is that the funeral director, whose presence at the side of the bereaved during the period of acute grief is mandated by his professional role, can serve as a counselor and give guidance that is limited only by the depth of his factual knowledge, the extent of his undergraduate and continuing educational training, his capacity for interdisciplinary colleagueship, and the soundness of his sensitivities as a caring human being predicated on cumulative experience.

16

The Funeral Director as Grief Counselor

Buell W. Dalton

"Grief is the pain of the soul," says one.

"Grief is a species of idleness," replies Dr. Samuel Johnson.

"It is dangerous to abandon oneself to the luxury of grief; it deprives one of courage and even of the wish for recovery," advises Frederic Amiel.

"The busy bee has no time for sorrow," says William Blake.

And Mark Twain puts the capstone on the attitude of the unimportance of death for some when he relates this story of his youth.

> After supper she got out her book and learned me about Moses and the bullrushers, and I was in a sweat to find out all about him; but by and by she let out that Moses had been dead a considerable long time; so then I didn't care no more about him, because I don't take no stock in dead people (Flesch, 1957).

Thus, the varieties of the importance of grief and the processes of its resolution are set forth for all people—from those for whom death and its consequent grief is a "pain of the soul" to Mark Twain's Huck Finn, who "don't take no stock in dead people."

For most people there are two sides to the experience of death: the person who is doing the dying and those who remain to mourn his death. Of this latter group there are, likewise, two different attitudes in their mourning: their empathy for the dying or the imagining of themselves in his or her place and, perhaps the more prevalent, their concern over their personal loss and their continued welfare without the contributions that the deceased made to their life.

It is not the experience of death itself that distinguishes man from other forms of life, for death is the ultimate common denominator of all biologic existence—zoologic and botanic. Rather, it is the characteristic of grief that a person experiences at the death of a significant other that makes him human. It is, therefore, to this latter group—those who are moved to grief at the death of a loved one, those who are more characteristically human—that the problems and processes of administering grief therapy should concern itself.

The fact is that the counseling of (1) those who expect soon to be in the midst of grief or, even more correctly, who may be presently experiencing anticipatory grief; (2) those who are in the immediacy of real grief; and (3) those who have just passed through the experience of the death of a significant other in their life is a project far different from expressing speculative theories and solutions about grief in an imagined or hypothetical situation. Therefore, the observations herein are the products of wide experience in actual pre-need, at-need, and postfuneral counseling.

A disturbing aspect of grief counseling relates to the one person nearest to those who are experiencing grief and the most logical one to offer help, the funeral director himself. When a family in the midst of grief comes to make the funeral arrangements, little or no help can be expected from the funeral director making the arrangements so far as grief counseling is concerned. There are two main reasons why this is so. First, there are so many statistical questions to be answered in order that the Bureau of Vital Statistics may be satisfied, and so many matters requiring decisions to be made now, and so many papers to be signed to make it all legal that one to two or more hours of time are consumed to get it all done. By this time the bereaved is mentally and emotionally exhausted by the details. The second reason, and one for which all the busyness of the first reason becomes a handy excuse, is that the funeral director is simply not qualified to do grief counseling. It is far better, therefore, that he refrain from any attempt to counsel. Few, if any, states require more than a formal high school diploma, in addition, of course, to a trade school certificate for licensing as a funeral director. The answer to this dilemma lies, not in the funeral director's seeking more opportunities, but in his being more sensitive and making himself more available to the opportunities that do come and in becoming better qualified to meet the challenge of each opportunity. In some measure both opportunity and challenge are present in every arrangement session. There certainly is no other single individual who is afforded a more natural opportunity for grief counseling than the local funeral director. In our segmented society the doctor is the one to whom we look for health and life; the funeral director is the specialist in death. We reason that, since grief is such a major part of the death process, his specialization should be complete. The real truth of the matter is that life and death are so inseparable that the doctor and the funeral director should be capable of dealing with both.

Effective grief counseling involves more than a one-shot affair. It is a process. To be effective, this process must include counseling in preparation for grief; it must include help and support during the experience of grief; it must include understanding and guidance and comfort during the period of recovery from grief. This is not the "comfort" of a hand on the shoulder and "keep a stiff upper lip" advice. It is "con" (with)-"fortis" (strength), and the Apostle Paul adds (11 Cor. 1:3–7) it is the kind of strength "wherewith we ourselves have been comforted." Perhaps this is the secret to the mystery of real and effective counseling. How can we be sharers of what we ourselves do not have or have not known? It certainly takes counseling out of the category of "couch sessions" and makes it an existential work of love, according to Kierkegaard.

Pre-need counseling or counseling in preparation for grief is done most effectively in group or lecture sessions where the individual has the opportunity for questions while, at the same time, his own individuality may be swallowed up in the anonymity of the group. When counseling is done on a one-to-one basis, the attention is centered upon that individual's particular problem. Human beings have a tendency to think of grief and death as statistical values that involve others—almost anyone else. We tend to turn it off when it becomes our own death or our own grief. Group sessions can be effective because they employ the process of "indirect discourse."

Pre-need arranging of funerals is a growing practice among thoughtful persons today. This is not limited to the time when a loved one is in the terminal stages of illness. Many a husband and wife, usually of middle age or past (whatever that is) and in good health will call for an appointment or simply drop in at the funeral home and ask to discuss their arrangements with a funeral director. What a wonderful opportunity for the funeral director to initiate pre-need counseling. In a sense these persons are asking for counseling. Perhaps, however, they had not thought of the possibility of pre-need counseling. Had they ever given any thought to the manner in which they would handle their grief when the time came? More than likely they had not even considered this, or as I have been asked the questions many times, "What can you do?" or "What can anybody do?"

The motives bringing persons to pre-need funeral counseling are varied but need to be understood. Primarily, perhaps, they stem from one of the basic fears of dying—that of losing the right of self-determination. By prearranging the funeral details, this person can extend his prerogative of self-determination even beyond life's final experience. Often this is true in the case of a person whose family is all gone and there is no next-of-kin, or at best there is only some distant relative who would resent the interruption and responsibility of such a task. Or the arrangements would be left to an executor or administrator whose major concern would be to save as much of the estate as possible for distribution—be it large or small.

On other occasions it may be a husband or wife who does not wish to leave the burden of such arrangements to be cared for by the survivor in a time of crisis and grief. This can be a devastating experience, particularly to a surviving wife who has not had a great deal to do with the management of the business affairs of the family.

Mrs. D's husband died rather suddenly about three weeks prior to the deadline for filing Internal Revenue tax forms. There had been no prearranging. He had always taken care of the family business. She could not even write a check or drive the car. Considerable property, investments, stocks, bonds, and other assets were involved in the settling of the estate. In my first postfuneral call on Mrs. D I found her almost distraught, not with grief, but with fear of what was going to happen to her if she did not get the federal tax forms filed by the deadline. Her great concern was that, in attempting to take care of the business, she might do it in such a manner that her husband would be proud of rather than disappointed with her. She brought me the tax forms he had begun to fill out before he died. I asked if she would like me to make an appointment for her with a friend of mine who is a certified public accountant. I called him from her kitchen telephone and arranged for an appointment convenient for both. About three days later I returned and took her to his office. Within two hours he had her tax report in the mail to the Internal Revenue office. I took her home with a great burden lifted from her mind. She was now ready and able to begin her grief work.

This is an illustration of the importance of prearranging funerals. It provides the funeral director with an opportunity to help, not only with dealing with the affairs of funeral arranging, but also, more importantly and if he is qualified, with understanding and executing the plans they can live with now in preparation for death when it comes.

Pre-need counseling may take many forms. In its least dimension it may consist of no more than reading a book or an article on grief. Rarely will pre-need counseling be performed in a one-to-one relationship in a client–patient situation. This is not to say that person-to-person counseling on this subject is not important. It is as important, if not more so, than the time spent in counseling on many other subjects. This does not mean, however, that we as a society are yet liberated from the stigma of death.

Pre-need counseling will be more readily accepted if presented on a group basis. Modern society is at a stage in its reversion to the acceptance of death that it will participate in such discussion so long as there is afforded the opportunity for the participants to think of death as something that is going to happen to others. This is not possible in a one-to-one relationship. In that situation it is ''our'' or ''my'' death we are talking about, and because it is so personal, it is an unwelcome subject for discussion.

Churches, in their program planning, have a natural opportunity to make pre-need counseling available to their congregations and the community through seminars on death. It has been my experience that these subjects attract those from the community who are not related to a particular congregation, or, for that matter, to any religious group.

Growing up in the mountains of Kentucky as I did, I am familiar with a culture in which counseling on death and grief was unknown and unnecessary. The entrance to any church in the community was through or past the cemetery where lay buried the friends and loved ones of those who passed by. Their graves had been dug with picks and shovels held in calloused hands of those who cared. The needs and welfare of the bereaved family were cared for cooperatively by a concerned community.

Some years ago, while serving as a pastor, I was pondering the program for the upcoming Lenten season. The idea came to me: Why not make it a seminar on death? The theme of the season lends itself quite naturally to the subject. It begins with the realization and preparation for impending death; it goes through the agony and the experience of death; it illustrates the differing grief reactions of those closely affected; it ends on the victorious note (in the Christian faith) of death's not being the end but the experience through which we enter a fuller, abundant, and eternal life. The sessions were conducted on each Wednesday evening during the Lenten season with an overwhelming and growing interest, attendance, and response.

Apart from the church, programs by community social groups such as the American Association of Retired Persons are always in demand. One-night programs can be made to be very informative and effective. These offer the community funeral director an opportunity to exercise public relations as well as for providing beneficial information.

The funeral director who misses the opportunity to introduce pre-need counseling during a session of prefuneral arrangement is missing the real purpose of offering his services to the public. How does one approach the subject? Certainly not by blatantly introducing the subject of counseling. This is a sure way to turn off any interest. There is still a stigma attached to any idea suggesting that one stands in need of counseling. Through "indirect discourse" one can inspire and evoke an interest, however small, and build on that beginning. This interest will be evident in the questions forthcoming about funeral arrangements and why some aspects of them are necessary. The content of pre-need counseling should give an opportunity for all kinds of questions to be asked and given proper answers.

Pre-need counseling, when dealt with promptly and effectively, can be rewarding to the counselor and productive of contentment to the survivors in the hour of death. The counseling funeral director can then join with the family in a great sigh of relief that such annoying details as "what was the deceased's mother's maiden name?" have all been taken care of before the time of death and the necessary at-need funeral arrangements. Economically speaking, pre-need funeral arranging and selection and cemetery costs are usually less when done then than when done at the time of need.

What Dr. Charles Hodges is reported to have said concerning the dying is also applicable to those who must deal with death. He said, "It is important that, when we come to die, we have nothing to do but to die." Likewise, for those brought into the experience of death, it is important that they have nothing to do but to deal with death.

"At-need" or "present-need" counseling is perhaps not the best of terms to use, since any counseling needs are always "present need." But in the frame of reference of grief counseling, "at-need" means those days or hours from the moment of the actual demise of a loved one through the days and experiences of memorialization.

The crises moments during this period are many. If the death occurs at home, the moment of removing the body from the home is the first real crisis. But even so I hesitate somewhat to say that this can be counted as an advantage of one's dying away from home and the family in a hospital or nursing home—or even a hospice. While it is only common courtesy to request that those most closely involved be relocated to another room while the removal is being made from the home, yet, the more readily and deeply one gets into the grief process, the more satisfying will be the outcome.

The call came about 5:30 A.M. By 6:00 we were at the address in a mobile home park. Mr. C, who had a history of heart trouble, had awakened about 4:00 A.M. complaining of not feeling well. He and Mrs. C were seated at the table in the small dining area of their mobile home when he suddenly fell out of his chair onto the floor. When we arrived, Mrs. C was sitting on the couch in the living room area, which was separated from the dining area and kitchen only by a room divider. A thoughtful neighbor had covered the body with a sheet. Mr. C was a rather large man, and the place and position in which he was lying promised to make the removal rather difficult to accomplish. Owing to the limited space it was impossible to get the removal cot or stretcher into the room. This meant that the body would have to be carried through the living room area and placed on the cot in the entrance area. The neighbor was asked to suggest that she and Mrs. C go into another room while the removal was being made. Mrs. C refused, saying that she had stayed by her husband's side for nearly 50 years and she was not about to leave him now. So she stayed. I believe that it was good that she did. In my postfuneral visits with her, I observed that she made one of the most wholesome adjustments I had ever witnessed.

Telling other family members of the death of a loved one is another crisis time. Well-meaning friends often offer to telephone news of the death to a son or daughter, father or mother. Though the bereaved may not be able to speak without crying, it means much more to the recipient of the news, to say nothing of the therapeutic value to the bereaved, if the news comes directly from another loved one. It binds them together in sharing a common grief.

The next crisis moment occurs during the memorial service. Be it religious, humanist, fraternal, or otherwise, it is nevertheless a ceremony of separation. During this ceremony the survivors look for the last time upon the physical form of one who has been a constant part of their life and has meant so much to them. It is the final opportunity for those grieving to perform an act of kindness and love. This is important. It is a wholesome opportunity for the working out of grief therapy and it ought to be exercised more. The funeral director, if he is really concerned with the resolution of the bereaved's grief, can suggest many ways in which this can be done.

The first impact comes when the survivors are escorted into the reposing room and look for the first time since the moment of death or before upon the deceased. Their reactions will depend in very large measure on how they have been counseled previously (pre-need) and on what they really expected to see. It has been the experience of most funeral directors that the next-of-kin will often decide to have the casket left open after viewing the remains for the first time.

This is, of course, the goal of the painstaking hours spent in the preparation and cosmetizing of the remains—to provide, not a death-denying, lifelike look, but a "memory picture" for survivors to take with them through life. Providing and preserving a pleasant memory picture is not, as it has often been spoken of, a selling gimmick for the embalmer's art. Anyone can reflect casually upon his life and realize that the experiences that are most readily recalled are the pleasant memories. It is with a great deal more deliberate effort and resultant anxiety that we recall the unpleasant experiences.

The deceased was the elderly mother of a wealthy widow. She had cared for her mother in her apartment until hospitalization became imperative. A night or two before her death, the mother had fallen from her bed onto the floor. The right eye and the right side of her face and head were terribly bruised and swollen. This was how the daughter had last seen her mother. The daughter decided that there would be a private viewing only for the immediate members of the family, and then the casket would be closed. I worked long and painstakingly at reducing the swelling and restoring the color. When the daughter came in for the private viewing, she was so surprised that she decided to have the casket kept open. When I called on her several days after the funeral, she expressed gratitude that I had been able to leave her with a pleasant memory of her mother's appearance.

Another case illustrates how important it is for the family to be allowed and even encouraged to participate in final acts of love toward the deceased during the memorial ceremonies. A father, 48, died suddenly of a heart attack. The immediate survivors were his wife and three sons who were in their early twenties. The wife, herself ill, requested that one of the sons assume the responsibility for making the funeral arrangements. He brought with him his father's brother and business partner. The uncle offered his advice when asked, but he wisely left the final decision to the son. In the selection room, as the son walked from one casket to another, I sensed that he was envisioning his father lying in this or that casket. Finally, crying and no longer able to speak, he came to the casket he wanted. He simply laid his hand on it, nodded his head, and walked away. I closed the casket, and we returned to the office to complete the arrangements. From the moment that I closed the casket until the completion of the arrangements, this young man was completely composed.

The casket was to be left open during the religious service in the chapel of the funeral home. After the service, when the family had been escorted to the cars, the flowers were being removed, and preparations were being made for proceeding to the cemetery, this young man came back into the chapel and said that he would like to close the casket. He asked if he might be left alone for a few minutes. All the funeral home personnel stepped into the hall and waited. After a few minutes, he came out and got into the car with the rest of the family. He was fully composed, for he had completed an important part of his life.

The character, content, and conduct of the right kind of counseling during this at-need period will seem strange to the traditional processes of counseling. The bereaved during this time will be consumed with grief. He or she will be passing through the stages of grief—denial, anger, guilt, compromise—on the way to realization and acceptance. At this time it is not unusual to witness depressive or even manic-depressive states. This is not a time for formal counseling processes, explaining how grief works, or trivializing the travail of the bereaved by saying, "he is better off" or "it's all for the best," or theologizing about the Will of God. Perhaps concerned friends are more in need of counseling at this time than the bereaved are. The best kind of counseling during this period is to be a genuinely concerned friend, not too liberal with advice or senseless words just to drive away the silence. To know when and how to keep one's mouth shut is a great achievement in counseling. Perhaps it is an occupational hazard that many professional counselors are so insecure within themselves or have such an overly exaggerated estimate of their own importance that they are uncomfortable in the presence of silence.

Simply being present, accepting, understanding without being maudlin, encouraging conversation about the deceased without insisting on it, allowing the bereaved to express their grief in their own way without insisting that it be done "our" way—these are the marks of a good "at-need" counselor. Those who are closest and wisest will make better counselors during this period than any professional counselor.

Whereas the format for pre-need counseling is that of supplying and gathering information and that of at-need counseling is basically supportive, postfuneral counseling takes on more of the traditional counseling characteristics; that is, it is of much longer duration and involves several sessions or visits. It seeks depth of expression and analysis; its therapeutic aim is to guide the individual to an awareness and acceptance of reality in a new and different dimension; it is deliberate rather than indirect in its approach. As to technique, many good books are available to help those who have had no formal training in counseling.

The fact that the funeral director makes a simple followup visit after the bill is paid has a tremendous effect on the bereaved family. If he is not trained in counseling art and procedure, he should not assume this role then or at any other time but should make a call simply as a concerned friend. The vernacular used in the establishment where I serve as both funeral director and counselor is to speak of the counselor as the "postfuneral visitor." However, the funeral director who is trained in turning a simple visit into a counseling experience will sense a more nearly complete fulfillment of this role. It might enhance the concept of the trade of funeral directing to the place where those engaged in it would bring into its practice those qualities that would justify its being termed a profession.

Postfuneral counseling is the area requiring training and aptitude. It involves a deliberate act and purpose on the part of the counselor. Here one encounters all types of personalities making all kinds of responses to an experience affecting persons in many different ways. Alertness in evaluating the situation in which one finds oneself is an important requisite.

As mentioned earlier, it is unfortunate that the extent of formal education required in most states for licensing as a funeral director is a high school diploma. It is encouraging that more persons who hold college and even graduate degrees in related and professional fields are entering funeral service practice out of recognition of its being an important area of human experience. It is also commendable that a trend of licensing agencies is toward requiring more formal education for licensing qualification. For the most part at present this may be no more that a two-year junior college degree; this, at least, is a beginning in improving the situation. There is also a growing insistence on some degree of continuing education for relicensing of those already engaged in funeral practice. This, too, at present, may mean nothing more than attending a one-or two-day state or county program featuring a speaker, perhaps no more qualified than his listeners, who addresses himself to some aspect of the funeral service, including counseling.

A serious drawback to this type of in-service training, particularly in the area of counseling, is that the atmosphere and content of the programs are in disproportionate balance in favor of management skills, merchandising ideas, pricing techniques, and office operations. Effective counseling skills cannot be taught or learned in this manner. An encouraging note is that former "mortuary science departments" in accredited colleges and universities are now known as "funeral service departments" with greater emphasis being given to social science disciplines in the curriculum.

This void in the funeral service is not caused by the deadened sensibilities of all funeral directors to human need. Many with whom I have discussed this matter were moved to great emotional heights when, on occasion, they said or did something during an arrangement session that brought expressions of appreciation from those families or persons who had been greatly helped thereby. When this happens, their countenance glows from the discovery that there is something more meaningful to be dealt with in funeral arranging than the gathering of vital statistics and the kind and cost of the casket selected. This experience of suddenly and unexpectedly being the source of comfort and help is so overwhelming that they wonder how they may drink more deeply and frequently from this well of satisfying experience.

Reference

R. F. Flesch 1957. *Book of Unusual Quotations*. New York: Harper.

17

Bereavement, Stress, and Rescaling Therapy

Tamara Ferguson, Calvin E. Schorer, Garfield Tourney, and Jack Ferguson

Early studies of bereavement focused on the emotional reactions to loss and found that most persons tend to follow a particular sequence of reactions. In his paper "Mourning and Melancholia" Freud (1957) stressed that the bereaved person had to go through a period of mourning before he gave up the person he loved, and Waller (1966, p. 478) stated that this proposition had been considered the central problem of bereavement. After an extensive review of the literature, Bowlby (1961, 1963) hypothesized three stages of bereavement: an urge to recover the lost object, a period of disorganization when the person faces the reality that interaction with the deceased is no longer possible, and a reorganization period when new relationships are initiated. When the urge to recover the lost object is prolonged, the subsequent stages do not take place, and anger may be repressed or displaced. Other studies examining differences in type of bereavement have found that the death of a spouse may provoke a set of reactions different from those following the death of a child, parent, or sibling (Marris, 1958; Parkes, 1972; Furman, 1974). In addition, bereavement began to be examined, not only as a unique event, but also as one of the stressful events in the life of an individual (Holmes and Rahe, 1967). By considering bereavement as a stress agent, it is possible to reconcile the many divergent responses it produces in different persons. Selye (1974, p. 27) notes that stress is the nonspecific response of the body to a demand, so that there would be an expected divergence in reaction to bereavement. It is also not clear to what extent the socioeconomic background of a person (Dohrenwend, 1973), her life history, other stressful events (Gersten et al., 1977), and her perception of the event as desirable or undesirable (Mueller et al., 1977) may affect her reaction to loss.

What is proposed here is an interpersonal theory of interaction that makes it possible to evaluate the biopsychosocial effects of a stressor and provide a structure and concepts that both therapist and widow can use to identify her problems and her mode of adaptation to them. The theory was developed during a survey of 100 widows who had been bereaved between four months and five years. Interviews lasted about two hours and were tape recorded and transcribed. It was found there that the type of adjustment made by the widow depended on the type of interaction she had had with her husband (Ferguson, 1970). Following this an interaction model was developed during subsequent research (Ferguson and Ferguson, 1977), and this is shown in Figure 17.1.

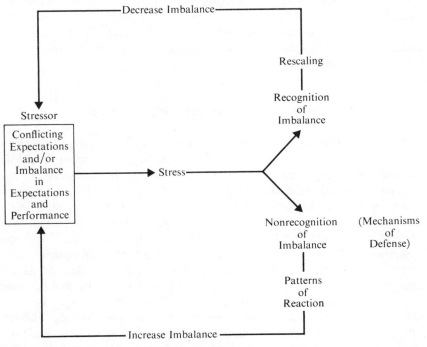

Figure 17.1. Response to imbalance in a life vector.

The basic elements of the theory are the person's expectations and performance within each of a defined set of areas of behavior, or life vectors. At an earlier stage of the theory (Ferguson, 1962), it was believed that an individual had to have positive expectations about herself and others if she was to interact successfully, but the study of widows and a later study on racism (Baker and Ferguson, 1972) showed that a person acquired confidence in herself and in others only when there was a balance between self-expectations together with her own performance and her expectations of others together with their performance.

Ideally, in a stable relationship between two persons, such as that between the widow and her late husband, her other expectations would correspond to his self-expectations, and vice versa, so that there would be complementarity (Parsons and Shils, 1951, p. 15). But in reality, most people have some imbalance between expectations and performance. What is proposed here is that this imbalance creates stress, and a person may be able to minimize stress by identifying her problems and trying to solve them consciously and rationally, or she may further compound her problems by not recognizing their nature and by reacting automatically in a nonrational manner.

Conflicting expectations within the individual also produce imbalance and stress because no performance can match the contradictory expectations.

Interdependence of Life Vectors

The survey findings showed that the death of the husband destroys the division of labor in the family. Left without a partner, a role model for young children, the young widow has to reconsider her expectations in all areas of behavior. She suffers a loss of status, her income drops considerably, and she may have to move, retrain, find a job, and build a new social life. She wonders if she alone can raise her children, whether or not it is ethical to have an affair, and she questions her own faith as she confronts mortality. Emotional problems such as shock, disbelief, anger, guilt, and loneliness exhaust her physically and make it even more difficult for her to make sound decisions. Everyone gives her advice, but the advisers may be self-interested or unaware of the scope of her problems. As this research progressed, it was realized that most of the young widows had, not just one or two problems, but a wide range of problems and that these had to be accounted for in a systematic way. The concept of life vector was proposed as a set of physiologic, psychologic, and social potentials for development, and the following sixteen were identified.

Life Vectors

1. Food	9. Education
2. Shelter	10. Sex
3. Health	11. Occupation
4. Motor Development	12. Finance
5. Speech	13. Parenthood
6. Social Life	14. Ethics
7. Art	15. Law
8. Politics	16. Religion

Life vectors have been derived from Malinowski's set of universal needs (1944) and Erikson's psychosocial crises (1958). The concept of life vector implies that expectations may cumulate continuously or spasmodically and may become activated at a particular period of development, at another period, or perhaps at several and that a problem in one life vector may trigger a problem in another. One widow used her husband's life insurance benefits to buy a new car without being aware that she would be unable to pay outstanding dental bills. Another widow was spending what money she had on her children's education without taking into account her own need for vocational retraining. This interdependence of life vectors led to the construction of a measure of total vector balance—the sum of balances of all vectors—and this was considered a major cause of the stress the widow experienced.

But how do widows cope with stress? The data showed that, after the initial shock of bereavement, there are two main modes of response. Some widows are able to consider their problems systematically and visualize the consequences of any action—both for themselves and their children. Others had undergone psychotherapy since bereavement, and explained their reactions in terms of Freudian defense mechanisms. Many of the other problems experienced in bereavement could be explained this way (Bowlby, 1961; Siggins, 1966; Miller, 1971; Furman, 1974; Kedz, 1977). In a tentative fashion we have interpreted widow's reactions in terms of defense mechanisms and translated them into the interaction theory.

Defense Mechanisms of Widows

Following Freud's formulation, we consider defense mechanisms to be the repression of certain expectations into the unconscious. The following defense mechanisms are tentatively reconceptualized in terms of the widow's expectations of herself and those of others:

Denial—The widow refuses to recognize certain expectations or performances. Following bereavement many widows refuse to believe that their husband is dead. They also often deny that their financial situation has changed and that they have to budget their income in a different way.

Repression—Certain expectations are forced into the unconscious. Some widows repress any negative feelings they formerly held about their husbands. (It may not be necessary to detail repression, since it is the general mechanism underlying the defensive process.)

Regression—The widow focuses on a set of expectations held at an earlier stage of life. Many widows become overly dependent on their parents or siblings in making decisions about their futures.

Rationalization—The widow forces her expectations to fit her behavior. Forty of the hundred widows bought a new car shortly after their husband's death and justified this decision as being economical despite contrary evidence.

Introjection—The widow adopts expectations of another person. Several widows were encouraged to give up their homes and live with parents or relatives. After the move the widows expressed the feeling that this was not what they really wanted.

Identification—Partly at a conscious level, the widow adopts the expectations of another person. A number of widows felt that they should not remarry and appeared to be following the behavior of their widowed mothers.

Projection—The widow attributes a derogatory expectation to another person that she holds herself. Several widows who were envious of those who had not lost their husbands commented that these other women were glad that they were widowed.

Displacement—The widow transfers an expectation about a person to another or to an object. Many widows transfer certain expectations they held about their husbands onto their sons or on themselves.

Reaction Formation—The widow replaces her original expectations with one that is the opposite. Several widows who had been very religious before their husbands' death turned against religion afterwards.

Sublimation—Partly at a conscious level, the widow substitutes a more socially acceptable expectation for a less acceptable one. Instead of considering remarriage, several widows planned to find a job or go back to school.

Somatization—The widow's expectation is transformed into a physical symptom. About 10 percent of the widows had developed identifiable psychosomatic symptoms.

Conversion—The widow's expectation is symbolized physically. Several widows believed they were developing the same illness, such as heart disease or cancer, that had killed their husbands.

Isolation—The widow blocks out new expectations. This could be maintained by a refusal to interact with anyone.

Undoing—The widow tries to extinguish certain expectations by overperforming another expectation. Several widows elaborately renovated their houses, even though they said that initially they would have liked to move.

Patterns of Reaction in Widowhood

We can only infer the mechanisms of defense from the interviews of the widows, but the description of their actual behavior allowed us to formulate four observable patterns of reaction to stress. They have been derived from Horney (1945, pp. 48–95), who suggested that anxiety leads the individual to move toward, against, or away from another.

Brutalization—The widow physically or verbally forces her performance on another person. The expectations and performance of the other are disregarded, and it is a one-sided interaction. Many widows were overly critical of their teenage sons' girlfriends and were also overprotective of their sons.

Victimization—The widow submits to the performance of another, even though this negates her self and other expectations. A number of widows unwillingly sold their houses or businesses to relatives, even though they were aware that these decisions were benefiting only the relatives. Other widows not only did their housekeeping but also unwillingly cleaned the homes of relatives.

Self-Brutalization—The widow physically or verbally forces a performance on herself. While this performance may be in accord with certain expectations, it is in conflict with others. Eleven widows either gained or lost 20 to 30 pounds after bereavement, and several others complained that they were drinking too much. Other widows spent money frivolously, even when they were aware that they were not financially secure.

Insulation—The widow refuses to perform, either by withdrawing physically or by refusing to talk about certain topics. A number of widows admitted that they had avoided former married friends so that they would not be reminded of their loss.

Rescaling: Recognition of Imbalance

When a person is faced with imbalance between expectations and performance and stress has been generated, there is a conscious attempt to modify either the expectations or the performance or both, so that a balance is regained. What distinguishes this behavior from the patterns of reaction is that it is conscious, rational, and not habitual.

Four months after bereavement, a 40-year-old widow whose husband had died in a factory accident was able to foresee the consequences of decisions over all of her life vectors. She felt that she would not remarry only for security, she wanted to work but would not take any job, and she was trying to decide between nursing and an office job as a new career. She preferred nursing but felt that she might not have the physical stamina. Because her children were young and still reacting to the death of their father, she thought that she would postpone for a few more months picking up either career choice. She was also postponing any decision about moving until these other problems were resolved. Although she felt that her status had changed, she went on seeing her friends and doing voluntary work.

Toward Rescaling Therapy

An understanding of Freudian defense mechanisms allows the therapist and widow to identify expectations that are not appropriate to her present situation, while an understanding of patterns of reaction explains why behavior is inappropriate to her present situation. A great deal more research is required, but the following therapeutic sequence is suggested:

1. Identifying imbalance between expectations and performances in specific life vectors
2. Type of imbalance:
   a. unrealistic self and/or other expectations
   b. conflicting expectations
   c. behavior in one life vector affecting another
3. Identifying the defense mechanisms affecting expectations
4. Identifying patterns of reaction affecting performance
5. Explaining the findings in interaction terms to the widow
6. Working out with the widow ways of changing her expectations and performances

The technique has been used experimentally with psychotic inpatients and has seemed to provide them with a structure to think about their problems constructively. Preliminary interviews were done by questionnaire. The identification of faulty expectations and performance does not guarantee that they can be corrected, but it is a necessary first step.

References

Baker, J. E. and T. Ferguson. 1972. *Identity and Separation Among College Students.* A Research Report prepared for the University of Detroit, Detroit, Michigan.

Bowlby, J. 1961. "Process of Mourning." *International Journal of Psychoanalysis* 42:317–40.

Bowlby, J. 1963. "Pathological Mourning and Childhood Mourning." *Journal of the American Psychoanalytic Association* 11:500–41.

Dohrenwend, B. P. 1973. "Social Status and Stressful Life Events." *Journal of Personality and Social Psychology* 28:225–35.

Erikson, E. H. 1958. "The Psychosocial Development of Children." In *Discussions on Child Development,* eds., J. M. Tanner and B. Inhelder, 3: 168–215. New York: International Universities Press.

Ferguson, T. 1962. *An Exploratory Study of the Repetitive Pattern of Maternal Deprivation.* Unpublished M. A. Essay, Columbia University.

Ferguson, T. 1970. *Conflict and the Young Widow.* Unpublished Ph.D. Dissertation, Columbia University.

Ferguson, T. and J. Ferguson. 1977. "Parental Transmission of Pattern of Behavior in Socialization." Paper submitted for publication.

Freud, S. 1957. "Mourning and Melancholia" (1915). In *Standard Edition of the Complete Psychological Works,* ed., J. Strachey, 14:243–58. London: Hogarth Press.

Furman, E. 1974. *A Child's Parent Dies, Studies in Childhood Bereavement.* New Haven, Connecticut: Yale University Press.

Gersten, J. G., T. S. Langner, J. G. Eisenberg, and O. Simcha-Fagan. 1977. "An Evaluation of the Etiologic Role of Stressful Life Change Events in Psychological Disorders." *Journal of Health and Social Behavior* 18:228–44.

Holmes, T. H. and R. H. Rahe. 1967. "The Social Readjustment Scale." *Journal of Psychomatic Research* 11:213–18.

Horney, K. 1945. *Our Inner Conflicts.* New York: Norton.

Kedz, D. M. 1977. "Understanding the Bereaved." *Archives of the Foundation of Thanatology* 6:81.

Marris, P. 1958. *Widows and Their Families.* London: Routledge and Kegan Paul.

Malinowski, B. 1944. *A Scientific Theory of Culture (and Other Essays).* Chapel. Hill: University of North Carolina Press.

Miller, J. B. M. 1971. "Reactions to the Death of a Parent. A Review of the Psychoanalytic Literature." *Journal of the American Psychoanalytic Association* 19:697–719.

Mueller, D. P., D. W. Edwards, and R. M. Yarvis. 1977. "Stressful Life Events and Psychiatric Symptomatology: Change or Undesirability?" *Journal of Health and Social Behavior* 18:307–17.

Parkes, C. M. 1972. "Health After Bereavement: A Controlled Study of Young Boston Widows and Widowers." *Psychosomatic Medicine* 34:449–61.

Parsons, T. and E. A. Shils. 1951. "The General Theory of Action." In *Toward a General Theory of Action*, eds., T. Parsons and E. A. Shils, Cambridge: Harvard University Press, pp. 1–29.

Selye, H. 1974. *Stress Without Distress*. Toronto: McClelland and Steward Ltd.

Siggins, L. D. 1966. "Mourning: A Critical Survey of the Literature." *International Journal of Psychoanalysis* 47:14–25.

Waller, W. 1966. *Bereavement: A Crisis of Family Dismemberment. The Family, A Dynamic Interpretation* (Revised by Reuben Hill). New York: Holt, Rinehart and Winston.

18

Organizational Complexity, Occupational Models, and the Role of the Funeral Director as a Counselor of the Bereaved

Vanderlyn R. Pine

This paper is a sociological examination of the major occupational counselor of the bereaved, the funeral director. It is a case study of the funeral directors who work in two diverse funeral homes. Using the same analytical framework as Pine's *Caretaker of the Dead: The American Funeral Director* (1975), I analyze some of the problematic aspects of the occupation of funeral directing, pointing out how differences in organizational complexity may influence people in death-related occupations. It is of particular interest to funeral directors and of general interest to other death-related fields such as medicine, nursing, social service, and counseling the bereaved.

The preparation of this paper was partially facilitated by a National Institutes of Health Fellowship No. 1 F01 MH3812401A1 from the National Institute of Mental Health. This is a revised version of a paper presented at the conference "Death Research: Methods and Substance," Berkeley, California, March 21–23, 1973, and supported by the National Institute of Mental Health, I R 13 MH22678. I am particularly indebted to Kathy D. Williams, Robert Fulton, Patricia P. Pine, and Derek L. Phillips for their efforts on earlier versions of this paper.

Two underlying assumptions serve as guides for the present study. First, the professional counseling by funeral directors is easily observable because they do their work primarily in the funeral home. Notably, funeral directors seldom leave their funeral establishments to provide services, unlike physicians who make house calls or hospital visits, or attorneys who conduct business in courts. Second, there is evidence that confusion and ambivalence exist concerning the occupational role and social status of funeral directors. This raises questions about what engenders these feelings. By examining the behavior of funeral directors in their everyday activities, it may be possible, not just to clarify their occupational patterns, but also to answer some of the questions about ambivalence and confusion.

Methodology

The methodology for this project involved multiple operations,[1] including participant observation, interviews with bereaved families and with funeral directors, and field observations in numerous funeral homes.

Field observations were made in two types of funeral homes selected because of their organizational structures.[2] The one was a corporately owned funeral home with a complex organizational structure, and the other was a family-owned and operated funeral home with a simple organizational structure. I was a "moderately participating observer" in the funeral homes,[3] and in this role, I performed certain requested activities to gain acceptance by bereaved people with whom I came in contact. However, I took precautions not to be classified as a "complete participant" by the funeral directors. Thus, I worked in the presence of funeral personnel who were conscious of my observer role and among bereaved people who may not have been aware of it.

At each of the two firms, I spent many hours on all shifts, talk-

---

[1] For an extensive treatment of the use of multiple operations in research, see Webb et al. (1966) and Pine (1975).

[2] Participant observation proved useful in studying the institutional treatment of dying patients; for example, see Fox (1959), Glaser and Strauss (1965), Sudnow (1967), and Kübler-Ross (1969). After death has occurred, however, the observation of survivors becomes somewhat more difficult. Namely, the bereaved generally leave the confines of the hospital and go about making funeral arrangements in a variety of places, most of which are not easily accessible to sociologists.

[3] For a discussion about some of the difficulties of participant observer roles, see Gold (1958).

ing, observing, interviewing, and participating in the activities of the funeral directors. I maintained an extensive diary and notes throughout the research process. In an attempt to increase the validity and generality of my findings, and because gaining access was not a problem, I made unobtrusive observations at other, similar funeral homes.[4]

I conducted informal interviews with about 50 funeral directors and more detailed interviews with about 25 others during my research. In addition, I conducted about 200 interviews with recently bereaved people while they were making funeral arrangements.

The following specific research questions emerged from theoretical and practical interests: (1) What common techniques are used by funeral directors to sustain and control the impressions of the situation concerning their occupational activities? (2) What common contingencies are associated with the use of these techniques? (3) How are these techniques affected by such things as the organization of the service practice? (4) What influence on impression sustenance and control does it have whether the funeral director is a solo service practitioner or a member of a bureaucratically organized practice? (5) How do funeral directors perceive their occupation in a general sense? (6) How do they perceive themselves as individual practitioners within that occupation?

Theoretical Background

An underlying assumption of this research is that major differences exist between funeral directors with a bureaucratic orientation and those with a personal service orientation. This assumption is based on three major premises. First, it is well known that the organization of an occupation influences the individuals within it. Second, the personal service model dominates the philosophy and orientation of most funeral directors and is an essential element of their education and training. Third, most of the occupational literature indicates that the most important aspect of funeral directing is to provide *professional* services at the time of death.

To assume that there are differences between funeral directors sets the stage; however, for such an assumption to be analytically useful, more conceptual development is required. Most people assess

[4] Such problems exist for others doing this sort of research; for example, see Webb et al. (1966). For a fairly complete reader about these and related concerns, see McCall and Simmons (1969).

their life in general (and their occupation in particular) in terms of specific models. Moreover, we all construct models of social phenomena and continuously use them to direct our actions and behavior in a given situation. Thus, we define a situation on the basis of the possession of common-sense conceptions of personally held models.[5]

There are clear-cut distinctions between personal servants and bureaucrats that are easy to recognize when we confront them. Our present concern is to delineate the differences between the models of personal service occupations versus bureaucratic occupations. Then we want to examine the differential influence of each on the perception of everyday occupational behavior.

Let us first define our notion of an occupational model. An occupational model is the constellation of beliefs, notions, and concepts that everyday people construct regarding the various occupations with which they are familiar.

Let us now define the differences between the two occupational models. A model personal service occupation is one whose practitioners provide a specialized service to a set of individuals with whom they have direct contact and personal communication but to whom they are not otherwise connected.[6] Most services are provided through settings that exist before servers and served ever establish their particular relationships; for example, a doctor's office need not be created anew for each person who falls sick; watch repairmen already have shops and reputations before new customers come to see them; funeral homes exist before people die. This means that "It is the client who becomes the guest."[7]

A model bureaucratic occupation is one whose members are organized within an extensive hierarchical division of labor, are technically competent experts who allocate time and effort according to rules governing the ways in which they treat those they serve, make a clear distinction between personal and business matters, and are not owners of the organization.[8]

---

[5] It is implicit that the individual actor defines these models for himself; however, since they are formed because of social forces, in general, they tend to be consistent within any given society. Even so, each individual makes his own subjective interpretation of a given situation by using the models he possesses at a specific time.

[6] This definition is based on the following sources: Parsons (1949, 1951), Hughes (1958), Goffman (1959, 1961), Smigel (1964), Vollmer and Mills (1966), Fulton (1967), and Freidson (1970).

[7] Goffman (1961, p. 332).

[8] This definition is based on the following sources: Gerth and Mills (1946), Merton (1949), Blau (1955), and Henderson and Parsons (1960).

It is not surprising that problems often arise when a service occupation is practiced by a bureaucratic organization.[9] Even though funeral directing is dominated by a professional orientation, it involves many tasks suitable to a bureaucratic organization. Most occupations with multiple facets solve their dilemma by separating the elements comprising them. For example, in medicine, the physician provides professional services, the hospital provides facilities and equipment, the pharmacy provides medicinal merchandise, and the ambulance service provides transportation. However, such a distribution of tasks is not found in funeral service. Rather, the funeral home customarily handles all aspects of funeral work. Of course, the size and organization of a funeral home influence the way in which the multiple facets are handled. The public may perceive the combined elements as if they were functions of a bureaucracy, regardless of the organization. Thus, the funeral director may be plagued by the problems common to any professional in a bureaucracy.

Findings

A distinctive characteristic of behavior in a funeral home with a simple organization is that all behavior is geared toward the totality, and efforts are made to render all aspects of the operation of the funeral home compatible with each other. Responsibility is borne by all members of the staff, who consciously strive to behave as masters of every facet of the firm. This emphasizes the distinctiveness of not having specialists for various tasks. Each member of the staff is capable of doing numerous tasks and duties. Thus, when people come for services, they are rendered by whoever is present at the time, for each person is capable of handling all clients. Implicit in such behavior is that the funeral directors have a service orientation. In addition to being concerned with the overall impression fostered by the funeral home, they are also concerned with appearing to be all-knowledgeable, all-capable service practitioners.

Another distinction of the funeral home with a simple organization is that each person does not merely exemplify the organization; rather, each person actually is the organization. Thus, even though several people may be providing services, each one does so as if she or he were the total organization. Questions and problems are dealt with individually as they arise and are not "referred" to some other

[9] For more nearly complete treatments of such problems, see Parsons (1949, pp. 193–199), Henderson and Parsons (1960, pp. 58–60, esp. footnote 4), and Goffman (1961, p. 345).

member of a hierarchy. It also means that the behavior of each individual at any given time is that behavior of the organization as a unit.

This trait also influences the behavior of the funeral directors in all aspects of their lives. Since the individual is the organization, and since the organization is service oriented, it follows that the individual funeral director is also service oriented. Moreover, the organization of the funeral home is such that it fosters the impression of providing professional personal services. Thus, the work setting in which one practices helps determine one's orientation toward one's profession.

Another important characteristic of the funeral directors in the simple organization is that they appear to have little awareness of the formal aspects of their organization. The members of the staff are not so much concerned with the distinctions between employer and employee, and the hierarchy of the organization is relatively unimportant to them. To be sure, a hierarchy does exist; however, it plays a very small part in a formal way. This means that to a great extent each practitioner is free to conduct himself as a full-fledged professional member of the organization without worrying about superiority or inferiority.

In addition, there is very little awareness of the informal aspects of organization. Again, this emphasizes that the members of the staff of the funeral home with a simple organization do not think of themselves as "part of an organization." Instead, they see themselves as individual (although not independent) service practitioners. This means that organizational activities are not seen as being formal or informal but all are part of the job of professional personal servants.

The personnel of the funeral home with a complex organization behave according to the specific area with which they are concerned. Counselors present themselves as counselors, funeral directors as funeral directors, trainees as trainees, and so forth. Hence, the way in which they conduct themselves is determined largely by the nature of their particular job. This does not mean that they do not have a conception of the totality of their funeral organization; rather they attend primarily to a specific area as part of this totality. Their primary concern is that each job is an integral part of the overall operation; as individuals, they are not nearly so important as is their actual work.

The funeral home with a complex organization is characterized by many limited specialists. Since there is enough work in each special area, each practitioner, though aware of the general operation, attends to his specialty as an expert. This is contrasted to the funeral home with a simple organization, where, in addition to being geared to the totality, there are no such specialists. The use of specialists helps foster a sense of one's job in such a fashion that the members of the firm, largely because of the way in which it is organized, come to believe in themselves as experts in a bureaucracy.

The funeral home with a complex organization has no "personality" in the same sense that the simple one does. The organization is the organization, and individuals are part of it in an almost anonymous way, and instead of exemplifying the organization, individuals are little more than workers in it. Of course, these individuals do not tend to see the organization in as personal a way as those in the other setting do.

In the funeral home with a complex organization, there is a keen awareness of its formal aspects. The hierarchy, table of organization, titles, positions, specific areas of competence, and rules and regulations are important to the way in which the individuals behave. Furthermore, the formality of the organization emphasizes its informal aspects. For example, individual personalities and the compatibility of colleagues are considerably more important than in the other funeral home. Informal control and sanctions considerably modify the effectiveness of the employees of the complex organization.

Service by those practitioners is accomplished efficiently. Little time is devoted to nonessential amenities, and bereaved people are dealt with as speedily as possible but without seeming haste by experts. Little effort is made by each specialist to provide services in other than his own aspect of the operation. This is different from the funeral home with the simple organization where every activity is seen as contributing to or being part of professional personal service.

Discussion

Although various professional situations conform to both models, the practitioner who conducts his practice as a service professional is less likely to experience problems than one who provides his services through a bureaucratic organization, behaving as a bureaucrat.[10] In addition, there are a number of unique features of funeral directing besides those common to the traditional professionals. For example, the labeling of funeral directing as a profession has been seen as a form of collective status seeking and mobility and an effort to elevate

[10] The problems of professionals working in bureaucratic organizations have often been analyzed empirically from the perspective of formally organized work units. For recent studies treating this general problem, see Miller (1967), Hall (1968), and Montagna (1968).

the funeral director in the eyes of the public.[11] However, since funeral directing also has its business elements, the values and practices of business are often at odds with those of the professional. For instance, businesses traditionally have a profit structure with mercantile overtones, while professionals are expected to provide services for the welfare of their client and then to "make their living" from their fees.[12]

Funeral directors in both settings must contend with this problem. In the simple organization the families served are considerably more aware of the funeral director's service provision than of his merchandise sales because of his personal involvement with each funeral. Therefore, to pay for his services, facilities, and merchandise conceivably might engender feelings of hostility because of the nature of the purchase, but it is not as likely to create adverse community feeling. Moreover, the funeral director in the simple organization, much like the solo medical practitioner, is seen as receiving financial reward for his provision of valuable services.

The funeral director in the complex organization is not so fortunate, because his personal involvement is so limited that the bereaved may never recognize his work as worth its cost. The anonymity and impersonality of the bureaucratic organization contribute to potential problems in terms of the profit structure of funeral directing.

Another problem for the American funeral director as a professional is that the educational requirements are minimal compared to, say, medicine, law, and education. In fact, some states have no education requirements for funeral directors, only for embalmers. Generally, the education required consists of one or two years of college plus one year of mortuary science courses and one or two years as an apprentice or trainee.

Education is not likely to have as great an influence on the assessment of the funeral director in the simple organization as on his counterpart in the bureaucracy. This is because the former generally enjoys high social status and prestige and is thought to be well educated and professionally trained for his field. Such thoughts may or may not be true for the latter, no matter what his educational background. The funeral director in a complex organization does not necessarily have high social status. Furthermore, he is usually not known intimately by the people he serves, and he is judged on the basis of how he carries out his work responsibilities. Once again, the prob-

[11] For example, see Bowman (1959, p. 78).

[12] To be sure, certain professions such as medicine and law have been severely criticized in recent years for allowing the profit motive to assume too great an importance in their practices; however, they still are seen as "providing necessary services for a fee."

lems confronting the funeral directors in the two settings are dissimilar, largely because of the type of organization in which they work.

Another problem for the funeral director in the complex organization is that, even though embalming requires technical and special skills, the firm does not treat embalmers completely as professionals. The task is handled as a bureaucratically allocated aspect of the job. Only a few of the practitioners do their work with enthusiasm or take pride in their craftsmanship as embalmers. For the most part their work is merely "part of the job." This problem is not faced by the funeral director in the simple organization, for each member of the firm is able to do embalming, and it is considered by all to be an important aspect of their professional services.

Unlike the traditional professions, the funeral director claims competence, not in a limited, well-defined area, but in many fields, including some for which he has limited professional training, such as grief therapy. In addition the brief duration of the funeral does not easily foster the development of the usual professional relationships. This is especially true for the funeral director in the complex organization. For the funeral director in the simple organization it is not too important that the funeral itself is brief, for he develops professional relationships with the public and the bereaved at times other than during a specific funeral. Because of his involvement in the total funeral operation and his extensive community participation, the funeral director in the simple organization enjoys traditional professional relationships. However, the funeral director in the complex organization may have a different sense of obligation to his clients than other professionals have. This is largely because he attends only to those matters that directly concern his location in the bureaucracy.

Whether or not the funeral director in either setting qualifies as a professional is influenced by the fact that he extends care to the human body.[13] Although there is no fear that the funeral director may "injure" the body as the physician might, the bereaved family implicitly (if not explicitly) believes the funeral director's professional competence is such that he will not "injure" the body and that he will do "no more than necessary" to perform his occupational duties. This lay vulnerability and professional right elevate the funeral director's occupational position to a height not easily attainable by other, similar business jobs.[14]

---

[13] For a fuller discussion, see Parsons (1951, pp. 451–465).

[14] For instance, his position is considerably different from that of hospital attendants, who merely move the already wrapped dead bodies to the morgue but do not do things to or for those bodies. Hughes (1958, p. 70) and Sudnow (1967) may be seen for a more thorough discussion.

Although it has business elements, funeral directing is not a typical mercantile business. The funeral director has certain unique advantages and disadvantages in the buyer–seller relationship. For example, the buyer may be vulnerable because of grief and because of guilt feelings regarding the deceased.[15] Even though this is the case, the funeral directors in both funeral homes did not appear to try to coerce, force, or cajole families into spending excessive amounts for services. The funeral director in the simple organization does not do so, because such behavior is inappropriate for a professional. The funeral director in the complex organization does not do so, because, even though sales records are maintained, the organization of the firm does not require him to make "good sales" for a commission. Clearly, even though the bereaved may be at a disadvantage, it is likely that they themselves bring about high expenditures that then may appear to be the fault of the funeral director.

The funeral director in the simple organization has advantages similar to those of professions such as medicine or law. For example, he often has a chance to look at the arranger's home when he removes the dead body or makes funeral arrangements. Thus, he may be able to assess the family's taste and potential spending ability. In this way the funeral director in the simple organization is rather like certain professionals, such as doctors or lawyers, who have the same kinds of advantages in assessing the ability of their patients or clients to pay for the provisions of their services. Most other businesses do not have such advantages in the sales situation.

All funeral directors labor under certain disadvantages that are not present in other businesses. For example, the bereaved arranger may uncomfortably speculate about and fear what will happen to the body of the deceased. Also, the market for funerals cannot be artificially stimulated. Furthermore, the nature of the "product" is a handicap in that the funeral director has nothing useful to repossess if the family later fails to pay. Finally, unlike most other businesses, the funeral director is caught between two pricing philosophies. The typical business operates on a quid pro quo basis, with "everyone paying the same." The funeral director, however, must also make special arrangements for the poor or indigent, a circumstance that is part of the noblesse oblige rationale of most professions.

In addition to such problems common to all funeral directors, there are other, less tangible but just as crucial ones that may place a strain on them. Long ago, funerals were performed by relatives and

---

[15] Bowman (1959, p. 32) argues that the funeral director takes undue advantage of this vulnerability.

neighbors of the deceased. With the increase of industrialization and urbanization, most interpersonal relationships have increased while primary relationships have decreased.[16]

This situation is often used to describe the plight of the American funeral director. The present findings indicate, however, that it is the case largely for funeral directors who work in a bureaucratic setting. The funeral director in the simple organization cherishes and nurtures primary group relationships with a wide range of people. Furthermore, his role in the community is such that it affords him status similar to that of the traditional professions.

It has been asserted that American funeral directors manipulate the American "way of death" in an undesirable fashion and that they generally force people into unpopular customs and decisions.[17] However, the present findings indicate that a high degree of individual satisfaction exists regarding funerals and funeral directors and that Americans tend to regard funeral practices favorably. Cultures develop unique funeral practices that may change from time to time, but their drastic revision or exploitation cannot easily or logically be blamed solely on a small group of individuals such as funeral directors.

Our findings also suggest that previous critical writings reflect a metropolitan, bureaucratic bias. Specifically, we found that many funeral directors who work in a simple, service-oriented organization do not fit the negative description. This may be contrasted with the plight of the funeral organization bureaucrat who often does fit the description and who tends not to enjoy the advantages of "professional" status.

Concluding Remarks

Our major conclusion is that the behavior of service practitioners depends on the organization of their firm, their orientation to the occupation, and the exigencies of the performance of everyday tasks. Such a thesis has two important ramifications. First, it suggests that service occupation behavior is as much a function of the setting in which such practitioners find themselves as it is of a certain orientation to the service occupation itself.

---

[16] Faunce and Fulton (1958, p. 206) explain that funeral directors reflect this and other tension-producing contacts.

[17] For example, see Mitford (1963).

Second, it suggests that segments of the general public may have problems dealing with those service practitioners whose firm organization and occupational orientation are such that they behave differently than expected. The way in which the funeral director acts depends on his definition of the funeral situation. However, this situation is not a singular, all-encompassing one that is identical in every case. Hence, service practitioners look for cues to help them define the situation appropriately.

Some practical implications of this study are pertinent to service practitioners in particular and all workers in general. It is important to be cognizant of the orientation one holds toward one's behavior, whether it be an occupational matter or not. Careless behavior has the potential of disrupting the overall interaction. By recognizing this potential, one can better understand how to attempt to act. Since this provides a greater measure of control over one's work, it should reduce some of the tensions that may exist.

In addition, there are implications for organizations as servers. Specifically, personal service firms, no matter what their organization, should recognize that their primary function is to provide services. This may seem redundant, since such organizations provide services. However, an important point emerging from the present study is that some service organizations tend to be organizations rather than servers. If such an organization is bureaucratic, certain service needs may be bypassed for the sake of efficient and expeditious operation. This is not necessarily problematic, except when it influences the ways in which the services are perceived. This means that, if people perceive "inefficiency" as indicative of personal service, it may be that, in the long run, inefficiency is more beneficial to the organization than is efficiency.

In the final analysis, organizations are represented by individuals who foster the impression of that organization. This means that training programs for positions in a bureaucratic organization must take into account bureaucratically relevant matters, as well as be geared to its occupational necessities. Put differently, it is not sufficient to have an extensive division of labor that is bureaucratically organized around an efficient hierarchy of offices to provide people with what they count as professional personal services. What is required has its roots in the personal service occupational model.

When the need arises for personal services, such as counseling the bereaved, people may be in a vulnerable position. Such lay vulnerability is not necessarily the result of the practitioners; rather it involves the severity of the need in question and the lay person's inability to cope with it alone. Such vulnerability can be attenuated only by increasing the public awareness of the everyday concerns of those caretakers who extend personal services. The converse is true that lay familiarity may reduce the effectiveness of the professional's work. This brings us to a final conclusion. The counselors of the bereaved must perform satisfactorily to serve the needs of the public without sacrificing the effectiveness of their services, and this is a difficult task.

References

Blau, Peter M. 1955. *The Dynamics of Bureaucracy*. Chicago: The University of Chicago Press.

Bowman, LeRoy. 1959. *The American Funeral*. Washington, D.C.: Public Affairs Press.

Faunce, William A., and Robert L. Fulton. 1958. "The Sociology of Death: A Neglected Area of Research," *Social Forces* 36(March):205–9.

Fox, Renee. 1959. *Experiment Perilous*. Glencoe, Illinois: The Free Press.

Freidson, Eliot. 1970. *Profession of Medicine*. New York: Dodd, Mead, and Co.

Fulton, Robert. 1967. *A Compilation of Studies of Attitudes Toward Death, Funerals, and Funeral Directors*. Minneapolis, privately printed.

Gerth, H. H. and C. Wright Mills. 1946. *From Max Weber: Essays in Sociology*. New York: Oxford University Press.

Glaser, Barney and Anselm Strauss. 1965. *Awareness of Dying*. Chicago: Aldine.

Goffman, Erving. 1959. *The Presentation of Self in Everyday Life*. Garden City, New York: Doubleday, Anchor Books; 1961. *Asylums*. Garden City, New York: Doubleday, Anchor Books.

Gold, Raymond. 1958. "Roles in Sociological Field Observations." *Social Forces* 36:217–23.

Hall, Richard H. 1968. "Professionalization and Bureaucratization." *American Sociological Review* 33(February):92–104.

Hughes, Everett C. 1958. *Men and Their Work*. Glencoe, Illinois: The Free Press.

Kübler-Ross, Elisabeth. 1969. *On Death and Dying*. London: The Macmillan Company.

McCall, George J. and J. L. Simmons. 1969. *Issues in Participant Observation*. Reading, Massachusetts: Addison-Wesley.

Merton, Robert K. 1949. *Social Theory and Social Structure*. New York: The Free Press.

Miller, George A. 1967. "Professionals in Bureaucracy: Alienation Among Industrial Scientists and Engineers." *American Sociological Review* 32 (October):755–68.

Mitford, Jessica. 1963. *The American Way of Death*. New York: Simon & Schuster.

Montagna, Paul D. 1968. "Professionalization and Bureaucratization in Large Professional Organizations." *American Journal of Sociology* 74 (September):138–45.

Parsons, Talcott. 1949. *Essays in Sociological Theory Pure and Applied*. Glencoe, Illinois: The Free Press; 1951. *The Social System*. New York: The Free Press.

Pine, Vanderlyn R. 1975. *Caretaker of the Dead: The American Funeral Director*. New York: Irvington Publishers, Inc. and Halsted Press, Division of John Wiley & Sons.

Smigel, Erwin O. 1964. *The Wall Street Lawyer*. Bloomington, Indiana: Indiana University Press.

Sudnow, David. 1967. *Passing On*. New York: Prentice-Hall.

Vollmer, Howard M. and Donald L. Mills, eds. 1966. *Professionalization*. Englewood Cliffs, New Jersey: Prentice-Hall.

Webb, Eugene J. et al. 1966. *Unobtrusive Measures: Nonreactive Research in the Social Sciences*. Chicago: Rand McNally & Company.

❧ 19

A Post-Funeral Counseling Program

Irene Sullivan

Care of the bereaved population has "fallen between the cracks" of designated services offered to specific populations, as responsibility for "aftercare" has been shunted among various agencies, institutions, and professional, business, and voluntary programs. The result has been either a total lack of services or minimally ambiguous, diffused, and ineffective types of services. Adding to the problems of the bereaved is the diversity of services they need.

Historically, funeral directors have identified the value of the funeral as the starting point toward mobilizing support systems and facilitating the grief process. Viewing the reality of death, the bereaved begin the course of psychologically burying their dead. In contemporary society, however, culture, religion, family, and rituals no longer supply the nutriments once mobilized during the funeral, forcing the funeral industry to reevaluate outdated services, to enrich them, while responding to changing demands. If the funeral industry is to continue emphasizing the value of the funeral while reaffirming its commitment to bereaved families, its direction must turn toward more significantly structured, organized programs to prevent increased economic plight, as well as mortality and physical and mental illness among the bereaved (Parkes, 1972). Bereaved families have the right to grief with dignity, and the funeral industry has an obligation and responsibility to facilitate and protect this right.

A model for funeral service's new responsibility was established in a postfuneral counseling program located in an urban funeral home. The purpose of this paper is to describe this program, which was developed by the author.

The program was organized along the following lines. Bereaved individuals, who made funeral arrangements at four branches of the funeral home, were referred for funeral counseling. They were encouraged to use the counseling program according to their needs, that is, counseling, financial assistance, legal assistance, mediation with other community resources, and so forth. If it was not possible to meet these families face to face, they were called on the telephone, or a personal letter extending our condolences and offering our services was sent. The bereaved were seen individually or with family members. Some preferred weekly telephone contacts with occasional home or office visits. Intervention lasted according to the needs of the individual. The program was free and existed for three years.

One of the advantages of locating the postfuneral counseling program within the funeral home setting was the opportunity it afforded to meet bereaved individuals and families during the funeral, or immediately thereafter, to facilitate the establishment of an identity as an empathic, professional resource person who would be available when the numbness subsided and the reality of the loss closed in. It permitted a natural extension of the services of the funeral home to include grief with dignity.

We had to recognize the inability of some funeral services to respond to the needs of many bereaved individuals. As a result various aspects of the funeral service were restructured. Conservative practitioners in the funeral industry have defended outmoded funeral practices and resisted innovative programs. They argue that the historical value of the funeral, as a way for friends and family to gather to grieve and remember, relieves the funeral director of the responsibility of including services to help people mourn when friends and family no longer meet these needs.

The issue of the positive, psychological value of the funeral has been raised (London Study, 1971) because the funeral service takes place too soon after the death, during the first week of bereavement, to constitute a successful rite of passage. The issue of the need for help in mourning has been investigated in significant studies by Gerber et al. (1975) and other investigators. Their findings concur with those of Caplan (1964) that, during the period of crisis, "a relatively minor force acting for a relatively short time . . . can mean the difference between a good and a poor outcome . . . mental health or mental ill health.''

Cadden (1964) has written, "Although the essential work of mourning, and the essential work of surmounting a crisis, must be done by the person who is most deeply involved in the trouble, he . . . needs real help from the people around him if he is to surmount the trouble and emerge from it in a healthy fashion.'' Unfortunately, "real help from the people around him,'' is viewed differently by those funeral directors who define "real help'' as "taking charge of the body while making all the appropriate funeral arrangements for the family,'' thereby regarding the burial or cremation of the deceased person as the completion of their work.

In contrast, the bereaved families contacted by our program felt that the burial raised all sorts of related problems (Parkes, 1972), emotional and concrete. The family with an understanding of what is happening during the bereavement, and what might be expected and why, will not avoid the pain, but they may not be as overwhelmed by the intensity of emotions or rendered as helpless and hopeless. The realization that the symptoms are temporal and universal responses to death can, in itself, offer emotional support for the bereaved.

The funeral director who incorporates a conceptual framework placing the focal point of the funeral with himself as the influential and responsible person in a hierarchical relationship with the vulnerable bereaved person during an extremely limited period of time and views his "real help'' as finished upon the burial or cremation of the deceased distorts the value of those services. He confuses the issue of who is really being served by the funeral, the deceased person, as argued by Mitford, or the family, as defended by the funeral industry. If, in fact, the family is being served, in order to receive "real help'' from the people around them, the focus needs to be on the bereaved family and not on the deceased.

The concept of changing the focal point from "the funeral'' to "the bereaved family'' allows us to organize phenomena on the basis of common characteristics of the bereaved population while responding to persons in their individual uniqueness (Compton and Galway, 1975). This results in a more effective identification of the needs we observed among the bereaved.

Mrs. T was a 71-year-old woman whose husband had died six months after his initial hospitalization. He was the father of their seven children. A retired executive, he was highly respected by his family and the community in which he had been actively involved. The large number of people who shared the family's grief during the funeral services suggested that Mrs. T would receive real help from the people around her. The funeral director had competently completed all the funeral details. Mr. T was buried, and the bill was paid, customarily discontinuing any further contact between the funeral home and the family.

However, the initiation of the postfuneral counseling program enabled us to contact Mrs. T to determine if she needed any further help from the funeral home. We found her extremely distressed. Although her children and the community had been very supportive, they had not been able to help her to handle her pain.

Mrs. T had given up her own profession when, in her late twenties, she married Mr. T. She "kept herself young" in her involvement with the children and their friends. She developed a very dependent relationship with her family. After her husband died, she expressed the fear of becoming old, isolated, and inactive, like the ladies on the park bench. Her seven married children felt threatened by her emotional dependency, as well as by her alternating bursts of interdependence and her own dependent/independent ambivilance. Intervention involved working with her family, on the one hand, and Mrs. T on the other, on an individual basis. They were helped to understand the impact of death on the family as a whole, and on their mother as a widowed person. Mrs. T was experiencing the affects of grief as confusion, inability to concentrate, waves of anxiety, psychological fear of economic deprivation, loneliness, fear of aging, and the loss of her role as a wife. Work was also effective with Mrs. T and the appropriate community resources. She became involved with the American Association of Retired People. This interaction enabled her to reach out to her past professional friends and renew their common interests. Identifying several community projects that needed her, she became encouraged to volunteer aiding disabled children. Helped to understand the grief process, Mrs. T and her children felt lessened anxiety and increased mutual support. Mrs. T became more confident in developing her potential for social usefulness and creativity. Even though she was widowed and aging, she still had much to contribute to a community that needed her.

We used the general systems theory to understand the needs of the bereaved population, to identify the variety of individualized services required, and to define how those services would be implemented. The systems theory "provides a framework for gaining an appreciation of the entire range of elements that bear on social problems, including social units involved, their interrelationships, and the implications of change in one as it affects all" (Compton and Galaway, 1975). The focal object was the stressful event of death, which "alters the situational conditions, structure and relationships" (Siporin, 1974). Our goals were to help the bereaved understand the grief process, to lend support while their adaptive capacity might be temporarily in a state of dysfunction, and to encourage them to "grow from the crisis by developing new adaptive modes" (Hartman, 1975).

When Mrs. B was 67, her husband died of lung cancer four months after he entered the hospital. Her grief was acute and incapacitating; the funeral director visited her home to make the funeral arrangements. No services were arranged, since she was unable to leave the house. Mr. B was cremated, and the bill was paid promptly. Further contact between Mrs. B and the funeral director did not seem obligatory.

However, we were able to extend the funeral home's service to include helping Mrs. B emerge from her crisis in a healthy state, physically and mentally. Mr. B had entered the hospital for treatment of pneumonia. After the physician diagnosed his more serious condition, he told Mrs. B to "be brave" and not tell her husband that he had lung cancer. Although Mr. B was a nonsmoker, Mrs. B was a heavy smoker. She neglected her health after her husband's death and showed visible signs of malnutrition, for example, sores in her mouth and a red, glossy tongue. She wheezed heavily and complained of the loss of her sense of taste, smell, and partial hearing. She fantasized about her husband's death, blaming government agents for pulling tubes out of his body. Mrs. B seemed inconsolable and threatened to overdose on the medication her doctor had given her. Mrs. B's doctor "advised" her that neighbors would have her "committed" because of her intensive outbursts. He wanted to send her to the same hospital in which her husband had died "at the hands of the government agents" for a complete examination.

Mrs. B's problems were exacerbated by her dependent, demanding, and hysterical personality; incapacitation of her coping mechanisms; her inability to accept or adapt to her husband's death; the doctor's failure to understand the impact of his admonition to lie to her husband, upon whom she was extremely dependent when he was dying; his insensitivity in choosing to send her to the same hospital in which her husband had just died; and her malnourished state. The unit of attention was the interaction between Mrs. B's hysterical personality and the interacting variables, that is, the death of her husband, isolation, aging, grief, the physician, the community, and our service.

Intervening with the physician on her behalf, we arranged to take her to his office for the examination. This partially relieved Mrs. B's anxiety. The x-ray and cardiogram were normal, and her wheezing stopped immediately. Support was continued throughout her intensive griefwork while she regained her health, and her sense of hearing, taste, and smell slowly returned. Continued encouragement helped her to develop her interests. She joined a bridge club where she enjoys socializing. She has learned to reach out in a less demanding manner and finds her friendlier approach is reciprocated. Her love of words and cultural background enhance her new creative activity. Mrs. B is writing a book about her past unique experiences, and

this keeps her interested, interesting, and active. Emotions which were repressed for many years are now being released.

Our population, predominantly an aged group, had to be helped
not only with mourning but also with making the environment "mas-
terable." We assisted families in coping with their new situation and
new problems, whether social, psychological, health, financial, or
legal, by using our own agency, linking them with the available
resources of other agencies, and thus personalizing the services of the
funeral home. Some of our families needed our help immediately,
while others evidenced need at a later date. We let them know that
we would be available whenever they needed us.

Mr. G died in the hospital eight months after his illness was diagnosed as
lung cancer. His widow was 71 years old. There were no children, and her
relations with in-laws were somewhat strained. She had no surviving
members of her own family, but she and her husband did have a close
friend, Mr. J, who was extremely supportive throughout Mr. G's illness and
after his death. The funeral went smoothly, Mr. G was buried, the bill was
paid, and the case would have been closed at this point by the funeral director if the postfuneral counseling program had not been active.

The opportunity to meet families during the funeral and offer those services even though the family did not need them at the time gave reassurance
that someone was available if help was needed. This was the case with
Mrs. G. She kept in touch with us for five months, just to say, "hello," to
give us her new unlisted telephone number, and to keep us posted on how
she was managing. Things seemed to go well, until medical problems developed. Her doctor arranged for her to be hospitalized. She was frightened,
wanted our help, and we responded. Intervention included helping her to
talk about her fears concerning the pending operation, while she was still involved in her unfinished grief work, and offering supportive counsel while
she faced an uncertain future.

The surgery resulted in partial removal of a cancerous lung. Supportive
counseling was continued in the hospital and during her convalescence. Mrs.
G recuperated rather quickly, in view of the seriousness of her operation,
and was able to enjoy a normal routine once again.

A year later, she was rehospitalized, and the prognosis was poor. Our
service worked throughout the crisis, caring, understanding, and supporting
both Mrs. G and Mr. J as needs arose. We were able to share and acknowledge with Mrs. G "when her moment of truth arrived" (Reeves, 1969),
supported her by sympathetically listening, helped her while she wept. And
helped her to grieve for herself. Supportive work with Mr. J resulted in his
ability to acknowledge Mrs. G's impending death and thereby establish
more meaningful communication between them. We also intervened in the
hospital setting to ensure appropriate care for her. After Mrs. G's death, Mr.
J continued to receive our support during his grief work.

Many families benefited from the security of knowing that someone was there if needed; others found themselves actually calling on our services when the needs arose; a large number were able to use our services immediately after the funeral in a variety of ways. A number of families were unable to solicit help for themselves, requiring that the postfuneral counseling program be an outreach program.

Mrs. P, a 45-year-old widow, blamed herself for the sudden death of her 70-year-old husband, because of her death wishes toward him. She arranged for a direct cremation. In the process of making the funeral arrangements and paying the bill, she contacted the funeral director many times by phone and in person. She was viewed somewhat as a troublemaker and a nuisance. Normally, contact by the funeral director would have been discontinued at this point.

The cremation arrangement did prevent us from meeting Mrs. A while she first evidenced a need for help in the funeral home. After several unsuccessful attempts to contact her by phone, we sent Mrs. A a letter. Primarily because we were not intimidated by her need to keep people at a distance, we were able to assist her. "What can you do for me, bring back my dead husband?" "No, we can't bring back your husband, he's dead. But, we would like to help you in other ways."

Mrs. A's maladaptive behavior as she sought help from neighbors and community organizations further isolated her and had prevented her from receiving the help she desperately needed. This was further evidenced when she admitted she was contemplating suicide. We worked with relieving the intense guilt she felt, partially as a result of her ambivalent relationship with her spouse, and tried to strengthen her ego capacities and functioning. Her basic mistrust of people (Erikson, 1950) had permeated into her relationships with family, neighbors, and fellow workers, while her maladaptive coping mechanisms kept her isolated, incapacitated, and without friends. Several times, she was in danger of losing her job, because of her verbal attacks on supervisors and co-workers. Much exploratory work was done to help her test reality and to function more appropriately. Dysfunctional family communication patterns were changed, resulting in better family relationships. Mrs. A and her brother, who had not spoken to each other for several years, because of destructive accusations and arguments following their parents' death, began talking to each other again.

We were able to suggest positive options that enabled her to make significant decisions for growth and change in the future. She resigned from the job she had disliked for so many years. She moved to a better location, near her brother. With his help, she found a job more suitable to her qualifications. Instead of negatively permitting things to happen to her as a result of her destructive approaches, that is, instigating her supervisor to fire her from a job she didn't like, she learned to effect more positive changes in her life and thereby began the task of repairing her damaged ego.

While face-to-face contact provides the advantage of observing facial cues and bodily expressions, telephone contact develops sensitivity in picking up expressions and voice intonations; it has been an extremely effective means of maintaining communication with those bereaved persons who preferred this type of communication (Battin et al., 1975).

Mr. B was a 59-year-old widower whose wife had died after a short period of illness and hospitalization. Mrs. B had been reluctant to seek medical attention because of fear of "what the doctors would find." She tried to regain her strength at home, and Mr. B struggled to follow her wishes, caring for her at home and maintaining his job. Finally, a cousin called an ambulance to take her to the hospital. She died shortly thereafter. The funeral was extremely painful. Communication between Mr. B and the funeral home would have ended at this point.

Shortly after the funeral, we were able to contact Mr. B by telephone. We encouraged him to talk about the circumstances of his wife's death. He was able to express his feelings of helplessness, inadequacy, guilt, and anger. We explained how normal those feelings were. Telephone communication was continued by Mr. B and ourselves throughout his period of grief work. He used the telephone communication to discuss his problems on his job and the problems he had adapting to his lonely new life, including his new role as cook and housekeeper. When he was ready to move out into the community, we encouraged him to join a senior center. The center provided him with inexpensive meals, as well as social activity. At first, he had many anxieties, but with much telephone support, he adapted quite well and enjoyed making new friendships. The effect of the telephone intervention was further demonstrated one year later. When he called us to let us know that he was fine, he thanked us for our intervention.

In the course of our relationship with Mr. B, we learned that he had experienced a psychotic episode several years before the crisis that he faced when his wife died. As our supportive work continued, it seemed to be particularly effective in preventing another such crisis.

Our services were directed toward working with both normal and pathological grief reactions. We developed sensitivity in identifying those persons who might have been in trouble. Immediate contact was established with certain individuals at high risk, that is, an isolated elderly person, a physically handicapped person, one suffering the death of a spouse.

By learning how specific bereaved individuals had handled previous losses or life crises, we could then identify those with ineffective problem-solving methods of behavior. During a crisis, maladaptive patterns can be altered in a relatively short period and may subsequently remain stable for a long time. "Crisis is a transitional period presenting an individual both with the opportunity for personal growth, and with the danger of increased vulnerability to mental disorder, the outcome of which in any particular instance to some extent depends on his way of handling the situation'' (Caplan, 1964). Our bereaved clients developed more effective problem-solving mechanisms, and these gave support to their personal growth even during this time of stress.

To be instrumental in effecting change during the transitional period of crisis, one must responsibly and firmly establish continuity of care for bereaved individuals and families in the funeral home. '' 'Social aftercare' should be defined as part of the funeral home's task; outreach programs should be built into the network of services provided; availability of and access to these services should be articulated in the way they are organized, located and delivered; the professional in charge should be held accountable for the provision of services'' (Caroff and Dobrof, 1975).

Crisis intervention requires three areas of expansion in a post-funeral counseling program: (1) Education, through lectures, workshops, groupwork and consultation services, with the purpose of raising the sensitivity level of those persons involved with the bereaved, that is, helping the funeral director to identify those individuals at risk; supporting legislation for required courses for the purpose of teaching the effects of grief, and related problems, with the material taught to be included in the examination for state licensing of funeral directors. (2) Appropriate use of varying methods of treatment for the bereaved. Individual, family, and group work must be available services. Individual counseling is more effective during the narcissistic earlier stages of grief, when the bereaved are more intensely involved in their own pain. After the first few months, group work is an appropriate method to help the bereaved understand they are not alone in their situation, since information is shared and new coping patterns are reinforced. (3) Community involvement to alleviate pressure and facilitate personal growth of the bereaved individual. This involved raising the level of knowledge of the community to understand the needs of the bereaved. That is, the senior center might have an outreach program for newly widowed persons who must learn to socialize without their spouse, educating the bereaved about available community resources. For example, a member of the American Association of Retired Persons might describe programs benefiting the senior group, such as half-fare tickets, rent control, food stamps, and inexpensive trips.

The expansion of responsibly and firmly established postfuneral counseling programs offering continuity of care to bereaved individuals and families calls for the firm commitment of the funeral industry. The industry is moving slowly toward such programs. An effective counseling program to extend and personalize funeral services is of inestimable value for the bereaved population, as evidenced by the overwhelmingly positive verbal and written responses our services received. The value of these programs must be appreciated by all in the funeral industry. Outdated funeral services are costly, and poor programs are destructive. Families will go where individualized services are provided. The funeral director has a responsibility to bereaved individuals, their families, and their community to provide these services.

References

Battin, D., et al. 1975. "Coping and Vulnerability among the Aged Bereaved." In *Bereavement: Its Psychological Aspects*, eds., B. Schoenberg, et al. New York: Columbia University Press.

Cadden, F. 1964. "Crisis in the Family." In G. Caplan, *Principles of Preventive Psychiatry*. New York: Basic Books.

Caplan, G. 1964. *Principles of Preventive Psychiatry*. New York: Basic Books.

Caroff, P. and R. Dobrof. 1975. "The Helping Process with Bereaved Families," In *Bereavement: Its Psychosocial Aspects*, eds., B. Schoenberg et al. New York: Columia University Press.

Compton and Galaway. 1975. *Social Work Processes*. Homewood, Ill.: The Dorsey Press.

Erikson, E. 1950. *Childhood and Society*. New York: W. W. Norton & Co.

Gerber, I., et al. 1975. "Brief Therapy to the Aged Bereaved," In *Bereavement: Its Psychosocial Aspects*, eds., B. Schoenberg et al. New York: Columbia University Press.

Hartman, A. 1975. "To Think About the Unthinkable." In *Social Work Processes*, eds. Compton and Galaway. Homewood, Ill.: The Dorsey Press. London Study. 1971.

Mitford, J. 1963. *The American Way of Death*. New York: Simon and Schuster.

Parkes, C. M. 1972. *Bereavement: Studies of Grief in Adult Life*. New York: International Universities Press.

Reeves, R. B., Jr. 1969. "To Tell or Not To Tell the Patient." In *Death and Bereavement*, ed. A. H. Kutscher. Springfield, Ill.: Charles C. Thomas.

Siporin, M. 1974. "Social Treatment: A New-Old Helping Method." In *The Practice of Social Work*, eds., Klenk and Ryan, 2nd ed. California: Wadsworth.

❦ 20

Grief, Grieving, and Bereavement: A Look at the BASICS

Joseph R. Proulx and Patricia D. Baker

Since one practical definition of education is reiteration without irritation, the general purpose of this paper is to look, once again, at a subject that has been defined, described, classified, categorized, examined, and explained. Although no claims are made for the originality of the content of this work, what is being proposed is a novel format for the application of knowledge relative to grief, grieving, and bereavement. The authors hope that this reworking of the familiar will be informative without being offensive.

With the development of thanatology as an interdisciplinary field of study, grief and bereavement have been the main staples of the burgeoning body of literature. Among the more recent and complete texts in the subject area are those by Parkes (1972), Schoenberg et al. (1974, 1975), and Glick et al. (1974). Despite this articulation in the literature, however, the actual confrontation of the professional care provider with the phenomenon of grief is usually beset by a host of problems—denial, defensiveness, fear, feelings of failure, guilt, and anger. These are natural human responses to difficult expressions of the human condition. But these responses may be modified to enable the professional care provider to deal more effectively with a grieving client. One simple and effective way to accomplish this task is to return to the basics in the study of grief.

To set the stage further for our thesis, consider the following case example:

Ada, the aging widow who lives in the apartment upstairs, seldom goes out. When she does venture forth she wears a wrinkled, ill-fitting, soiled black dress. It's always the same: her mourning clothes. Inside the apartment each evening, just before retiring, she very carefully lays out her dead husband's pajamas. At first she washed and ironed them every week; she only does it once a month now. Ira her spouse had died some five or six years earlier.

Shortly after Ira's death from a brain tumor, Ada began experiencing headaches of such intensity that she remained confined to bed, often for a day or two. Despite the passage of time and the attention of her doctor (though only at the insistence of her son), these headaches continue to besiege her at sporadic intervals. Her physician has assured the son that everything possible is being done, that the problem is not serious, and that the cause is, of course, emotional in origin.

Ada is also beset by disturbing thought processes. She continues to reflect that Ira always wanted to sell the family business and move to Florida. "If only I would have listened to him. It was all my fault that he took sick. The store was vandalized twice in one month . . . he started to have headaches . . . we could have moved away. Why did I insist on staying?" Time passes and both life and Ada go on.

The Model

In reflecting about the introductory case example, one can see that it is representative, in one fashion or another, of the phenomenon known as grief. It can also be seen that these descriptions of Ada are distinct and represent different manifestations of the global concept. The model being proposed addresses the individual components of grief, as well as their sum total. Advances in science and medical technology have led to increased specialization, which in turn results in fragmented care to the clients. Although prescriptions to "treat the whole person" abound, nonetheless the sorry plight that persists in actual practice is that these exhortations are largely inoperative. In dealing with the phenomenon of grief in man we must recognize that every grieving or bereaved individual is an acting, feeling, sensing, imagining, and thinking human being. As such, then, to engage in effective grief work, each of these modalities can and should be explored; they are viewed as essential components of the whole.

The specific purpose of this paper is to illustrate and apply a multimodal behavior modification model for use in dealing with the grief stricken and the bereaved. It is suggested that this model is universal in light of its applicability to all grieving clients and catholic in view of its possible use by all care providers regardless of their distinct disciplines.

BASIC is an acronym referring to behavior, affect, sensation, imagery, and cognition. It is a truncated version of BASIC ID,* a model first developed by Lazarus (1973) for use in behavior therapy. A multimodel model was proposed originally because of its potential for effective treatment within and across a broad range of traditional schools of psychotherapy.

One advantage of such a paradigm is that it tends to ameliorate the tendentious, and thereby self-limiting, approach of specific schools of thought (Lazarus, 1976). Similarly, this advantage may be paraphrased to include a truly interdisciplinary approach to the treatment of the dying, the grief stricken, and the bereaved. Although chaplains, nurses, physicians, and social workers may choose to use a variety of theoretical underpinnings in their individual interactions with clients, any helping discipline can readily incorporate the multimodal framework into its plan of care.

Another advantage of this approach is its firm foundation and tested empirical base, that is, learning theory.

This lies within the province of learning principles, and, more especially, social learning, cognitive processes, and behavioral principles for which there is experimental evidence. We assume that a major portion of therapy is educational, and that the questions of how and why people learn and unlearn adaptive and maladaptive responses are crucial for effective therapeutic intervention. Thus, the major thrust in multimodal therapy is didactic (Lazarus, 1976, p. 4).

Grieving is a normal process. However, if carried to extremes, it may become dysfunctional at best or pathological at worst. The professional roles in dealing with grief are to assist the client through the normal process in as constructive a manner as possible and, obviously, to alter or modify behaviors, feelings, and thoughts that tend toward the destructive or abnormal. Recall that this model was designed originally for work in behavior therapy, and the use of learning principles undergirds its clinical application. The professional, then, helps the client to learn more comfortable and appropriate ways with which to deal with his or her grief.

---

*For the purposes of this paper the ID (interpersonal relations and drugs) portion has been omitted. Interpersonal relations was not included, because of the already extant body of literature available, and drugs, because of the highly specialized nature of the subject. This is not, however, to negate the importance of these components in dealing with the grieving client.

A third claim for the multimodal approach is its specificity, which is, in fact, a hallmark of this paradigm. Describing clients engaged in psychotherapy, Lazarus (1973, p. 404) stated that "patients are usually troubled by a multitude of *specific* problems which should be dealt with by a similar multitude of *specific* treatments." As mentioned earlier though, this framework is also universal and global in its application. All grieving persons behave in certain fashions. The bereaved are beset by a variety of feelings. Grief is usually accompanied by concomitant physical sensations. Imagery is a common phenomenon, and the grief stricken often suffer from irrational thought processes. Using the BASIC approach, professionals from all disciplines may be able to identify and treat specific problems that hinder effective grief resolution.

Lastly, the model is both simple and sound. The acronym itself may serve as a mnemonic device enabling students and professional practitioners to readily grasp the necessary essentials of their clients' reactions to grief. The model is authentic in that the modalities of behavior, affect, sensation, imagery, and cognition constitute the basis of human personality or man in his wholeness. "These specific dimensions are all interactive and yet sufficiently discrete to preserve their own locus of control" (Lazarus, 1976, p. 5). A systematic approach to treating the whole person is suggested in that a change in any one modality will influence every other dimension (Lazarus, 1976). Notwithstanding the Gestalt admonition that the whole is greater than the sum of its parts, we suggest that the whole becomes more meaningful when examined in light of its constituent components.

Applications of the Model

The multimodal format may be used with equal ease in the classroom and/or the clinical setting. Since dealing with grief is usually an anxiety-producing experience we have found that a relatively secure and nonthreatening introduction to the model involves the review of thanatologic literature. This classroom exercise asks the learner to identify, interpret, and distinguish the modalities as they appear in writing. In this manner several educational objectives—comprehension, application, and analysis of the multimodal framework—may be met satisfactorily.

For the purpose of illustration we have selected a few excerpts from the work *A Grief Observed,* by the distinguished English theologian and author C. S. Lewis. The work, written under a pseudonym (N. W. Clerk), represents the author's reflections following his spouse's lingering death.

The opening paragraph quickly gives evidence of three of the modalities: affect, sensation, and behavior. "No one ever told me that grief felt so like fear. I am not afraid, but the sensation is like being afraid. The same fluttering in the stomach, the same restlessness, the yawning. I keep on swallowing" (Clerk, p. 7).

In a number of places in the text Clerk revives images of H, his deceased spouse. The following passage recalls his wife's mental processes and their influence on him.

> For H wasn't like that at all. Her mind was lithe and quick and muscular as a leopard. Passion, tenderness and pain were all equally unable to disarm it. It scented the first whiff of cant or slush; then sprang and knocked you over before you knew what was happening. How many bubbles of mine she pricked! I soon learned not to talk rot to her unless I did it for the sheer pleasure—and there's another red-hot jab—of being exposed and laughed at. I was never less silly than as H's lover (Clerk, p. 8).

The experience of death must be faced and its place in the divine scheme probed. The matter and question of faith, particularly for a theologian, represents an ideal example of the cognitive aspects of one's personality. In addition, the following excerpt illustrates Clerk's experience of the vivid imagery of abandonment.

> Meanwhile where is God? This is one of the most disquieting symptoms. When you are happy, so happy that you have no sense of needing Him, so happy that you are tempted to feel his claims upon you as an interruption, if you remember yourself and turn to him with gratitude and praise, you will be—o.k. so it feels—welcomed with open arms. But go to Him when your need is desperate, when all other help is vain, and what do you find? A door slammed in your face, and a sound of bolting and double bolting on the inside. After that, silence. You may as well turn away. The longer you wait, the more empathic the silence will become. There are no lights in the windows. It might be an empty house. Was it ever inhabited? It seemed so once. And that seeming was as strong as this. What can this mean? Why is He so present a commander in our time of prosperity and so very absent a help in time of trouble. (Clerk, p. 9)

Very often a number of modalities appear jumbled together in the literature. This might produce a rash of individual interpretations as different reviewers posit varying opinions. However, with adequate discussion and guidance, individual interpretation is seen, not as a weakness, but rather a strength of the model. Attention is constantly called to the interdependence of the modalities, as well as to their sui generis character. The literature review exercise offers the learner an opportunity to gain skill in recognizing the hallmarks of personal grief and also to become more aware of their interplay in the empirical setting.

The paradigm may be used in the clinical setting to guide care for the grieving and/or bereaved. Obviously, the extent to which the model is used depends on the amount and type of interaction the student or practitioner has with the client. However, even in the most restricted and superficial contacts the multimodal approach can be effective in beginning a plan of care. A brief outline of this BASIC format appears here. (For more detailed interpretation the reader is referred to Lazarus, 1976, pp. 25–47.)

Behavior refers essentially to exhibited coping mechanisms on the part of the client. Examples might include crying, anorexia, insomnia, unkempt appearance, aimless activity, withdrawal, and mumbling speech. Key questions to be considered in this modality, which are also basic to all other modalities, consist of the following:

When did the behavior begin?
What was happening at that time?
Where were you?
Who was with you?
How did you feel about reacting in this fashion?

The behavior must also be examined in terms of frequency, intensity, and duration. In addition, the importance of opposites should not be overlooked. Examples are the following: When did you not behave in that fashion? Who was not with you at the time?

Affect concerns the feeling tone being expressed. One place to start is to ask the client how he or she feels when exhibiting certain behaviors. Observation and inquiry may be made relative to the absence or presence of feelings; to their experience as pleasant or unpleasant. The affective content should also be explored. Are these feelings of anxiety, anger, guilt, and so forth?

Sensation probes the sensory or physical component of grief. What sights, sounds, smells, tastes, and touches are distressing? Is the client aware, unaware, or perhaps overly sensitive to certain sensations? Visceral complaints and organic pathology may also be subsumed under this rubric.

Imagery deals with the "mental pictures" formed by the grief stricken or bereaved. Places, people, and specific experiences shared with the deceased predominate, often in the form of eidetic imagery. Clients may report being in the presence of the deceased or even conversing with him or her. Specific details of earlier losses may be vividly recalled, and special, comforting, hiding places (often used during childhood years) may be mentally reconstructed.

Cognition represents thought processes that often consume the grieving or bereaved. The faulty or aberrant substance of these thought processes usually deals with demanding prescriptions and themes of denial. Examples of the former might be: "I must not cry," or "I should be brave," or even, "It was all my fault. . . ." Examples stemming from the latter are: "I refuse to believe that he has died," or "There must be something else you can do," and "I can't go on living without her."

In concluding this abbreviated outline of the multimodal framework, it is necessary to stress two points. First, quantification is extremely important; the frequency, intensity, and duration of behavior, affect, sensation, imagery, and cognition serve as a baseline for determining the extent of the problem (Lazarus, 1976). Second, it is imperative to remember that "each modality interacts with every modality" (Lazarus, 1976, p. 35). Recall, however, that two of the original modalities, namely, interpersonal relations and drugs, have not been addressed.

The BASIC model is essentially a problem-solving tool encompassing specification of problems or goals, specification of treatment techniques designed to address the problems or goals, and an ongoing evaluation of the effectiveness of treatment (Lazarus, 1973). Specifically, a modality profile—which necessitates the integration of the processes of assessment, the setting of objectives, and the specification of treatment techniques—may be constructed for each of the following: the client, the family, and even members of the health care team if so indicated. This format may be used in working with anticipatory and conventional grief.

Since the multimodal therapeutic approach is problem centered, its similarity to, and compatibility with, the problem-oriented medical record (POMR) should not be overlooked (Weed, 1968). The pinpointing of particular client problems, deficits, and maladaptive responses could easily elicit the appropriate matching therapeutic intervention from a variety of care providers. Thus, an interdisciplinary team approach is suggested for the development, implementation, evaluation, and modification of a more unified and cohesive plan of care.

Finally, although the central purpose of the model is designed to assist the care provider in identifying and treating negative or troublesome client responses, this tool may also be used in the recognition and strengthening of appropriate or satisfactory coping mechanisms to acute grief.

Grief is a universal human phenomenon. Each grieving person is an acting, feeling, sensing, imagining, and thinking individual. By addressing these essential components of the personality, professional care providers and/or students may offer more effective assistance to grieving clients in coping with their loss.

BASIC is an acronym referring to behavior, affect, sensation, imagery, and cognition. It is an adaptation of a multimodal behavior modification model first developed by Arnold Lazarus. Human reactions and responses to grief often include deviant behaviors, unpleasant feelings, negative sensations, intrusive images, and irrational beliefs. The model offers a sane, simple, and sound approach to meeting the needs of the whole person by exploring problem areas within and across these modalities.

Because of its inherent simplicity and universal applicability the model lends itself with equal ease to both classroom and clinical work in dealing with acute grief.

References

Clerk, N. W. 1963. *A Grief Observed*. Greenwich, Connecticut: The Seabury Press.

Glick, I. et al. 1974. *The First Year of Bereavement*. New York: Wiley.

Lazarus, A. 1973. "Multimodal Behavior Therapy: Treating the BASIC ID," *Journal of Nervous and Mental Diseases* 156 (June):404–11.

Lazarus, A. 1976. *Multimodal Behavior Therapy*. New York: Springer.

Parkes, C. M. 1972. *Bereavement: Studies of Grief in Adult Life*. New York: International Universities Press.

Schoenberg, B. et al. 1974. *Anticipatory Grief*. New York: Columbia University Press.

Schoenberg, B. et al. 1975. *Bereavement: Its Psychosocial Aspects*. New York: Columbia University Press.

Weed, L. L. 1968. "Medical Records That Guide and Teach," *New England Journal of Medicine* 278:593–600.

Part IV

Acute Grief and Survivor Expectations

❧ 21

Acute Grief and Survivor Expectations

Royal Keith

An increasing number of persons in today's society who experience the death of a significant other are groping for ways to cope with their acute grief. This is paradoxical inasmuch as it is now axiomatic that more has been written and taught in the last decade on dying, death, and bereavement than at any previous period in our history. Is it possible that efforts in death education have failed to focus on the acute grief crisis? Are societal changes, such as family dispersion and depersonalization, placing acute grief sufferers in a form of solitude? Is there a growing reluctance to rely on the ritualized responses to a death because of criticism that implies they are meaningless and valueless? Is there a lack of information on acute grief and an absence of experts on whom the survivors can rely during the acute grief experience? These questions should be explored if the confusion and uncertainty of acute grief sufferers are to be replaced by positive expectations of help and counsel in their crisis.

The Focus in Death Education

There is no doubt that the proliferation of articles, books, and courses on the broad subject of dying, death, and bereavement has largely remedied the lack of death awareness that existed in our society a decade ago. The original excitement of exploring and developing a new education field is gradually being replaced with some introspection and doubts about the quality, content, and expectations of death education. Conventional wisdom has held that death education would remove the taboos and provide information to assist a person as he coped with a death crisis or with his own mortality. Great value can be received from reading, studying, and discussing death. But a caveat is necessary lest one get the impression that this intellectual exercise will significantly lessen the emotional trauma of a life-threatening illness or the death of a significant other. A reappraisal of the goals of death education and death-related literature is both timely and necessary.

Part of this evaluation should be directed at the lack of emphasis on the needs and emotions of those experiencing acute grief. This area has been substantially unexplored by writers and researchers outside of funeral service, since they have concentrated on the dying patient and his relatives during the dying process. What happens to the survivors immediately after the death has to a great extent been ignored. The information contributed by funeral service on this issue has often been disregarded because it has been anecdotal or experiential. Suffice it to say here that this contribution needs to be supplemented and expanded by others.

There is a further consideration regarding death education and its impact on those experiencing acute grief. Among those who study and read about the subject of death, there is an expectation that they can immunize themselves from the impact of a death and thus can escape the feelings of acute grief. As an example of this attitude, the following excerpt from a paper written by a student in a college death course is cited: "[By studying death, a family] works out a certain amount of their grief long in advance of a death, and can be prepared to accept death in a rational manner. . . . Death is accepted as part of the day's living, and there is no need to go through the five stages of grief mentioned by Kübler-Ross. The loss of the 'loved one' is just as acute as ever, but having worked grief out as an anticipatory factor over a period of time allows the family to proceed rationally." The disturbing element in this attitude is the emphasis and reliance on rationality, as if to deny the existence of emotion. This student failed to recognize the coexistence of rational and emotional natures in man.

According to Pine (1977), "It is possible for courses in dying and death to be so abstract or lacking in a humanistic perspective that the courses themselves become a means of denying. By believing that death education can insulate against the pain of loss and grief some teachers and students may use such a course for purposes of deny-ing.'' The expectation by some survivors that knowledge and reason have a potential for curing or preventing the hurts of grief poses a challenge, not only for those in death education, but also for those in a caring role with the survivors of a death.

Societal Changes and Acute Grief

Many clichés of the 1960s and 1970s have revolved around the theme of change and the necessity for a person to adapt to that change. The impact of these changes on those experiencing acute grief cannot be ignored. The mobility of the American population, the dispersion of a family to different geographic locations, and the change in emphasis regarding individuality have had a profound effect on many persons' ability to cope with a close death.

In most cultures there has been reliance on a grief support sys-tem at the time of death. This system included a close family unit (psychologically and geographically), a caring community providing a social fabric of reinforcement, a deep-rooted philosophical or re-ligious attitude toward the death experience, and the continuity and stability provided by known and repeated ceremonial forms. Within contemporary American society much of this support system has been modified or eroded by change. Because of this, acute grief is becom-ing more complex and its resolution more difficult.

While the erosion and modification of the support system should be acknowledged, it is equally important to recognize that the needs of the survivors necessitating that system are still present and valid. It is incumbent on those in a care-giving role with survivors to encour-age alternate or revised forms of that system rather than allow the needs to be unfulfilled. Even though a family has been separated by time and distance, basic elements of support can come only through the uniting of the family at the time of death. Those who counsel the bereaved often hear a widow request her geographically distant son not to come to the funeral because he had just visited his dying fa-ther. If the son does not come, most observers sense in the widow an unspoken emptiness that will never be filled. In spite of the disper-sion of the American family and some premature speculation about its demise as the basic social unit, it must continue to be regarded by grief experts as the key element in any support system for the be-reaved.

Revision and alteration are more feasible with the community and religious elements of the support system. During a long terminal illness, ties to the familiar community have frequently been cut. When the death occurs, the most meaningful support may come from those directly involved in the death process, including nurses, doctors, and other patients and their families who have established a close relationship with the family of the dying patient. Many funeral directors are observing that the presence of the nurse who was particularly involved in the death process may be more meaningful than the presence of a friend of 50 years. The point here is that the community giving the survivors social support at the time of a death can be different from what was important to them at other stages in their lives. However, the presence of someone to show care and concern is an essential element.

For most individuals the religious element in the support system is significant. For those without an organized religion as a base for that support, key persons during the death process such as chaplains can fill this role, even if only temporarily. More than in any other experience, those suffering acute grief need a philosophical basis for understanding and coping with their crisis. The need is there and becomes even more apparent for those who move away from institutionalized religion and a philosophy of life and death.

The final element in the support system, known and repeated ceremonial forms, is still intact for most bereaved. There are, however, repeated criticisms of contemporary funeral practice as being a meaningless and valueless element in the support system. These criticisms are leading many survivors to anticipate that postdeath activities with a ceremonial or ritualistic form can be eliminated without any detrimental effects on the resolution of acute grief. In some instances a person gives instructions to his family that he wants no ritual or ceremony following his death. These instructions might disregard the feelings and needs of his family when his death actually occurs. Although unintentional, this can impose a dilemma on the family. They cannot ignore his instructions, nor can they completely ignore their personal feelings and needs. What had been done for sound intellectual reasons may have detrimental consequences for the emotional well-being of a family.

It would be erroneous to generalize that all people surviving a death need a funeral to resolve their grief. But it is even more erroneous to deny that for most people there is a meaning and value in the contemporary funeral experience. According to Margaret Mead (1972):

A good ritual is very much like a natural language. The important thing about a natural language is that it has been spoken for a very long time by very many kinds of people—geniuses and dullards, old people on the verge of dying and children just learning to speak, men and women, good people and bad people, farmers and scholars and fishermen. It has become a language that everyone can speak and everyone can learn, a language that carries overtones of very old meanings and the possibilities of new meanings. I think we can describe ritual in exactly the same way. . . . The essence of ritual is the ability of the known form to reinvoke past emotion, to bind the individual to his own past experience, and to bring the members of the group together in a shared experience. . . . Ritual also gives people access to intensity of feelings at times when responsiveness is muted.

At a time when man needs stabilizing behavior patterns more than ever to resolve grief, it is ironic that there are efforts to minimize the ritual and context of responses to a death. As the other elements in the support system are being eroded and modified by societal changes, the funeral experience is becoming a more critical element as a certain time and place to bring together the family, community, and religious and philosophical support elements.

It appears that serious tampering with any element of the support system for those in acute grief is not justified unless there is a readily available substitute system that could provide an equal or higher level of support. An adequate and proven substitute has not been forthcoming from the critics of the funeral. Further, Lorenz (1974), argues that "being enlightened is no reason for confronting transmitted tradition with hostile arrogance." To attempt to eliminate or significantly change any custom or ritual is precarious for all of society, for once a tradition has been destroyed, it is difficult to restore. Lorenz writes: "Not only highly developed rites or ceremonies [as in funeral ceremonies] but also simpler and less conspicuous norms of social behavior may attain, after a number of generations, the character of sacred customs which are loved and considered as values whose infringement is severely frowned upon by public opinion."

The Variations of Acute Grief

The manner in which people respond or react in acute grief normally includes behavior patterns that have been learned or observed in others. In addition, several models have been proposed to assist in understanding the variables of acute grief responses to different death situations. These models have been based on how the person died, the time available to the survivors to adjust to the potential death (anticipatory grief), the closeness of relationship to the deceased, the stages of bereavement, prior death experiences, and so on. However, little attention has been focused on the fact that when a person dies there are many different survivors with varying physical and emotional needs and with different levels of intensity of the acute grief experience. This complicates the role of those who attempt to counsel the many survivors of a given death, particularly as it relates to immediate postdeath activities that would have meaning and value for all of them. What may be unnecessary for some may be essential for others. A funeral with the body present may have meaning and value to some survivors of a death but have little meaning and value to others.

An important goal for those who counsel the bereaved is to reconcile these differences so that each person's needs are met, particularly those who have the most acute needs. Sometimes, however, it is difficult to ascertain who among the survivors is suffering the most acute grief and who will have the most difficulty resolving grief. To help identify those who may experience grief more intensely, it is suggested that three groups of survivors can be distinguished in most situations following a death. They will have varying degrees of needs and emotional responses to that death and can be referred to as the primary, secondary, and tertiary survivors of a death.

A hypothetical example may be helpful to illustrate this concept. A 45-year-old man dies after a three-year battle with cancer. His family includes his wife, two sons, a brother, and his parents. They would normally show all the symptoms of acute grief, as described by Lindemann (1944) and others. The sense of irretrievable loss, somatic distress, disorientation, denial feelings, and hostility are some of those symptoms. They would be the primary survivors of his death.

The man had several intimate friends with whom he shared much of life's experiences and the closeness of human companionship. They would experience some of the symptoms of acute grief, including the feelings of denial, irretrievable loss, and possibly hostility, but probably would not experience the disorientation and physical symptomatology of the primary survivors. For them, life would go on normally after some grief work had been accomplished. They would be the secondary survivors of his death.

The man had been an active member of his community and had

many social and business acquaintances with whom he had shared some experiences. They would probably suffer none of the feelings of acute grief, with the possible exception of feelings of denial. However, his death would give them a disturbing reminder of their own mortality and would cause the generalized sense of loss expressed by John Donne: "Any man's death diminishes me, because I am involved in Mankinde." They would be the tertiary survivors of his death.

Generally, caregivers in a grief situation should concentrate their efforts on meeting the acute needs of the primary survivors. Even among the primary survivors, however, there are variations in needs and responses to the same death. Funeral directors and other professionals who counsel the bereaved should be sensitive to these variations. In the example just given, the wife and one son may have been closely involved during the illness and may have minimized their needs through anticipatory grief. The other son, however, lived a great distance away and had not been with his father during the death process. His need for a support system at the time of death may be very intense. Yet, if his mother and brother choose not to avail themselves of the elements of the support system, that is, family solidarity, community sharing, positive philosophical attitudes, and funerary procedures, what is left to support the second son as he begins his grief work? There is evidence to suggest that those who attempt to resolve their grief in solitude, without any elements of the support system, will have the greatest difficulty in adjusting to their loss. A part of the caregiver's role to that family unit should be to point out this potential problem. It would be a normal expectation of the wife and son that the other primary survivors would have the same feelings and reactions as they had to the death. Explaining the potential harm of this erroneous expectation should be a responsibility of those who counsel the primary survivors of a death, especially the clergy and funeral director.

There is a further complicating factor in identifying those who have the most acute needs following a death. In the example just given, a close relationship had developed between the man who died and another patient in the hospital. In many ways, he may exhibit signs of acute grief normally expected only from the primary survivors. Yet these signs may go unrecognized and his needs unresolved. Hospital chaplains and health care professionals should be particularly sensitive to this situation. The patient usually will be unable to participate in the funeral process, but the other elements of the support system should be made available to him.

For different reasons the support system can be helpful even to those who are the secondary and tertiary survivors of a death. Again, variations in grief responses occur within these two groups, but there is one common factor that should be noted. A few times in our lives will we be the primary survivors of a death. Frequently, however, we will be involved as secondary or tertiary survivors. With the exception of exhaustive study or perhaps painful introspection, there is no procedure or process whereby we can prepare or condition ourselves for the eventual role as a primary survivor. It is suggested here that a person can obtain some valuable insight into this role because he can observe as a secondary or tertiary survivor the behavior and responses in primary survivors. To some extent the secondary or tertiary roles become the only rehearsal stage or practice field for the inevitable role of a primary survivor. If this concept is valid, then trends toward privatization of postdeath activities may be depriving many people of important preparation and rehearsal activity for their own acute grief experience.

Those who counsel the bereaved must be cognizant of the multiple variations of acute grief. They should be sensitive to different needs and to the various levels of intensity. They should focus their caring role on those intense feelings and needs. But they should not disregard other survivors who also have needs that can be effectively fulfilled by the elements of the grief support system.

The Funeral Director and Survivor Expectations

The variety of needs and responses requires many decisions and choices by the primary survivors. It is imperative that society provide reliable experts in grief during the difficult period immediately following a death. Most frequently the primary survivors look for help and advice from those to whom Kastenbaum (1972) refers to as the "professionals in our death system," that is, physicians, nurses, clergy, mental health specialists, and funeral directors. But Kastenbaum observes that these professionals have not given "the participants in the death situation . . . effective answers and emotional support." This observation merits serious discussion on every professional's role as a caregiver in a grief situation. This paper deals, however, only with the observation as it relates to the funeral director as a grief expert.

The societal changes and the alterations to the grief support system discussed earlier in this paper have expanded the role of the funeral director in the acute grief crisis. Some people are highly critical of this expanded role because they feel the funeral director is not qualified and his objectivity as a grief expert is related to economic motivation. At the same time other people commend the funeral director as the most helpful professional during their death crisis. Meanwhile, a significant portion of society is neither critical nor complimentary and view the funeral director as neither a positive nor a negative factor in the ''death system.'' This latter group, however, has heard of the controversy regarding the value of the funeral director. When a death occurs in their family, their expectation that a funeral director has sufficient expertise to ''cure'' grief can be just as detrimental as the expectation that a funeral director has no reliability as a caregiver.

Funeral directors must accept some of the responsibility for the confusion in survivor expectations regarding their role in a grief situation. A few funeral directors have been less objective in asserting that a traditional funeral with the body present is necessary for all survivors following a death. Some have not kept up with the new and expanded literature available through their professional associations and from the various information and research centers on bereavement and thanatology. An isolated few have placed financial considerations above the needs of the survivors. By their lack of professional objectivity, their lack of professional growth, and their lack of professional responsibility, they have increased the uncertainty regarding the quality of help the survivors can expect from a funeral director. Fortunately, strong efforts by funeral service leaders to upgrade the professional level of funeral directors is beginning to show some positive results. Symposia, continuing education programs, and seminars are but some of the significant educational opportunities having substantial impact on the professional growth of the funeral director.

The critics of the funeral profession must also bear some responsibility for the growing confusion and uncertainty about what the survivor should expect from a funeral director. Some are less than objective when they assert that there is little or no value in the funeral and that the funeral director is not qualified to be of any significant help to those in acute grief. If we are to provide survivors with realistic expectations, this position of the critics must be explored.

Much of the criticism of contemporary funeral practices is based on costs. Greatly ignored, however, is the critical issue of whether there is value received for the funeral expenditure. With significant frequency families express to their funeral directors that the funeral experience was the key factor as they began to acknowledge and work through their acute grief. If the survivors failed to use this element of the support system, it would be difficult to ascertain the cost to them in terms of maladaptive behavior, repressed emotion, or a lengthy period of death denial.

It was mentioned earlier that a key element in the grief support system is the continuity and stability provided by known and repeated ceremonial rites. For most people a funeral ceremony fills this need. Those opposed to contemporary funeral practices suggest a memorial service as an alternative to meet survivor needs. Although this may provide the support for some people, there has been no evidence presented to suggest that this form would fill all the needs of most survivors of a death. It is generally accepted that the immediate needs of the survivors that should be satisfied by a ceremony include the need to accept the reality of death; the need to express the emotion of grief; the need for human companionship and support; the need for philosophical, religious, or spiritual support; and the need for a finalization of the relationship with the deceased. Although a memorial service or other alternates to the funeral can fill some of these needs, they have potential deficiencies that should be acknowledged.

These deficiencies include a lack of opportunity to face the reality of death and to finalize the relationship with the deceased. In the experience of this writer, most primary survivors begin to accept the reality of a death only when they see the person who died. Although the critics of the funeral with the body present refer negatively to the custom of viewing, no substitute procedure has been provided by them that would allow primary survivors the opportunity to fully face the reality of a death. In addition, many who have experienced a memorial service have observed that it was an appropriate setting for the intellectual acknowledgment of death, but it seemed to be an inappropriate setting for the emotional expression of grief. Again, the important dual nature of man must be emphasized. Grief is an emotion that must be expressed. If the opportunity for expression of that emotion is not given during the immediate postdeath period, then the possibility grows that much of the grief will be repressed. For some survivors, in certain grief situations, these potential deficiencies may not be significant. But serious detrimental effects could result if all survivors of deaths have the expectation that a memorial service will fill all their needs.

The criticism that the funeral director has no qualification as a grief expert ignores some significant facts. The ''in service experience'' of the funeral director in grief situations should not be discounted as a source of knowledge and expertise in assisting the survivors of a death. He is the only "death system professional" whose primary experience is exclusively involved in the grief crisis. His daily professional practice involves dealing with persons who are struggling with their feelings regarding a pending death, with persons who have just experienced a death in their family, and with persons who are still working through their grief long after a death has occurred. Because of this daily experience, he has learned to recognize the variations in grief responses and the different needs of survivors. Even though it is frequently anecdotally and experientially based, the expertise of the funeral director in the field of grief deserves to be acknowledged.

In addition, most funeral directors today do not rely on experience as their only teacher. They are also expanding their professional expertise by attending seminars and symposia and by reading and studying the increased thanatologic literature. They recognize that they are being relied on as key supportive persons in an acute grief situation. Most are accepting this role responsibly so that the expectations of survivors can be fulfilled.

Moreover, the differences, the changes in attitudes, and the rising expectations of survivors have placed demands on the adaptiveness and the ability of today's funeral director. Four observations can be made to help illustrate this point.

First, for years many families would select a funeral director because of his facilities, his cars, and his record of prior services. Today, more and more people are now saying these criteria are not enough. They are now expecting the funeral director they select to have a high level of professional expertise. They expect him to possess a trained skill for listening to and caring about survivors' individual wants and needs. In addition they expect him to evidence concern about the impact of the death crisis by being involved in community education on dying, death, and bereavement.

Second, the mobility of the American population has resulted in many families' calling a funeral director because of the convenience of location, particularly in urban areas. As a result, there is not the close personal relationship that existed when the funeral director had served the same family many times. In these situations the counseling role of the funeral director is even more sensitive and complex. Even though chosen because of location, the funeral director has an even greater responsibility to fulfill a family's expectation that he will evidence care, concern, and competence in meeting their needs and desires.

Third, because of their differing needs, wants, desires, and demands, the various survivors of a death expect a wide and diverse range of choices in the kinds of services and merchandise offered. The funeral director must have an adaptive pricing schedule that fairly and equitably responds to different family requests—from a traditional chapel service to a simple memorial service, from a service in a church to a service on the banks of a river, from an involved graveside service to none at all. In the same way a wide selection in the merchandise offered must complement the diversity in the services provided. To limit their choices is to limit each family's unique and individual way of working through their grief. After listening to the family, after communicating experience and knowledge, after assisting them to transform their feelings into action, the funeral director must then respond to their decisions and be as supportive as possible, regardless of the manner in which the family has chosen to express their grief.

Fourth, there is a growing desire by many families to be more involved in the funeral process. This desire is expressed in many forms. The widow may wish to write something special to be printed on the memorial folder. A family may wish to play a song recorded by a granddaughter who was unable to attend the service. A son with woodworking skills may wish to make the casket for his father. A daughter may wish to read special comments about her father's life. The challenge to the funeral director is to be sensitive to this need for personal expression and involvement. Often this need is not expressed voluntarily. Only through skilled listening can the funeral director ascertain that one of the primary survivors could be helped through grief if he could be more personally involved.

The signs are encouraging that most funeral directors are responding and adapting to these changes and differences in the attitudes of the survivors of a death. In doing so, their caregiving role becomes even more vital and important as they meet the higher level of survivor expectations of help, counsel, and support in the acute grief crisis.

Conclusion

The early efforts in death education have focused insufficient attention on the impact of acute grief. Societal changes have caused some erosion and modification of the grief support system that has been essential to survivors. The variables in acute grief and how different survivors of a death are affected deserve more study and attention. Survivors are becoming uncertain about who can be relied on in their grief crisis. These developments pose serious challenges to those in a caring role for the survivors of a death.

To meet these challenges, efforts should be intensified toward better understanding of acute grief, its complexities, its unique characteristics, and its resolution. Care should be taken that the description of acute grief in thanatology literature is not stereotyped or generalized. There is a need for an emphasis that reduces the expectation that acute grief can be avoided if one knows enough about it. All the caring professionals must recognize not only the significant impact of acute grief but also the critical importance of reliable and proved procedures to be followed in its resolution. The increasingly important role of the funeral director in the grief resolution process needs to be recognized and acknowledged. The funeral director, in turn, must accept the substantial responsibility this recognition imposes on him to be qualified for that role.

In most crisis events in life, people have an expectation that there will be helping and caring professionals with a proven body of knowledge to assist them through the crisis. For most people, one of the greatest crises will be the death of someone loved. It is imperative that a caring and informed professional be present to fulfill the expectations of a survivor who seeks help and counsel in his acute grief experience. A professionally competent funeral director can fill that role.

References

Kastenbaum, R. 1972. *The Psychology of Death*. New York: Springer Publishing Company, p. 79.

Lorenz, K. 1974. *Civilized Man's Eight Deadly Sins*. New York: Harcourt Brace Jovanovich, pp. 61–65.

Mead, M. 1972. *Twentieth Century Faith*. New York: Harper and Row, pp. 127, 159.

Pine, V. R. 1977. "Socio-Historical Portrait of Death Education." *Death Education*, 1(1): 79.

Sudden Death, Acute Grief, and Ultimate Recovery

Roy V. Nichols

On Friday, April 29, 1977, Larry walked outdoors, said "I'm sorry" to the world, molded his lips around the end of his twelve-gauge shotgun, and then pressed the trigger. He was free forever of the torment and turmoil that had stalked him throughout his life. Intermittently under psychiatric care for years, he was tired, worn out, and alone. The psychiatrist had told Betsy, Larry's wife, that she could expect little change in his condition and that she should decide a future for herself, their two daughters, and Larry on that reality. A week before, Betsy, Heidi, age 6, and Erica, age 5 had gone to Texas. They were considering moving there—without Larry—so that they might find some tranquility. Larry knew that and made their decision for them.

My first meeting with Betsy, as the funeral director she sought, affirmed what my years of experience had taught: Survivors of sudden death often seek an avoidance and protective behavioral pattern. It was on Saturday, April 30. Betsy had returned from Texas that day, placed her two girls with a friend (not telling them why) and came to me that evening. She wanted me to bury the body quietly and with little involvement with her community. That is easy to understand. Pain hurts. Suicide implies guilt and shame. Children should be happy and protected from the nasty world. Besides, how could she possibly explain the psychiatric disorder from which Larry suffered and of which only a very select few were aware?

I listened carefully as Betsy talked and talked and talked. She was intelligent, fluent, and well read. After a couple of hours, when the rapport seemed right, I asked Betsy to do what I have asked many families to do in recent months—and with dramatic results: to enter into a period of 24 to 30 hours with me during which time she would make no decisions whatsoever. With a quizzical look, she asked "Why?"

"Because what Larry has done has tremendous and critical long-range implications for your mental health and that of your girls, and the way you three will go on together. It's extremely vital that the decisions made this week be right, and that takes long and serious deliberation." After some discussion, Betsy understood and agreed to no decision-making for a full 24-hour period. We spent the rest of the evening talking.

What unfolded was an involved week of crisis intervention. Sunday, Betsy sent for her children so that the family could experience the death together. At the time of his death Larry had been covering their home with rough sawed cedar lumber. Along the way he had remarked that he wanted to be buried in a shipping crate. Betsy, Larry's two brothers, and I, built his "shipping crate" of rough sawed cedar lumber. Betsy brought his pillow and blanket from home. The girls drew several pictures and picked fresh flowers from the yard to be placed with their daddy's body.

The funeral, held Tuesday evening so as to be accessible to more people, was heavily attended. Elements of his illness were explained and illustrated with music of the kind that Larry used to listen to. Amidst the aroma of newly sawed cedar, the torment was explained and Betsy and the girls were buoyed from suspicion, shame, and guilt. After the service, for those who chose, the cedar box was opened, and many saw the reality for themselves. Betsy, Heidi, and Erica now affirm that experience. On Wednesday—five days after Larry died—he was buried. No lowering device or green matting hid the grave. Only a tent was there to keep us from getting too wet as Betsy, Heidi, Erica, and a host of others shoveled dirt into the grave.

During my 15 years of experience in funeral service I have observed a somewhat consistent phenomenon regarding sudden death. When death is sudden, catastrophic, unexpected, and interruptive, survivors are more inclined to short-circuit the intervention possibilities of the funeral experience. Closed caskets, absent bodies, no viewing, private services, graveside services, and no services are more frequent than when the death is not sudden. Seemingly, the greater the trauma, shame, guilt, insecurity, and disorientation, the greater the tendency for denial, avoidance, retreat, isolation, and escape. Certainly, the desire for denial is understandable and justifiable. Denial serves a needed and critical purpose for a period of time. Too much reality too fast could be psychologically overwhelming to some, and to impose reality on denial when it is needed could be a gross error.

The question is who needs how much denial for how long? This is a fascinating one that can be answered only in the individual case in point. My sense is that most usually seek more denial than is needed and that many caregivers are prone to encourage denial through protecting the client and through functionary roles rather than through facilitating and enabling roles.

The attempt to delay or avoid grieving is commonly reported as a primary cause of bad response to loss. How long can one sustain the attempt to delay or avoid? Again the true answer lies in the individual circumstance and case in point. It appears that occasionally someone can sustain a very long denial period with little apparent psychological maladaptation or distortion to the psyche. Parkes (1972) and Gorer (1965) have placed a two-week limitation in their writings; beyond that point, they report, the possibility of maladaptation increases as time passes. This approximate time period has been affirmed by several researchers in conversation. Surely the deeply set maladaptations and distortions from loss that highly skilled therapists attempt to alter have a great deal to do with the length of time the psyche has had to develop a distorted pattern of adjustment. At the moment a sudden death occurs, survivors have no maladaptation or distortion caused by the death. What is needed are caregivers who can engage with the survivors immediately and who, in that brief period of time, can design an intervention system of experiences that facilitates the grieving experience and, in the long term, minimizes the maladaptive response to the loss.

Undoubtedly, we grieve and, consequently, adapt to loss. Of that we have no choice. The choice we do have is *when* and *how* we grieve and adapt. Whether we adapt in a normal or a distorted pattern has a significant consequence on the degree of pathology with which we all live on without those we have loved.

That we do grieve, that the attempt to delay or avoid grieving is risky, and that a two-week limitation is valid for most people have led to a different management approach to sudden death in my funeral practice. Compounding the sense of that responsibility is the further fact that the cleric and the funeral director are most likely to be the only two caregivers involved at the crisis time. If neither is able to intervene significantly and appropriately, the possibility of pathology is increased. Furthermore, when death is sudden, usually little of major significance occurs during those first two weeks except the funeral period. The funeral period, then, takes on critical implications in its impact on the ultimate recovery of the survivors, and the cleric and the funeral director must, as caregivers, work in unison toward common goals. With that understanding of the professional roles in sudden death, we have met with most of the clergy in our area and have discussed the team approach. Usually, we are able to work as a team; we try to urge the family to wait 24 to 30 hours after sudden death during which time no decisions are made.

During that period, several areas of concern are explored with both the total family unit and its individual members. The discussions are disjointed, erratic, impatient, sometimes explosive, and irrational. Sometimes the whole approach fails. What emerges are bits and snatches of information, ideas, and insights that, when collected and integrated, serve in the formulation of objective concepts of persons and of a family. By working out of those concepts, approaches can be designed to provide meaningful experiences for the family and its members, so that each person may be accorded respect and each person may be given an opportunity to examine various approaches to ease recovery.

Attempts are made to determine how the family has handled prior crises and losses. Do its members function as a unit—or does that unit fracture, with the members going their various ways? It is also necessary to determine how the individuals respond to crisis and loss; one must learn what their grief timetables are: which of its members are resilient and thus able to return to stability more quickly. Then, too, one must determine which are the prominent emotions and behaviors (anger, depression, guilt, etc.), and determine who needs how much closure with the dead person (since sudden death always leaves relationships in suspension). Finally, one must discover who is willing to work toward closure, and which members of the family want to be involved and to what extent: who wants support? who wishes to go it alone?

A working definition of what the family and its individuals want to be one year hence is attempted. This usually takes on words such as settled, well, happy, comfortable, productive, and the like. Thought is given on how to move toward that goal. Ways of facilitating grieving as a family unit and as individuals are discussed. One of the critical concepts often difficult to convey is the reality that the family must grieve as a unit, and each of its own members needs to grieve as an individual. A family grieves as a unit as determined by their historical model from past crises and losses, and each person grieves in his own way according to his historical model as a person. It is critical that each person in the family fully appreciate that each must grieve in his own way and the family must grieve in their way. Conflict may arise when one interferes with the other. Ways of supporting and facilitating each other are discussed.

Historical models are determined by examining past crises and losses in the family, for example, when a pet died, a child went to college, a parent moved out, a retirement was imposed, an employee was dismissed, a change occurred in the community, a member was cut from the basketball squad, a member failed to make the cheerleader squad, or a family member lost a political race. Central and recurrent themes, behaviors, and emotions are discovered. These determine the grief pattern to be used in responding to the current crisis and loss. If dissatisfaction is expressed in the past models, an attempt may be made to alter the response model.

Having determined in a loose fashion some or a few of these—that is, having discovered historical models and future goals in adjustment, discussion of the here and now may proceed with some wisdom and consideration of various decisions. The heightened awareness of the importance of death in the family, the nature of crisis management and its long-range implications on mental health, and the impact of today's decisions on tomorrow's recovery have often resulted in families' and/or individual's becoming more rather than less involved in the funeral experience as an intervention system.

Peyson died on May 16, 1977, at 51 years of age. A corporate executive, he collapsed in his office of a sudden cardiac arrest and was dead on arrival at the hospital. Sally, his wife, was 35. Their children were Shepperd, age 13; Kimberlee, age 12; and Brent, age 6. Sally was accompanied to the funeral home by two business associates who had come to tell her that Peyson was dead. They had not telephoned ahead, and they arrived in midafternoon. Don, my associate, met them. In a few minutes he had learned of the children and their ages. Sally had asked a friend to meet the school buses and take the children away. Don intervened and said, "What we have to do here can wait. Go home, be there when the kids get home, tell them the truth, and be with them. We'll talk later." Sally did.

Peyson's children had not yet experienced death in the family. They had no foundation upon which to begin a recovery. Don is familiar with principles of crisis management, the child's developmental concept of death, and the developmental fear of death; he is also sensitive and gentle. He explored with Sally, Shep, Kim, and Brent what Peyson's death meant to them. Peyson died on Monday. On Tuesday, the five of them did a lot of talking, with their minister present as much as possible. On Wednesday, the children explored the funeral home, got hot chocolate, gumballs out of the machine, saw the preparation room, crawled into the back of the hearse, and generally experimented with a strange world. Brent spent a long time in a casket, lifting the pillow, crawling under the blanket, having the lid closed, and trying to understand what the box was about. Having been given permission by Sally and by Don, the three were free to ask any questions, look behind any door, and explore for themselves. Spontaneously, with no adult suggestion, they set the letters spelling their dad's name on the register stand, and in typical child's scrawly handwriting, wrote their dad's name, dates, and other family information in the register book. One child decided, since his daddy always rested with his legs crossed, that he should lie so in the casket. Without asking permission, he pulled one of his father's legs over the other and then went to get mommy to show her what he had done.

The minister helped Sally determine goals for the ritual ceremony. One of them was saying "I love you" before it is too late. Music was selected to facilitate the goals, and the words were duplicated so that all could read them as the music was played. When the children arrived for the funeral, they decided it should be their task to pass out the songsheets. Several articles, letters, and pictures were put with Peyson's body that morning. The minister had carefully prepared his message to convey the goals and to establish where the hope was. En route to the cemetery, Sally, the minister, and Don were in the front seat of the hearse. The three children rode in the rear with the casket and body. If you have to go to the cemetery because you are dead, what better way to go than with your children and spouse taking you? At the cemetery only a lowering device was used. No green matting covered the rich earth and no tent hid a beautiful blue sky. They stayed until Peyson's body was in its grave. Brent threw in a clump of dirt.

The early emotions and behaviors that characteristically accompany sudden death are reasonably predictable. One would expect numbness, shock, disbelief, disorientation, bewilderment, and stunned silence. Once these begin to thaw, active behaviors usually prevail. People need to do something! Panic, anger, fear, revenge, feelings of being cheated, and desires to strike back motivate the grieving person. Giving direction to the activity in some expressive therapeutic and functional ways is critical or the behavior may take on a scattergun pattern that has little purpose and may not be based in reality. Being able to function against what appears insurmountable assists in warding off feelings of helplessness, bitterness, hopelessness, and self-pity. Learning that one can continue to function, to fight, and to perform assists in minimizing the debilitating effects of passivity, depression, meaninglessness, and isolation. The family, moving as a unit, tends to bring along those who would become passive. It is critical that caregivers (in this instance, funeral directors and clergy) not contribute to the passivity of survivors of crisis and loss by being the sole functionaries in the crisis; rather they should share the performance of tasks so that survivors, too, can learn that not all is lost.

If a continuum is drawn with "do nothing" at one end and "do everything" at the other end, I fantasize removing myself entirely from the functional role and finding others (family members) to perform every task. Occasionally, while counseling, the do nothing–do everything line is drawn on paper, and the client is asked to strike a mark on the continuum expressing the desire for involvement in the experience. That guides me in my role as I become the caregiver who will guide the intervention experience. Some want no involvement. Some want intense involvement. Too often, when sudden death strikes, the surrogate sufferers (those who would suffer in place of the sufferers so that the sufferers need not suffer!) are summoned. The coroner, police, funeral director, and cleric respond to the call, and the survivors are left in a passive position of answering questions and being told when to be where and how to behave. The constriction of behavior can be limiting on the freedom of the sufferers to suffer without delay so that the suffering may be moved through and be ended. Suppose there were no funeral directors, clerics, or anyone else to perform the tasks except the family? Suppose the family had to arrange the entire proceedings, build a box, dig and fill the grave, notify friends, and deliver the funeral message of meaning and hope to the community? I believe they would understand the nature of life and death more clearly, would develop coping strategies earlier in life, would formulate workable and meaningful philosophies of life and death that would sustain them, would talk more, would move beyond denial sooner, would grieve more rapidly, would express emotions more readily, would recover from the loss with less maladaptive and distorted risk, and would find peace sooner. It is toward that end that I strive to engage a family in the management of sudden death.

A word of caution is critically important to guard against the overextension of a person in the experience. The art of permission-giving so that persons are free to engage actively in the crisis is a delicate art that must be monitored constantly when one is guiding persons through an experience so that no one engages when it is not his free choice to do so. To bring someone into the experience "because he should" or "because it is good for him" or to instill obligatory feelings conveying behavior that is expected could be psychologically harmful to the person. Such guidance on the part of the caregiver would be most unprofessional and dangerous for the grieving person. To safeguard against such overextension an approach using deferred judgment is employed. Any task offered to the grieving person is offered well in advance (hours or the day before, if possible) so that the person has time to consider the decision. Immediate decisions are usually made in an avoidance pattern. Decisions that are deferred have a higher frequency of moving into the experience. When persons have ample time for consideration and have permission to engage or disengage with the experience without judgment on the part of the caregiver, the caregiver has assurance that the mourners are not overextending themselves in the experience and are behaving in an entirely voluntary manner.

Jerry, less than three years old, died in about six hours one day of acute necrotizing epiglottiditis. The night before the funeral, Jaye, his mother, had difficulty sleeping. Words kept tumbling through her mind, formulating a poem. This pattern has become well known as an example of how rapidly one can identify, crystallize, and focus the confusion of feelings we all experience at sudden death. The opportunity to take time, consider, defer, and invest oneself at the crisis time facilitates crystalization of grief issues so that one has a better sense of where grief work needs to be done. This poem emerged the day before Jerry's funeral and was read at the funeral.

With His Playclothes On

You lie there sleeping, my little son
    with long dark hair
    and your playclothes on.

How many times I'd pray that you'd sleep—
    one more hour—a day—a week
    so I could wash, or clean, or bake—
    a pie—some cookies or a cake.

How many times when the house was clean—
    I'd get upset because you'd spill your juice—
    or crumble a cookie—
    or drip your bottle all over the steps.

If only you'd wake up in my bad dream
    and throw your bottle
    or stand there and scream.

If only we could see you smile—
    or spill your cereal on our new tile.

Dear God—
    Give me strength
    to forget the bad days I had—
    when I got upset with this little lad—
        with his long dark hair—
        with his curls and his smile.

Who lies there sleeping
    with his playclothes on.

One final example. Truth and reality come slowly, sometimes ever so slowly, to one's full awareness—purposefully and rightfully so. Is it not true that we all would collapse under too much reality too fast in the right circumstance? The following example illustrates how it is not possible to move the human psyche faster than it will allow so long as the experience of the psyche is not pushed beyond its willful place. The intervention system in this example was very extensive. Yet the recovery of the parents is at their pace. The unanswered question in the example is how much longer would the recovery have been delayed and how much more distortion might have developed if the intervention system had not occurred swiftly in the parental bereavement experience?

Fourteen-month-old Marcia was riding in the car seat. Paul, her father, was driving, and Rae Ann, her mother, was riding with her in the front seat. Three-year-old brother, Greg, was riding with his grandfather in another car. An unfortunate circumstance suddenly occurred on the road causing Paul to cut the car sharply to the left. The car rolled over and the roof caved in. Paul was shaken but unhurt. Rae Ann dislocated her shoulder. Marcia died in a few seconds of head and neck injuries.

The emergency room staff at the hospital had recently had an inservice program in the management of sudden death. Paul and Rae Ann were offered the opportunity to be with Marcia's body. They did so—picking her up, holding her, telling her how beautiful she is/was, and how she had taught a lot of people how to love. They wanted to take her home that night. Later when asked why, Rae Ann said, ''I wanted to get out of there because when I got home both kids would be safe in their beds. This was all a dream and Marcia was at home in bed.'' When asked what they would have done if they had taken Marcia home, Paul and Rae Ann indicated they would have put her pajamas on, held her, rocked her, and would have done what they would have done if death had given notification in advance.

Later Rae Ann, Paul, and Greg dressed their Marcia. They combed her hair, put on what little cosmetics they wanted, put a tiny silver cross on a necklace around her neck, and cried a lot. All that took a long time. Greg, when putting Marcia's booties on her, asked, ''When Marcia is done dying, can we take her home with us?''

The grave was a naked hole. After the minister finished the commitment, he invited those who wanted to stay to witness the burial to do so. Several stayed along with Paul and Rae Ann, and the body was put in the grave. Rae Ann, on her knees at the edge of the hole, dropped a pink baby rosebud onto the casket lid. They left.

The grave now has a tree planted on it. Several toy windmills turn constantly in the breeze. The marker has Marcia's picture on it with the inscription, ''Step softly. A dream lies here, for God needed another angel.'' Three months later, when asked if they go to the grave often, they responded, ''It's down to about three times a week now. We were going every day.''

The absolutely incredible truth that is so elusive for those who have never had a Marcia die suddenly is the interplay and struggle between belief and disbelief. The polarizing powerplay between the two takes weeks? Months? Years? The internal tug-of-war pulls first one way, then the other. Even with their intellectual awareness that Marcia was dead, these parents struggled with intense emotional forces that tried to deny reality. Internal dissonance goes on and on and on. Marcia died on May 23, 1977. On August 29, 1977, a tape-recorded interview with Paul and Rae Ann revealed that continuing dissonance between belief and disbelief. After an extensive week of intervention, all of which has been affirmed by Paul and Rae Ann as voluntary on their part and which included seeing Marcia dead at the scene, interacting with her body at the hospital, dressing her body at the funeral home, meeting with hosts of friends and neighbors, and witnessing the placing of Marcia in the grave, Rae Ann spoke of her concern regarding her new pregnancy (the conception having taken place before Marcia's death). ''It hasn't registered on me yet. Sometimes it does, but 90 percent of the time I still consider her in the room,'' or, ''even though I'm not busy because she is not here to keep me busy, I still think I am putting too much into this baby, thinking that this is going to be her reborn. I'm trying to talk myself out of it because it could be a boy and it could be completely different and I can't classify this baby as an imprint of Marcia.''

Later, she continued in speaking of her initial impulses in the first few days as they relate to where she was in the interview, ''I really didn't think at that time I would not see her again. I wish I would have spent more time with her and I knew I could come down here [the funeral home] at anytime, but I stayed at home thinking she was going to come to me. I've been waiting three months now and she hasn't and it's starting to go through my mind that she is not coming home. I wondered when we moved (planned before Marcia's death) if she would be able to find us. A lot of times I feel her inside me. I don't know if that sounds funny. But I feel her and I told Paul many times she was talking, yet I hear this 'I'm all-right now, Mommy.' I keep hearing that and that keeps me going because I feel that she is all right for now. I have my moments when I don't.''

An interesting contrast exists between Paul and Rae Ann. Within the past four years Paul had faced his sister's homicidal death and his father's sudden death from a heart attack. Rae Ann had never had to integrate tragic loss, even as a child. Her pets were just taken away. Paul finds himself more patient with himself and with others—even trying to help them understand. Said Rae Ann, ''It's all new to me.''

References

Gorer, G. 1965. *Death, Grief, and Mourning*. New York: Doubleday.
Parkes, C. M. 1972. *Bereavement: Studies of Grief in Adult Life*. New York: International Universities Press.

23

The Clergyman Also Mourns

Steven A. Moss

It is common knowledge that a clergyman is more often involved in death than the average person. This image of the clergyman is so widespread that some people see him as the harbinger of death. This kind of reaction greets me when I walk into a patient's room and he looks up and says, "Oh, I suppose you are here to say last rites?" Or it has been reflected in my conversation with a man as we were standing in a cemetery. After I had said, "I hope that we can meet somewhere else on a better occasion," he answered. "But this is one of the only places you meet a Rabbi, isn't it?"

These generalizations are not completely unfounded. As a clergyman, I participate in an average of 15 funerals a year. That I have a small congregation implies that other clergymen with larger congregations perform many more of such rituals. Each year I perform nearly the same number of dedications of grave stones. I am regularly involved with hospital work and visiting of nursing homes. In these facilities I visit both congregants and noncongregants. I have been involved in counseling the terminally ill. I have been present at the time of death of many people, and at times, I have accompanied the family immediately to the funeral home to help them make the funeral arrangements.

Knowing of this intense involvement with the dying and the bereaved, many assume that the clergyman becomes "used" to these crises in peoples' lives. The bereaved assume, and sometimes desire, that the clergyman does not or should not mourn, even for those with whom he has a close and intimate relationship.

As I have visited in a hospital room or at the house of the bereaved, I have often been greeted with the words, "We are sure that you have heard a story such as ours many times before." To these people, their experience of anxiety, of grief is new and fresh. Their words indicate to me their hope that their experience is not unique, for if it is, who will be able to console them? These words also reflect the hope that, because I have dealt with such a crisis so often before, perhaps I have an objectivity that can be of help to them now. But these words also express an attitude toward the clergyman's professionalism, saying that, no matter what he says, his objectivity has put him at a distance, and, therefore, the question raised is, "Can he really understand?"

These expectations in regard to the clergyman's role bring him closer to, yet put him at a distance from, the bereaved. These expectations both want him and not want him to mourn, to express his actual feelings, which might not be totally objective. The needs of the dying and then the bereaved call for both of these attitudes. The bereaved need to feel the uniqueness of their grief, as well as the hope that someone else can help them, through his past experiences, by his objectivity, as well as by his sensitivity.

But what of the needs of the clergyman at these moments when he becomes involved with the crises in people's lives? Do their needs and his needs work against each other or do they work together?

I have found that each clergyman becomes involved with the people he meets on different levels of intensity. The close or distant relationships he establishes are for the most part influenced by his own personality. There are some clergymen who, out of their own inability to cope with the death of others, make their professional role one of coldness and distance. Such a distance protects them from being hurt when death comes. The separation that death brings triggers the feelings of mourning, feelings that need an outlet and an expression. If the clergyman does not see an expression of feelings as appropriate or possible, he can use his professionalism to create the distance that forestalls and suppresses them. But such a distance also obviously affects his ability to help the dying and bereaved, for his relationship with them is not totally open.

The clergyman who wishes to become involved with people in their living and their dying must understand his role and his feelings in regard to those he is trying to help. Understanding can aid his effectiveness in helping those facing their own death and those facing the death of others.

As a member of a congregation becomes sick, the involved clergyman becomes intensely involved with the patient and the family. He visits them in the hospital, and then when death comes he must minister to the needs of those bereaved people who might be like members of his own family. He attends the funeral as a clergyman but also as a friend of the dead and the bereaved. The clergyman in this case is there as both mourner and comforter. But to which role is he to be true? Is there a possible mixture of the two, so that he meets his needs as mourner and their needs as comforter?

I believe that such a mixture is possible, in that his very ministrations can be cathartic rituals for his own grief, just as they are for the dying and the bereaved. When I visit the sick, my prayers, words, and physical actions are as much a comfort to the sick as they are a reflection of my own feelings toward that person, and they thereby satisfy my own needs. At times, to cry with someone during their distress is all right, is useful for both clergyman and patient/congregant. At other times this kind of action is neither appropriate nor needed. It becomes necessary, therefore, for the clergyman to recognize his feelings toward this dying person. Then the feelings can be channeled into a more acceptable response, such as prayer or a physical "touching." The physical is an especially valuable response. I have often squeezed a hand, hugged, or even kissed persons as their hearts poured forth their deepest emotion.

These physical acts were meaningful responses to the needs of the person who needed that "shoulder" to cry on, who needed to know someone cared. But they were also meaningful responses to my needs, my feelings, which needed a positive and constructive outlet.

From my own experiences I have found that the first step the clergyman needs to take is to realize that he too mourns. He must understand that he too grieves. Often he sees himself as the proverbial "rock," who can show no feelings or emotions. Many religious traditions hold such a role as a model for its adherents. Certain clergymen take on this demeanor as they attempt to fulfill their tradition's aspirations for the religious life. But others use it to maintain distance. Being a "rock" allows them not to grieve either before other people or even to themselves. As the bereaved's "rock," they can insulate themselves against the hurt that death brings. Using the clergy's role for such self-protective purposes is neither healthy nor productive. Once the clergyman accepts his own feelings, he can then use them positively in his own life and in the lives of those he cares for. It is his very role that can become an outlet for these feelings.

That the clergyman mourns is beyond a doubt. Once he takes the step of involvement in peoples' lives, he must feel the separation that death brings. Sometimes his relationships are of short duration, as they often are for the chaplain visiting patients in a hospital setting. At other times, and for most clergymen, the relationships are created over years of interaction with congregational members. Such relationships are those whose severing are most strongly felt, for he becomes close to these people.

When a spiritual leader is in a congregation for 10, 15, or 20 years, he participates in the life cycles, the social, intellectual, and spiritual moments of his people. He must mourn the death of his congregants. He must feel. This is the first step for him in helping the dying and then the bereaved. He needs to use his role as clergyman and the various acts of his tradition to help satisfy his needs and the needs of those he is helping.

In my work with the dying I have always been aware of the natural guilt reaction to death. Guilt comes about from unclosed relationships, deeds not done, or words not spoken. With this awareness I try as best as possible to minimize possible guilt reactions for myself through my actions and words. Such moves also help the patient, for they also meet his needs. I minimize my guilt reactions by trying to do all I can possibly do for the patient, on all levels of involvement. I try not to leave a room with words or feelings not said and not expressed. If I know or sense that a visit might be the last visit before death, I express a final goodbye by a kiss or through words. I would not speak directly to the finality of the visit, but I would express my feelings, admiration, respect, and love for that person. The "right" saying of goodbye minimizes guilt reactions on my part as clergyman.

When I have been able to express myself in this way, I have walked away from such a relationship feeling "good," knowing I have helped this other person, by binding together our lives at the end of his life, and I have also helped myself. I have accomplished this through my office of clergyman. A final "shalom," or word of prayer, a kiss, or expression of true feeling can mean so much. These are actions that at times can come only from a clergyman.

This same process can be put into effect in helping the bereaved. The clergyman also mourns. He can, of course, express his condolences to a family through words of comfort and through his presence during the mourning period. These rituals and actions are the expected and appropriate behavior for the clergyman. They can be most helpful to the needs of the bereaved. But they are not necessarily beneficial to the clergyman in expressing the needs of his grief.

As with roles these rituals during mourning can be used by the clergyman as a barrier between himself and the bereaved. He can just perform his functions with competency and professionalism. And though these rituals, when performed this way, might be helpful to the mourners, they put a distance between them and the clergyman. He establishes this barrier, for it allows him not to have to place his emotions on the line, not to release his truest feelings.

Such rituals, on the other hand, can be cathartic for the clergyman. When I receive a call to officiate at a funeral, I never say "no" (unless it is impossible for me to attend). I will not say "no," for aside from the help I can give this family, I can also help myself. To me, the eulogy I write, the prayers and rituals I say and do, are the last deeds of farewell I can perform for another human being. I feel good about doing them, not depressed or sad, because they are actions I, and only I, as a clergyman, can take. They are my own special farewell to the deceased. They thereby also become my unique way of honoring the dead, through comforting the mourners. They are my gift to the dead.

The funeral and mourning rituals serve these functions for me, whether I am officiating at the funeral of a family I know well or of a family I have just met. In this way I have found a cathartic usage of ritual. This usage was especially important and useful for me when I officated at the funeral of my grandmother. My work as clergyman was my gift as a mourner to my loved one.

It is this cathartic function of the role of clergyman that I have found to be useful in my own work with the dying and the bereaved. Such a function allows me to be true to my own feelings while helping fulfill the needs of others. I believe that, by being true to myself, I have been most successful in these regards. I, as a clergyman, need not be afraid to mourn, and that is good. I hope that others will be able to do the same.

Having the Courage To Care

Kermit Edison

An eight-year-old child died following open heart surgery. Born prematurely with a defective heart, Mary had experienced long periods of hospitalization, including more than one attempt to correct her malfunctioning heart. This time the prognosis was excellent. But Mary died. In a large city, very distant from home, her parents were shocked and at a loss what to do. During their flight home, they talked about a funeral for Mary and considered the following questions: Why not have a funeral in complete privacy? Why not request the omission of flowers? Why not have a funeral at church?

When Mary's parents arrived home, they called me to their home to discuss these questions, as well as other alternatives predicated on the premise that privacy was not in their best interest. Mary's parents and the entire family were religiously oriented. The choice of a funeral in the church where a religious rite would be held was quickly resolved.

The immediate problem concerning the church service was the absence of their regular pastor. Who would officiate? I suggested a pastor whom I knew to be a very understanding and empathic person, capable of providing proper spiritual comfort while centering his message around the life that had been lived. With him, Mary's parents planned the church service. The pastor supported my contention that privacy precluded sharing, and Mary's parents rejected the idea of privacy with the stipulation that they would limit their own participation to an hour at the funeral home the evening before the funeral. Like generations of other families who experience the value and comfort of sociability in a period of crisis they discovered that with Mary's death came new dimensions of possession. Now Mary belonged to those whose lives she had shared, as well as to her immediate family. The responsiveness of those who felt the loss was so great that five hours passed before they left the funeral home. Mary's parents expressed their gratitude: ''The visitation at the funeral home gave our friends the opportunity to tell us how much Mary had been loved.''

Mary's parents needed someone to open the door to grief work, to take the first step with them. The events following Mary's death illustrate how a funeral director can aid those experiencing acute grief. Moreover, he is willing to accept grief reactions, have the courage to offer counsel, and open the door that allows for grief work.

The funeral director must accept irrational behavior, expressions of hostility, and acts of disappointment as natural phenomena in the acute grief process. He must realize that logic and reason are not always solutions to acute grief. He recognizes that impractical notions and unusual behavior are justified as essential components of grief work.

There is a direct correlation between counseling in funeral matters and opening the door to grief work. Helping people help themselves in grief work is clearly the essence of funeral service. Through the funeral, grief work is accomplished by flexibility and adaptability to the various circumstances surrounding individual and collective needs. Some needs are so personal one hesitates to comment on any observations for fear of violating a trust. (To assume there is acute grief associated with every death is a fallacy, and to counsel the nongriever in a manner that is appropriate for one experiencing acute grief is equally wrong.)

What is wrong with privacy in acute grief situations? Privacy does suggest relaxation and diminishes the fear of formality. Mary's parents had reasoned that privacy would be less burdensome and, consequently, would lessen the ''hurt of this loss.'' If I had agreed that privacy was in their best interest, they probably would have been extremely grateful. Yet, as a caring funeral director, I could not sit by confident that the family could handle their grief in private. The decision not to counsel is an easy one to make, for it eliminates the possibility of having one's sincere motives impugned. There is risk in presenting diverse alternatives to previously conceived notions regarding privacy. When the concept of genuine care prevails, one cannot consent to privacy in acute grief situations, because it is contrary to the proved theory of social support as an effective way to open the door to grief work and emotional release.

Grief work is letting hurts hurt. Emotional hurts are not healed by privacy, denial, pills, or alcohol. Emotional wounds are healed by expression, by facing reality, by visual confrontation, by social support, by sharing feelings through conversations, by personal concern. With that kind of involvement it is impossible to make believe that nothing happened. The story of "what happened" is told over and over and eventually the hurt person accepts what he or she has said.

Mary's parents did not regret having opened the door for others, because they discovered a special solace as their own personal needs were met. This aspect of my counsel was perceived dimly at the outset but took on special significance as time passed. They expressed appreciation for my advice. While Mary's entire family, friends, teachers, and classmates rejoiced that they had shared a part of Mary's life and funeral, they recognized that this relationship and experience had provided a new perception of life and death.

Funeral directors can provide resources in acute grief situations if they have the courage to suggest the appropriate and if they have the courage to care.

Poets and prophets seem to have special insights into feelings, as well as a special ability to express these feelings. As he examined the idea of sharing grief, Oscar Wilde wrote:

> If a friend of mine . . . gave a feast, and did not invite me to it, I should not mind a bit . . . But if . . . a friend of mine had a sorrow and refused to allow me to share it, I should feel it most bitterly. If he shut the doors of his house of mourning against me, I would move back again and again and beg to be admitted, so that I might share in what I was entitled to share. If he thought me unworthy, unfit to weep with him, I should feel it as the most poignant humiliation, as the most terrible mode by which disgrace could be inflicted on me . . . he who can look on the loveliness of the world and share its sorrow and realize something of the wonder of both is in immediate contact with divine things and has got as near to God's secret as anyone can get.

❦ 25

The Funeral Director in His Community

J. Robert Belmany

In the past the funeral director (or undertaker as he was known then) was called upon at the time of death to prepare the body and direct the funeral. Today the funeral director is obligated to go far beyond those duties; "the man in black" must also be something of a psychologist to counsel the dying patient and his family.

Our physicians rarely have the time to counsel patients and their families once it is known that death is imminent. However, someone must be ready to fill this need. It is to be the nurse or some other professional counselor? More and more, funeral directors should be prepared to assume these functions along with their many other duties. Naturally, it follows that the educational standards of funeral service must be raised to meet these challenges.

In an illustration of this need, the following case study is presented: One morning a young lady in her late thirties entered my office weeping profusely. I assumed a death had just occurred. When I was finally able to quiet her, I learned that a death had not occurred, but it was imminent. However, my problem was compounded greatly by what her husband's doctor told her: "Honey, you had better buy a cemetery lot and see an undertaker. He's going to die."

After talking with "Mrs. Doe" for two sessions, I obtained the doctor's permission to counsel with the patient and his family. There followed several meetings with members of that family. The first two sessions were intended to give the wife a realistic look at death and to prepare her to handle the situation when she and her husband met again. The next two meetings included the husband alone with me. He was then told that he was going to die. The patient's reaction and comments were: "Do you think I am that dumb, even though I have not been told? I could watch any soap opera and know that radiation therapy is a good hint that death is predicted." The goals of the two meetings with this patient were to support his religious attitudes toward death and thereby achieve his realistic acceptance of these. When people whom we counsel are not churchgoers, a minister is called in. The patient is not only prepared spiritually but also is urged to teach his family not to be dependent on him. In this case John taught his four-year-old son how to tie his shoes, among other things. The wife was instructed in handling the bank account, home affairs, and literally to take on a new role in life before the patient died so that she could feel some confidence in her own abilities.

The husband and wife were brought together. For the first time they shared the realization that death would occur soon. A tear was shed, an embrace given. From here on, however, they began to think seriously "What do we do? How much time is left to us?" Two more sessions followed, during which the mother said to their children, "Daddy will die soon!" Preparing children is most important. Older children will not accept death as easily as the younger ones. Each child is distinct in personality and must be dealt with individually. More than two sessions with the children are sometimes needed.

The family in its entirety were now brought together for the final two sessions (ninth and tenth). This included the patient, his wife, and their children. At this point the family as a unit had begun to accept the fact that death was to be a reality in their lives. By this time the family had some religious, legal, and psychological ways of viewing death.

The reward for me was the knowledge that the surviving family members would be stronger and better able to cope when the death occurred.

❧26

The Funeral
as a Therapeutic Tool
in Acute Bereavement

Irene B. Seeland

During ten years of working with terminal patients, their families, and the hospital staff I have become increasingly aware of the problems that surround dying in the hospital. Particularly outstanding is the isolation of the terminal patient during the last days or hours of life. Limitations in visiting hours and hospital regulations make the participation of other than the closest family members difficult, if not impossible, and never enable children to be more than distant observers of an event that will deeply affect their lives and future.

Often patients die in the hospital alone, or in the company of a nurse or an aide. Usually, the family is notified shortly before or after the actual death; in some hospital settings, family members may be able to come to the hospital room to say goodbye to the deceased. Many times the body is removed to the hospital morgue as quickly as possible, partly because there is a functional need for the hospital bed, partly because the staff do not want to upset other patients, and partly because they want to remove the dead person from sight. Often a funeral director who may not be personally known to the family is notified. He then assumes the responsibility of taking the body from the morgue to the funeral home where he and his staff take care of all necessary preparations. The visit to the funeral chapel during specific hours enables the bereaved to spend some time with the body, and ceremonies appropriate to the religious belief and customs of the family usually take place in the chapel or at a later time in a church or temple.

The question of whether a more active participation of family members in the preparation for a funeral might be therapeutic in their own process of bereavement began to emerge during these years. The role of the funeral during the acute bereavement period of a family's life came very strongly into personal focus when, over a period of nine months, I experienced the death of two persons who were close to me, as well as to a large number of friends.

My husband, a 43-year-old director of an international educational institution, became acutely ill with acute lymphoblastic leukemia in July 1975. After an initial three weeks' hospitalization marked by serious complications, a short-term remission was achieved, and my husband, after extensive discussions with his physicians and family members, chose to proceed with the proposed lengthy chemotherapeutic treatment on an outpatient basis. Treatments continued over a period of 13 months, with three separate hospitalizations for central nervous system involvement and treatment. The illness progressed rapidly and remissions became increasingly shorter. Side effects of the chemotherapeutic agents added to complications of the illness, and during the last four months of his life my husband was nearly completely paralyzed and needed 24-hour nursing care. His wish to remain at home was fulfilled and made possible by the dedicated care of a group of five friends who took turns with me in providing the necessary intensive home care. This group consisted of two psychiatrists, a lawyer, a medical student, and a psychology student, all of whom had been our close friends and co-workers for several years. The medical and nursing skills of these people improved quickly with the assistance of the primary physicians and several private duty nurses, and this team soon proved to be adequate to the rapidly growing medical and nursing care needs of my husband as his illness progressed. His two physicians, after some initial concern about whether adequate care could be provided in his home setting, did everything in their power to assist in this process and helped to overcome institutional barriers in providing medication, blood transfusions, and other means of support.

Throughout his illness my husband remained mentally alert and active and provided much-needed emotional stability and support to those caring for him. Friends, co-workers, and children had easy access to him, and he openly shared with those close to him his own process of preparing for his death, which he anticipated and accepted, yet which he did not give into without "putting up a good battle first."

He died at home after 13 months of illness at the age of 44. A 24-hour period of coma preceded his death.

Two months prior to his death, when chemotherapeutic treatments were becoming increasingly ineffective, he had suggested to me that I should find a funeral director and begin to explore funeral arrangements. His only specific wish was to be cremated. He had no other particular preferences regarding funeral arrangements, but he agreed completely with the following suggestions: to have the body remain at home following his death until the time of cremation; to have a small, informal ceremony conducted in the home and not at the cemetery; and, in general, to keep the process simple.

Through friends, I made contact with a funeral director and discussed the situation with him. During the first meeting the specific wishes of my husband and our family were explored to see if they were possible and feasible. Our family's wish for the body to remain at home prior to cremation and to allow a minimum of 24 hours for a wake made embalming necessary. The funeral director, trained in home embalming by his father in an old Italian family business, felt that this could be done in a private home. Details regarding choice of other funeral arrangements, the casket, cremation site, and expenses were discussed and made final during this meeting. My husband was relieved to know that arrangements had been completed and that there would be no need for our family to deal with these issues, either shortly before or after his death when the stress of the situation would be taking its greatest toll on everyone.

On the day when my husband's death was obviously approaching, the closest family members and friends stayed with the comatose patient, spending the time in reflection and preparing for the death. Other friends were notified, and those who expressed a wish to be with the patient for a while were encouraged to do so. Our oldest son, nine years of age, and the seven-year-old son of close friends joined at the bedside for a brief period, with the clear awareness that it was to say a final goodbye. Our younger son, eight-years-old, who had been quite overwhelmed by the destructiveness of the illness on his father's physical appearance, felt unable to join but asked me to say goodbye for him.

After my husband's death those closest to him stayed with the body for a while before notifying the physicians and the funeral director, all of whom had previously been alerted to the impending death. When the funeral director arrived, I requested permission to remain with the body during the embalming process. When the embalming was completed, friends helped to wash and dress the body and assisted the funeral director in placing the body into the casket.

The open casket was placed in a large room that is used to exhibit some of the art pieces my husband had collected during his life, and it was surrounded by flowers and candles. This room, large enough to accommodate 40 people, was to become the central point for the family and friends over the next 36 hours. During the first night several friends offered to stay with the body so that the persons who had spent the last few months in taking care of my husband could rest or get some sleep. Some friends stayed to take care of the children, and others prepared food and notified friends and co-workers who had not yet been advised of the death.

On the next day there was opportunity to spend time in small or large groups with the body. Later in the day, when other friends and co-workers arrived, people were invited to read from scriptures, poetry, or other sources meaningful to them or to sing songs my husband had loved. Two of the children participated in most of these proceedings. Our younger son again felt too overwhelmed to participate, and his wish to share in the events only from a distance was respected.

During the second night small groups of family members and friends shared the wake. They found in these quiet hours an opportunity to acknowledge the reality of the death and to begin the process of dealing with their own grief. In the morning of the second day a brief final goodbye was said, and the casket was closed and taken to the crematorium. Only our family and our most intimate friends accompanied the casket. In the chapel of the crematorium we said a final prayer to send the body on its last journey.

Six months after the onset of my husband's illness, one of his closest friends, a 72-year-old, single woman and professor of education, had become seriously ill with metastatic ovarian cancer. After surgery she was placed on chemotherapy and had an excellent remission for a period of seven months. She participated in my husband's funeral with the full awareness that she was the most likely person to follow him in death.

After the relapse and fairly fast progression of her illness a few months later she also expressed a wish to spend as much of her remaining life as possible at home and not in the hospital. Since her only direct family was an elderly brother and his wife living in California, both of them retired and physically infirm, friends and co-workers decided to make use of the experience gained in taking care of my husband, and, with the assistance of an excellent Jamaican nurse's aide, they were able to provide 24-hour nursing coverage at the patient's home. This time the group of people caring for the patient was larger and included a number of younger people, as well as older friends, several of whom had had no previous close exposure to serious illness and death.

This patient's progression toward death was slower and less dramatic, and she spent three weeks in a state of alternating semicoma and alertness before she died following a deep coma that lasted three days. Earlier in her illness she had expressed a wish to have a funeral similar to that of her friend, and so some time was spent exploring her specific concerns and wishes about funeral arrangements.

The patient died surrounded by all those who had cared for her, and her death provided a deeply moving experience for them. In particular, those people who had never previously witnessed a death and who were not likely, at least in their professional fields, to be part of the dying of another person expressed gratitude to be able to be present at her death.

The funeral, wake, and cremation mainly followed the process of the first funeral. Because the patient's studio apartment was too small for a large gathering of people, it was decided to use my home for the wake. Before this decision was made, the question of what impact a second funeral in the home would have on the children was explored. In view, however, of the fact that the patient was a very close friend of the family and godmother to my oldest son, we felt that the children would understand the relevance of having the funeral in their father's home, especially since this had been the patient's hope.

During the wake, friends and co-workers again had time and opportunity to reflect on the life and the work of their friend, as well as to allow the reality of the loss of another close person, one who had contributed so much to their lives, to sink in. The two children who had participated in the first funeral joined again and shared actively in the wake and the periods of being together. My younger son initially stayed away from the room where the open casket was placed and stated that he was too frightened of the body to join the others. A brief exploration with me about his fears seemed to have little impact. Yet shortly thereafter he offered to escort a newly arrived friend into the room and joined the other people for the rest of the day. He stated with great relief that his fantasies about what a dead person looked like had been proved wrong, and he brought his most treasured toy, a toy raccoon, to keep his old friend company.

The rapidity and intensity of events during this period did not leave much space for reflection on and understanding of what impact the illness, death, and burial of these two persons had on the lives of those who had participated in some or all aspects of their care. In retrospect, however, it has become clear that much was gained and learned during this time, and during the many explorations following the death of these two people the essence of the learning process emerged. Learning had taken place in several fairly distinct processes.

The Illness

The decision to take care of both patients in their own home environment confronted every person involved with the process of progressive illness and the deterioration of the body on a day-to-day basis. This proved to be a painful and stressful experience for everyone, but acceptance was made possible through the unusual emotional equilibrium, sense of humor, and perspective that both patients demonstrated. Nevertheless, both patients were also subjected to periods of severe physical stress, pain, and sometimes discouragement and shared these as willingly with those around them as they had shared their times of peacefulness and resolution.

In both cases there was little doubt that the illness was incurable and would lead to death in the near future. The time available was, however, used intensely and was limited only by the progressive impairment of the patients' physical function. The fact that both patients knew their diagnosis and probable prognosis from the beginning of their illness made possible open communication, exploration, and planning for all concerned.

Funeral Arrangements

As the illness progressed and death approached, the reality of having to plan for a funeral became clear. The patient, his family, and friends had no particular precedent to follow, nor did they feel any social or specific religious obligations that might determine the format of a funeral. The freedom to plan without a prescribed form made it possible to allow an organic process to take place that expressed the needs and took into account the life realities of those participating in this life process. The willingness of the funeral director to be open to somewhat unconventional plans and to put his professional skills into creative use did much to allow arrangements to proceed without conflict or complications during a stressful time. The meetings with the funeral director several weeks prior to the actual death of the patients alleviated much anxiety and concern and also established a rapport and trust that proved to be invaluable at the time of death. At that point the funeral director was no longer a stranger and "businessman" proceeding with "his business" but a friend who had been willing to listen and offer advice and help.

The Death

At the time of death of both patients, those involved in their actual physical care were gathered around their bed for several hours and shared the actual death process. The fact that this took place in the home environment contributed much to making this a peaceful and constructive experience. It also enabled people to give each other support; to reflect on the life, the illness, and the death of the patients; and to begin slowly to prepare psychologically for the time after the death.

The actual moment of death was deeply experienced by those present and transmitted to everyone a strong sense of transition, not an end.

Some time after the death was spent in quietness and individual prayer. After this time the task of beginning with the more functional aspect of preparing for a funeral was taken up: notification of physicians, the funeral director, and friends and family members who were not in the immediate vicinity. Until the arrival of the physicians and the funeral director, we again spent time in quiet togetherness, sitting by the bedside of the deceased, allowing a process of accepting the long-anticipated and now finally actual fact of the death of a beloved person to begin. My decision to stay with the body during the embalming in both cases came from a strong feeling of not wanting to leave the bodily remains of these two close people without company during this time, and it was a purely personal choice.

After the embalming process several friends rejoined me, and together we washed and prepared the body for dressing. Although none in their lives had previously helped with this type of task, they all experienced a sense of participating in a beautiful, ancient ritual, and they all felt that they could express one more time their love for the deceased by this last act of care. Upon completion of the dressing and placing of the body in the casket, the open casket was placed in the room chosen to function as the place for the wake for the next 24 hours.

The Wake

The decision to hold an "old-fashioned" wake had emerged from a sense that there was need for an opportunity to spend time with the body, to reflect, and to say personal goodbyes. A period of several hours during the next day was set aside for other friends and co-workers to come and join. This allowed for more private time for closer friends and immediate family, as well as for some time to be shared with other people.

The fact that the body of the deceased remained each time in a home setting made it possible for friends and family to spend time with the body between periods of rest; to take care of other people, especially the children; and in this way to allow for a more continuous and more natural process of accepting the fact of death. For the individual it gave space to sit by the body and review past times together, to deal with unresolved issues, to have times of sorrow and peacefulness—all in the presence of the body—and at all times to find confirmed the fact of death. The process of the wake in the home proved to be especially helpful to the children, who had an opportunity to approach death at their own rate of acceptance, to be with the body, or to be with the family not too far away from the body. They entered into a process of becoming familiar with death and observing others in their own process of dealing with it, all in their own familiar environment. In the case of the younger son this process was slower and more painful, and yet it came to a point of successful resolution at the time of the second death that the child had had to experience within nine months.

Those friends who kept watch at the casket during the nights expressed later that those hours had been very precious to them. When the time for ending the wake arrived, a feeling of completion had emerged, and the last moments with the body before closing the casket gave them the feeling of having said a final goodbye to a friend who was going on a long journey. At that point there was also a strong sense that what was to be cremated was not the old friend but only the physical remains.

The Funeral Service

The drive to the crematorium, both times in glorious sunshine, and the brief time in the crematorium's chapel were characterized by a feeling that a long and painful process had been brought to a point of completion. There was a strong sense of fullness or wholeness and a shared feeling that this process had left its participants richer.

The days and weeks after each death confirmed the impression that the events surrounding and immediately following the death of these two persons had contributed much to help the bereaved to enter into their own process of acceptance, of separation, and of transition into a life now without these two friends who had contributed so much to everyone's life. The mourning process continued in its normal fashion with periods of sorrow, remorse, aloneness, and depression, and yet it was much helped by the fact that an important human experience had been shared with several people during the illness, death, and funeral of these two friends. During later times of exploration many of the friends expressed their own intense experience of participating in an aspect of human life that had added new and unexpected dimensions of understanding to their perceptions of life and of death.

One month after the death of these two people, a child was born to two other friends, and the continuity of life was confirmed in this joyful event.

The events described here were in some respects specific to particular life situations and sequences of events. They were also an expression of the people who participated in them and of their lives and their work together. It would be difficult to extract these events out of the lives in which they occurred and develop them into a "model" for patient care or for planning for a funeral.

There are, however, certain aspects of the described process that may be an expression of more universal human needs and experiences and may, therefore, have greater relevance to other people. Active participation in the care of a terminal patient can have a variety of impacts on the participants. It creates the possibility for more closeness and openness, sharing of previous times and events, and a mutual giving. It may also bring into the open underlying conflicts and unresolved issues, both in the patient and in those around him, and, if dealt with appropriately, it can facilitate the resolution of these issues before the patient's death and thus alleviate guilt and remorse in the survivors. Close participation in the physical care of the patient can relieve the feeling of helplessness and at the same time bring the progressive physical deterioration into clear perspective and give opportunity for the family to prepare themselves for the impending death of the patient. Death may then be experienced as a welcome and well-deserved release and respite for the suffering friend.

To be present at the death of a friend or a family member, which used to be a frequent occurrence in the past, enables the participants to witness for themselves the passage of the dying and often may confirm the idea that death is only a transition, a release. It may also help alleviate unrealistic fears and fantasies about the "agonies of death," for many patients die peacefully and not in a terrifying struggle.

Active participation in the preparation of the body for the funeral gives an opportunity to express a last act of care and love to the dead one. This also permits one to become familiar with the effect that death has on the human body. There is little chance to "make believe" that the dead person is only "sleeping," as the euphemism goes, when one assists in the washing and the dressing of a body; it confronts the participants with the finality of death, allowing them to move toward the next step in their mourning process. This confirmation of death continues for an extended period of time, during the process of the wake as the family and friends spend time with the body and have an opportunity to work through in themselves their own feelings, thoughts, and memories while still in the presence of the body.

Two other aspects of the two funerals seem to have a particular importance and deserve to be mentioned. The availability of the funeral director as a human being, as well as a helping professional, added much to the therapeutic effect of the funerals on the bereaved. His willingness to help plan and assist in arranging the funeral in such a manner that it could become an organic expression of the family's needs and wishes, made him a friend and caring helper instead of a distant outsider to whom a business was delegated. As emerged in later discussions, the participation of the family and friends in the preparation for the funeral also had a deep effect on the funeral director himself, who felt that he was included in the process that the family was undergoing and that he was invited and allowed to give of himself beyond his professional skills. A business transaction became a human interaction instead, and it enriched his own life in addition to giving a greater meaning to his professional activities.

The participation of a number of friends and co-workers in the care of the patients and in the preparation for their funerals provided much human support for all involved. It made possible periods of respite for the family and closer friends who carried the major burden of the physical care and who were also under serious psychological stress because of the impending loss of two important people in their lives. It allowed the growth of closer human bonds, and, as became evident after the death of both patients, it welded people together in the shared intense experience of caring and giving and participating together in one of the most important events in life.

The two funerals described here proved to be of deep human relevance for all who participated in them. They are looked back upon as cherished memories, and there is a consensus that they allowed for a resolution and healing. They were much more than an expression of grief and loss; they were a true celebration of the lives of those who had died by those who would go on with the task of living. Just as the process of giving birth has, in the last decades, lost much of its threat and has become a process in which both parents increasingly and consciously participate and which they experience as an intense and meaningful event in their lives, so there is hope that death similarly will lose its terror for man and begin to be shared as a meaningful and intensely experienced event of human existence.

❦ 27

Why a Funeral Home

Clarence Novitzke

As it exists today, the funeral home is a reflection of former and current social and cultural desires, requests, and expectations. The funeral home and the personalized services it provides have evolved as a result of constant adaptation to existing demands. What is traditional is carried over from the past to the present. The values of rites and ceremony are carried into succeeding generations and continue to serve the living. Funerals link the past with the present. As we cannot forsake the past, neither can we refuse to advance from it. A funeral home has evolved from the past to the present as a unique community facility, designed to serve a specific purpose.

Architecturally, the funeral home is constructed to portray stability and sensitivity. It must portray stability, but at the same time not be inconsistent with change. It is directly connected with the rate of change in society, and this societal change may be slow or rapid. But stability is ensured by maintaining order, preserving the traditional, and filling current needs, as well as by adapting to innovations. It is designed to encompass the ethnic customs, community culture, and individual philosophies. The funeral home serves the individual and his community as a vital resource. Concerned for individuals, the individual funeral home recognizes the unique dynamics surrounding each single death. Individual sensitivity is necessary, for there is no one funeral for everyone.

Funeral homes exist in both urban and suburban areas. Each funeral home serves and is an intimate part of its particular community.

Within the confines of these types of localities, funeral homes are restricted to serving the residents of a specific area. In most cases it is not economically feasible nor is it appropriate to attempt to serve beyond the arbitrary community limits.

Generally, the inhabitants of the community refer to the funeral home in a possessive way. There is no financial investment, but there can be an element of personal and emotional interest. However, a building and its location do provide a community with nothing but a source of revenue in the form of taxes. Competent staff is required to provide services and to fulfill a vital role.

Public relations professionals theorize that good public relations are not what you are but what people think you are. This may be true for a building and its location, but the staff must ensure stability and demonstrate sensitivity. The funeral home is a facility within which the practitioners perform their technical and professional skills. The staff members must exhibit stability and sensitivity as a symbol of their ability to assist individuals of the community to cope with their fears and frustration about death. In the area of technical skills they must be knowledgeable and competent in embalming, restorative art, public health concerns, and compliance with laws and regulations. There must be evidence of sound business ethics in providing merchandise and services.

Professional skills are varied and complex. The practitioner must be able to perform in crisis situations. The definition of a crisis is debatable, and my use of the word may not adequately describe the total emotional impact following the death of a family member, but to the survivor the postdeath experiences are as traumatic as they are varied. At this point competent help contributes to the eventual recovery from trauma caused by death. Competent help identified with the funeral home is a symbol of that resource.

The survivor usually exhibits an inability to meet problems that accompany and follow a death. Emotions must be dealt with at the time they are being experienced. The catharsis of talking about emotions is essential. In counseling the survivor there is no model or format to follow. No single method offers a magical single answer. The diversity of methods is matched only by the diversity of the crisis situations.

"Why a Funeral Home?" is a question that many people struggle with. Those who have never experienced a death in the family find it easy to shrug off the thought of death. They seem to regard the funeral home with awe. During times of visitation they can be seen directing their empathy toward people entering or leaving the building. Across the street from my funeral home is a school bus stop. On cold and rainy days the children seek protection in our entryway. It is closed in on three sides with a good view to the bus stop. For many years there has never been any form of vandalism; this must have meaning.

A young girl who had lost her father wrote the following essay for her seventh grade English class:

Funeral Home

The car stops in front of a place I've always dreaded. I get out and stand there wondering if I dare proceed. I do and the stairs seem endless. I open the door and a creak of death comes from the brass hinges. It was time now to face my father as I have never faced him before. I proceed on into the lounge and wait with coldness until I am called. The time comes and I stand firmly, waiting for something I have never longed for. I walk in and with one glance I break down. A tender arm reaches kindly around me—which is my brother's. I hesitantly glance again and I stand there numb—for where is the smile my father always had? Gone. I stand by his side picking out the strange things that I never knew before and then I realize why I never knew because of death. I walk away knowing that I'll never see his smile or touch him ever again. I never realized how much I loved my father until I lost him.

The very act of writing and delivering this essay was an essential part of working through the experience that began at the funeral home. The funeral home was essential for her to resolve her fear and anxieties. In the process she accepted reality.

The elderly bring to the funeral home many wholesome and interesting revelations. An 84-year-old lady made funeral arrangements and then remained seated in her chair with a twinkle in her eye and a contented smile in her facial expression. After a moment she made the following remark. "You know, my husband was always quite concerned about the place he wanted to be buried and the funeral home to call. I used to tease him about it and I always told him that he could bury me in the backyard or anywhere for that matter. Now that I am a little older I have a better understanding and I can see why he was concerned."

A call came to our home from a woman who was interested in information about cemeteries and funerals. We talked at length in a friendly manner. Finally I asked her, "Whom am I talking to?" She replied, "We just retired and moved to this area. I don't think that our name is important at this point."

These anecdotes reveal four individuals' common concern about the funeral home. The gentleman who had died accepted his eventual death at an early age. His wife, in her words "Now that I'm a little older," accepted her eventual death later in life, and the lady caller and her husband were making their acceptance. These attitudes emphasize that the funeral home provides physical evidence of service and access to assistance when these are needed.

Attitudes are established through observation and acquiring information. The funeral home, its staff, and the services rendered are under continual observation. Information is secured through contact with qualified funeral home personnel. Their training and the nature of their work place them in the role of a consultant.

It is a common assumption that the operation of a funeral home is strictly a business function. This is true to a certain degree, but the commitment and responsibility to serve the living dilute the commercial aspect. A significant amount of staff time is devoted to giving counsel to people.

Each day the business community and its professionals provide merchandise and render services to individuals. In the merchandise and service transaction, exchanges are made to the mutual satisfaction of both parties. The widget is provided and the service is rendered. The exchange is consummated.

The services of a funeral home become more involved. The funeral home is also a place where information is sought by those who are not affected by a loss. At the funeral home all answers to questions about funerals are submitted as points of information. The funeral home personnel are fully aware of the importance of individual needs and confidentiality. The interactions among individuals result in search and discovery. Through interaction individuals are enabled to make wise decisions consciously, deliberately, and intelligently and to analyze the value of the alternatives after counseling. This interchange of ideas and information provides a foundation for constructive attitudes.

When a death has occurred and the funeral home's services are requested, it serves the living in a quasi-business capacity. Here again, advice and counsel are of major importance. The griever most often feels strange and different as if an abnormality existed. There is also the feeling that no one will understand. A lady described this feeling by saying, "It's like trying to describe a headache." Within this framework the funeral home and its staff create stability. The mourner is in a situation different from any other daily encounter. The stabilizing influence of the staff gives the grievers support in extricating themselves from what they think is unreal into what is real.

Participation in the planning of a funeral is the first step the survivor takes in recovery from a crisis situation.

In bereavement, people exhibit an inability to solve the problems that accompany and follow death. Personal needs of those in grief must be met and steps must be taken to plan a funeral that is meaningful for them.

In most personal service professions, services are rendered without contact with another discipline. In the process of funeralization the funeral home and its staff are in cooperation with many other professionals, various governmental agencies, and the business community. A review of the average funeral reveals the following contacts, usually in this order:

the medical doctor or coroner

the hospital or other institution

the clergy

the business community

the local law enforcement personnel

the attorney

the federal or state agencies

It is conceivable that in many occasions the contact with additional professions is essential or mandated.

The funeral home personnel act as personal representatives of the survivors in coordinating postdeath activities. In life situations we promise according to our hopes and perform according to our fears. Neither condition is applicable in a crisis situation. The entire process of funeral planning is reality testing for the survivor. Throughout the planning session the griever begins to identify emotions and make adjustments to them. It is axiomatic that individuals, in grief, be relieved of certain obligations and responsibilities.

The funeral home serves the residents of a community in crisis situations. Each funeral home can be classified as a crisis prevention center. Few, if any, people suffering grief consult a physician or a psychiatrist. Only those who grieve to such an extent that they become physically ill eventually seek medical help. Without usurping the roles of medical personnel, the funeral home intervenes in crisis situations. The very nature of its purpose puts it in direct contact with people in any of the stages of grief. People come to the funeral home expressing emotions. The expressions on their faces telegraph a message. They appear to be helpless, confused, and frustrated.

The funeral home, through its service, gives dignity to man.

Usually people assume that such reference to human dignity means dignity to the deceased or the survivors of the deceased. But the funeral home's service makes every effort to consider the human dignity of others. Every funeral brings people together, frequently in large groups, sometimes only in limited numbers. Nevertheless, in every group those assembled have a common, natural attribute: human dignity. Dignity knits people together and through this value systems develop.

To those affected by the death, the funeral home becomes a place where individuals meet, in a group, with a common purpose. Yet, within this group, the individual personal needs are diverse. Within the confines of the facility, the griever is exposed to an environment conducive to individual expression and to the release of pent-up emotions. A strong desire to help is evident, and confidence in funeral home personnel develops. The grief is accepted with understanding. Out of what appeared to be chaos comes an identifiable sense of direction.

The funeral home, as we know and see it, is a result of constant adaptation to individual personal needs. The future will surely require further adaptations to assist families and communities in life-and-death situations.

28

The Therapeutic Value of the Funeral in Post-Funeral Counseling

R. Jay Kraeer

Although abundant writings and research have been done in past years regarding the therapeutic value of the funeral as it applies to the survivors in personal and societal context, I attempt to identify and define one aspect of the grief process that seems to be most crucial to recovery, on the basis of a program of post-funeral visits in 3,000 homes over a period of three years. I suggest that we conceive recovery, or rediscovery of life, as "reorientation," demanding adjustment in personal concepts, as well as in societal role relationships. In addition, I consider what are commonly noted as the "stages" of grief to be rather *characteristics* of the grieving process. In this context the funeral is considered as those specific formalized ceremonies in which the body is present.

Is there a common denominator in grief expression that seems basic to a successful reorientation process? Ever since a well-known educator remarked in conversation, "I'm beginning to believe one never gets over it (the death of a loved one)," to which was replied, "The whole name of the game of life is *how* we handle our memories," I have come to believe that this may be the common denominator we seek. If so, then it is crucial how we handle the memories, how and when the stimulation of this process occurs, and in what environment and social situation it takes place. In our post-funeral visitation program we have found that the funeral rites not only verify to the grieving family and community the actuality and finality of the death but also initiate and accelerate the memory image process. The sooner this screening process is initiated by these formalized social rites and accelerated by subsequent time spent alone by the grieving person in familiar circumstances, the sooner confusion gives way to the reassertion of the self. Meaningful communication face to face with a caring, empathic listener adds impetus to the screen-image process and shortens the initial grieving period. Therefore, it seems, that the memory recall process handled wisely and well can be a bridge between the relationships of the past and the building of new value structures, attitudes, and relationships for the future.

A composite screen image of the deceased must form in the griever's "memory bank," an image compatible with the survivor's own self-concept. All of us have heard remarks such as, "He looks so peaceful"; "He looked twenty years younger"; "She looked just like I remembered her ten years ago." Invariably, those we served found some bit of consolation (a compatible memory image) in this phase of our service. Those who cannot bring themselves to view the remains are those who are unable to handle the idea of their own death, who may have an incompatible screen image of a previous grief experience, or who may have some psychologically unendurable screen-image patterns (deep guilt, for example) in relationship to the present decedent. The initial days of grief carry with them, as with any expensive or major change, the confusion of the orienting cues that help us distinguish reality from illusion; yet under these very circumstances the griever begins to sift and adapt recalled situations and experiences to meet his deepest psychological needs.

How does this composite screen-image operate? As time spent alone brings to bear the finality of the death, certain observed mementos, furnishings, clothing, and so forth recall to the survivor the attitudes, likes and dislikes, habit patterns, personal relationships, and shared experiences. Each time one of these memories penetrates through the disorientation, causing a ventilation of the emotions, a partial image of the deceased is imprinted on the survivor's memory bank. One by one, these fall into place—modified, selected, arranged—until the composite screen image is complete. The resultant image may underline the value of the past and, in a socially satisfying and personally fulfilling manner, give the opportunity to reorient to the new role demanded of us for the future. Or the image may be so modified that the survivor may abrogate the past and "start a new life.'' Or the image may be distorted in such a way that the survivor can live with himself or herself and assume new roles and relationships satisfactorily. We all have heard such remarks as, "My Arthur was a perfect husband!" "You couldn't ask for a better man!" "He was *always* so. . . ." And finally, the emerging screen image may be so distasteful as to be rejected in order to preserve the self-image of the survivor. This rejection, however, may surface later in a subsequent less demanding stress situation as tension and trauma. Any but immediate and temporary denial patterns are extremely dangerous psychologically. The demands of the dying for direct disposition may be psychological suicide; by the same token, the demand of the living for direct disposition may be a form of denial, indifference, or hatred. All of these may lead to later psychosomatic complications. In the case of sudden, accidental, or untimely deaths, the grieving—and often guilt-ridden—survivors have a tendency to resent the memory-screening process as a subconscious threat to their own survival. "I don't want to think about it" has a familiar ring. They may fall victim to morbid and chronic depression, obsessed with the idea of death, or taking on the characteristics of the deceased's last illness. Such persons need immediate professional help to rediscover their self-identity.

It is important for feelings to be expressed and ventilated during the memory-screening process. When one experiences his feelings without hiding them, the feelings pass more quickly and drain one less. The grieving person who stifles the free flow of feelings has a tendency to become fixated in the reorientation process, with certain characteristics becoming dominant—anger and hurt, fear (aloneness, futility), depression with somatic complications. The funeral, with the viewing of the body, is a time-proved means to initiate the memory-sifting and screening process, no matter how deep the hurt and anger, and to provide the means by which the reinforcing of caring persons can penetrate through confusion to the consciousness of the mourner. A record study of 800 visits in 1975 revealed that, of those who had no services (direct disposition), 34 percent showed signs of arrested progress in grief recovery, with chronic anger, fear, depression, and social withdrawal manifesting themselves; 22 percent of those who had some kind of formalized rites, limited in nature, were unsuccessful in the reorientation process, while only 12 percent of those having full funeral service had "hang-ups" in working through to new and/or modified life relationships. These percentiles were relatively constant in both high- and low-volume funeral homes. Of these 800 visits, 6.5 percent had no services, 3.5 percent had private ser-

vices, 1 percent had memorial services, and 89 percent had full services. Those with memorial services seemed to take longer to work
through the initial stages of grief stress. Those with no services, who
may have had previously unresolved crises of stress, had alcoholism
problems, deep hate and anger held for longer periods of time, high
tension levels, attempts to "escape," need of marriage counseling
because of deteriorating man–wife relationships, and psychological
and social withdrawal tendencies. Those requesting private services
showed signs of noncommunication verbally, aggravated and increased alcoholic consumption, and compulsive busyness, so as to
avoid "thinking." Those having full funeral service had major
reorientation problems, but these seemed to be more diffused. All
those having difficulties showed the widespread use of "uppers" and
"downers" in order to cope with their immediate feelings and situations. These may have been taken by medical prescription and needed
temporarily, or may have been provided by well-meaning friends.
But I am of the opinion that these can complicate the situation, hinder
the coping mechanisms later, and deepen and extend the struggle to
rediscover life with its new and rewarding roles. Full-service funerals
help to clean out the wound and treat it so that healing may occur.

We make the following conclusions. Nothing in human experience is more shattering, more temporarily devastating, than the loss
of one who has been deeply loved; we are never quite the same
again. We are all different; it is not a matter of accepting or facing a
situation so much as it is of finding our way through it all. Self must
be perceived as of worth and importance apart from the deceased
before life can be seen as important apart from the deceased. Those
with incompatible screen-memory images tend (1) to become reclu-
sive and/or vegetative; (2) to be maladaptive to new life patterns and
to demonstrate cynicism, bitterness, or negativity; and (3) to become
increasingly dictatorial and aggressive with others. The goal of postfuneral counseling may be conceived as the extension of the healing
process, which has been initiated, facilitated, and reinforced by the
funeral.

During this counseling process any question or suggestion that
stimulates verbalization about the shared past, in which the bereaved
deems self as important, will stimulate the acceptance of one's self as
important in new life-oriented roles. This helps in the reestablishment
of the survivor as a person of self-worth. The caring counselor keeps
communication channels open between himself and those in grief
stress; he gives suggestive direction for reorganization with hope,
making no room for morbid preoccupation, which is an enemy to

growth. But in the final sense, "No one else can give meaning of my life to me (the griever); it is something I alone can make. The meaning is not something predetermined that simply unfolds; I help both to create it and to discover it, and this is a continuing process, not a once-and-for-all" (Mayeroff, 1971, p. 62). I am convinced that the secret is, not in abrogating memories, or in living with memories without new experiences, or in becoming obsessed with them, but in learning how to handle them constructively; one just accepts them as the bridge from the past to the values of the present for the enrichment of the future. Because of this, the formalized ceremonies and customs of the full-service funeral have a pivotal place in our life and value structures.

My studies, as presented here, are by no means exhaustive but are designed to stimulate further observation and creative evaluation. Rather than generalize or oversimplify I hope I have found in the simple and observable an insight that is both cognitive and profound. It is always a mistake to abandon social customs and values for new norms without careful consideration and scrutiny of both. The funeral lays a foundation upon which the wise counselor may observe reactions and emotions concurrent with such ceremonies. Using this and familiar nonverbal communicational cues, the counselor may be able to assist the individual to find again the path to self-fulfillment.

References

Mayeroff, M. 1971. *On Caring*. New York: Harper and Row.

Shneidman, E. S. 1976. *Death: Current Perspectives*. Palo Alto, California: Mayfield Publishing Co.

Viscott, D. 1976. *The Language of Feelings*. New York: Pocket Books.

29

The Psychosocial Value of a Funeral in the Home

William A. Tari

In our complex society there appears to be an underlying need to break away from the common or traditional, from conformity. People seek ways and means of doing that are personalized and allow for the full expression of the individual. Yet society still clings to the old ways and means, for these have been tested by time and by their very continuance have demonstrated that society has accepted the security they afford.

Toffler (1970) pointed out that it is not change that makes society anxious but rather the rapidity of a certain change. Whenever change occurs, it takes time for society to set up the systems necessary for its members to find security in the new way. Although the change may satisfy the individual's needs on the psychological level, without concurrent or relatively immediate subsequent social support and approval, the change will prove to be sociologically unsatisfactory for the individual. The exceptions to this are those individuals who are either totally autonomous or totally anomic. In most cases adjusted individuals find it difficult to cope without the support of society.

So a dichotomy exists: the psychological need for individual expression through new, personalized means and ways and the sociological need for support through a continuance of old, time-tested mechanisms. Change must satisfy the individual need but at the same time possess identifiable intrinsic characteristics allowing for social acceptance and support.

Any alteration of what is considered contemporary represents change. In both the degree and content of the alteration society judges the validity of the change. The type of alteration may take forms that modify the contemporary situation with the interjection of the historical or old, the modern but not contemporary, the combination of two or more existing contemporary means, or a totally innovative concept. In general, society seems more at ease with the first three types of change because they have features immediately identifiable as workable. Resistance is usually met when the concept is completely new and extensive and demonstrates little or no evidence that it will succeed. Finally, society views any change from its segmented perspective on what is culturally relative. Consequently, the changes are weighed differently by different subgroups within the society. Therefore, if the contemporary funeral rite is to be altered, adapted, or in any way changed to meet the individual and different needs of each client family, which it must if it is to have true value, the funeral director and the client must work jointly to ensure that any such adaptation will have psychosocial value.

The knowledgeable funeral director has the potential of assuming the role of a therapeutic person. Since the client family may have had no previous experience with death or have had experiences that have not had value to them, they look to the funeral director for guidance. The direction they are given should not be myopic but rather should allow a broad view of alternatives from which may be drawn the most suitable avenue of approach. With this in mind some particular case material dealing with the funeral at home may be explored.

The funeral in the home is not in and of itself a new concept. What is new is the contemporary era in which it might be applied. Since it is a deviation from the norm today, the funeral in the home must be considered an alteration of what is contemporary and, therefore, an adaptation of those funeral customs presently accepted in our culture. The question is, "Does the funeral in the home truly possess the necessary characteristics to adjudge it as beneficial to the client family?"

In general, in our culture there has been a depersonalization of the funeral rite, a tendency to divorce the rite itself from the active participation of the client family members. I do not mean to imply that the only or the most beneficial way of personalizing the funeral rite and actively involving the client family is to have the funeral in the home. Nor do I foresee a wholesale movement toward the funeral in the home; however, it must not be excluded as an option for the client family.

The funeral director must keep in mind that a funeral in the home in this era does not involve the amount of necessary paraphernalia as was once the case. Just to give one example, in today's society, color and daylight are more readily acceptable as they are concerned with the trappings surrounding the funeral rite itself. The traditional funeral in the home where the funeral director had to set up a particular funeral environment, supplying draperies or lighting, is no longer necessary. In the modern household the funeral director finds a setting suitable for the placement of the casket without a great deal of adjustment. Moreover, the use of a dimmer-type switch in the living room areas of the home permits the funeral directors control of lighting, if this is desirable.

Experiences encountered in two successive home funerals demonstrate the positive features of a funeral held in the home. Although not directly related by blood, the two individual client families did have a close social bond of friendship.

In the first case the wife of the decedent was the person who made initial contact with the funeral director prior to the death of the husband. The contact was made through a mutual friend of the funeral director and the wife. Knowing that this friend was familiar with a number of funeral directors because of his role in funeral service education, the wife had inquired if he knew of a funeral director who might be empathic to the particular set of circumstances that existed. A meeting was arranged.

The husband was terminally ill and was being cared for at home by his family and friends. This closely knit social group had in their ranks sufficient expertise in the area of medicine to permit this to be done properly.

The initial meeting between the funeral director and the wife took place in the office of the funeral director, with the complete knowledge of the husband, and as a matter of fact with his personal wishes in this area being considered totally.

The first area of discussion was the question of whether or not the funeral could be held in the family home. The funeral director explained that this would not pose a problem.

The question of embalming was discussed. The wife asked if embalming was necessary, since the final disposition was to be cremation. The funeral director told her that embalming is not required by law in most cases, no matter what the method of disposition was to be. However, because a viewing period was being contemplated and because the time of death or the climatic conditions at that time could not be predicted with any accuracy, the decision on whether or not to embalm would have to be reserved for the time and place of death. The wife was assured that if the death were in the home and embalming were necessary it could be performed in the home so that her husband would not have to be transferred out of the home and then back again. Since the wife had a medical background, the funeral director suggested she could be present at the time of embalming if it should be necessary. She agreed that she would like to be present.

During a conversation exploring the specific requests of the wife, the husband, and the social unit of friends, vital information was transmitted. The funeral director observed almost immediately that a continuance of the caring role that the wife, the friends, and the couple's young children had assumed during the long illness of the husband must be maintained throughout the funeral rite. Moreover, it was evident that their involvement should be as active rather than just as passive participants. With this in mind the funeral director allowed the wife to discuss her thoughts and those of husband, their children, and friends in this area. The funeral director's ultimate goal was to allow the client family to adapt the funeral rite to their particular needs and wishes. He gave only guidance and did not attempt to make decisions for the client family. When he perceived a problem that might arise, he would advise the wife and offer some alternatives in keeping with the priorities already established. Those priorities may be summarized by the funeral director's interpretation of what the wife was saying, in essence: "My children and I want to be involved. Our friends wish to participate actively. Don't close us out!"

The funeral director asked the wife to describe the physical layout of her home, so that together they might establish a plan of action for the actual mechanics of the funeral. Moreover, with this information he would have an idea of what equipment would have to be brought to the home at the time of death. An attempt would be made to use as much of the existing facility as possible with the least use of alien accoutrements. The funeral director would have preferred to visit the home at some time prior to the death, but the wife felt that this was not warranted.

The wife wished to have a continuing visitation period, extending from the time of death for about 24 hours. The funeral director explained that this period might be longer or shorter, depending on the time of death, since with cremation certain clearances would have to be obtained from the proper municipal offices.

The first discussion ended with the consideration of a suitable casket. A simple unfinished pine casket was chosen. The funeral director assured the wife that each detail would be followed as closely as possible, and the consultation period ended.

It was only a few short months after this meeting that what was planned had to be implemented, when the husband, aged 44, died.

In the early morning hours of a day in August, the funeral director was summoned to the home. He arrived with an assistant, the necessary equipment, and the casket.

Upon entering the home he found the wife seated at the dining room table. She informed him that her husband had died shortly before the funeral director had been called and that friends were with him. She asked if they might be allowed to stay for a time with her husband before the funeral director began his work, and this was done. During this period the funeral director was able to speak to the wife and meet the children and some of the friends.

The wife, the funeral director, and his assistant entered the husband's bedroom a short time later. The friends were gathered around the bed discussing the deceased at times and at other times allowing their silence to speak for them.

Because of the time of death and the warm weather it was agreed that embalming would be necessary if the rest of the plans were to be followed. Cremation could not take place for some 36 or more hours. The embalming was performed on the bed, with the wife present and in a few instances actually participating in an assisting role. Upon completion of the embalming the friends returned and assisted the wife in washing and dressing her husband's body.

The casket was brought into the room and placed on a portable bierhich that had been brought by the funeral director. At this point it seemed that the funeral director had been totally accepted into the social group, if not on an actual basis at least on an honorary one. With the friends he helped arrange a material they had acquired for placement around the casket. They then placed the deceased in the casket, and the casket was relocated in the center of a large living room area. The area itself was designed in the round, so that it lent itself to conversation. Lighting was dimmer controlled, and candles were used in a candelabra at the head of the casket.

The deceased remained in state for a period of about 36 hours while a continuous stream of family and friends moved in and out freely. While some slept, some would keep vigil. So it went until the afternoon of the procession to the crematory.

On the day of the funeral, and at other times when he was in contact with the client family, the funeral director's attire could not be considered the sterotypical garb many people expect funeral directors to wear. As with other facets of this funeral, the funeral director took his lead from the client family. His dress reflected what the client family had communicated through word and action. The use of colors was accepted and even preferred. Although his attire was always proper, he did not wear black. On the day of the funeral the funeral director dressed in a cream-colored vested suit. The client family also wore light colors throughout the funeral rite.

A short service at the crematory consisted of both spontaneous song and verbal tributes to the deceased by the wife and friends. Although no clergyman was present, the service itself was religious.

Throughout the funeral rite a tight bond between the funeral director and the client family developed—to such a high degree of personal commitment that they were able to freely demonstrate support through touch, embraces, and kisses of friendship. An air of fulfillment and satisfaction seemed to be felt by all present.

What was demonstrated to the funeral director and the client family was that a funeral rite can be adapted to allow for the personal expression of the participants and at the same time retain the social support needed to maintain it as a social function. Also demonstrated was the value of the director as a therapeutic person; in this role he did not usurp anyone else's role. The funeral director's role should not be one of script writer, choreographer, or principal actor but rather one of demonstrating to the client family that he welcomes their active participation.

Evidence that this type of adaptive funeral was accepted on a psychosocial level is the fact that within one year there was a second death within this same social group. At that time the same type of service was requested. The second case followed closely the procedures of the first, except that the subject was a single female, 77 years of age.

Their second case offered a degree of further adaptation. It was the deceased's request to be held in state in the same round living room. Since friendship ties were so strong, this was easily arranged. After embalming in her own home, she was transferred by the funeral director to the home of her friend, the widow of the man in the previously mentioned situation. Once again the objective of the funeral director was to involve the client family as totally as possible. This was accomplished.

Although these experiences may not be what is considered ideal funeral rites by many people, they demonstrate the high degree of cultural relativity within the social group that opted for them.

Reference

Toffler, A. 1970. *Future Shock.* New York: Random House; paperback ed. New York: Bantam, 1971.

30

The Expanding Role of the Funeral Director as a Counselor

C. Stewart Hausmann

All funeral directors are informational and situational counselors. The only question to be raised is whether they are good or bad counselors. Counselors need not be professional psychotherapists with extensive academic credentials. When matters related to death are discussed with or by a funeral director, he, in essence, becomes a counselor to those to whom he imparts advice and information. Since most professional funeral service persons accept this axiom, there follows a natural desire on the part of most practitioners to improve their counseling skills and the insights underlying those skills.

The funeral director should be challenged to identify new counseling areas beyond those regularly considered part of a funeral service and, by filling those voids, should provide better service to those seeking his help. Because the role of the funeral service practitioner is expanding to open new vistas and new opportunities, it is developing greater justification for his professional existence and bringing more profound satisfaction in his service to the community.

Traditionally, a funeral director's professional, technical, and business skills have been confined to at-need situations. He enters the scene as a crisis intervenor at the time of death. Historically, the vehicle of the funeral has been used as an experience of value to help the bereaved accept the reality of death. The period of the funeral has allowed time for the community to share the loss and offer social support to the grieving family. The attendant ceremony, the procession to the place of final disposition, and the committal service have engaged the family in activities that many psychologists feel are necessary. During the whole funeral process the family has been attended carefully by a caring funeral director, one who performs his traditional functions well.

Today, however, traditions are crumbling about us, including some of those involving the funeral. No longer are family and community units intact to provide social support. The dying and bereaved may live in crushing loneliness, in the midst of saturated metropolitan areas or isolated into hospitals, extended-care units, or retirement villages, separated from family or others of significance in their lives. A traditional funeral may be dysfunctional or possibly just too expensive for many surviving bereaved. Life-styles have dictated changes in social customs and ethnic mores. The three-day funeral, as a tradition, is eroding and alternates to the funeral are evolving.

Despite these changes, however, the psychological trauma of death has not lessened. Feelings of guilt, shock, and denial seem to be even more profound in today's death environment. Yet those experiencing these emotions have fewer of the traditional supports from which to derive solace and help. The challenge for funeral directors emerges from these changes in our society.

It may be true that other professionals are available to render advice and assistance, but none is as readily available or is as openly consulted at the time of a death than the funeral director. Quite naturally, he is the first-line counselor and upon him falls a new responsibility and opportunity. It is up to him to identify the opportunity and seize it. The result is a more sensitive service to the bereaved and a new function for the practitioner. The more training and experience the funeral director has in counseling, the more readily he identifies counseling opportunities. Modifications in the funeral service curriculum are providing the background of knowledge necessary for this skill.

The funeral director need not hesitate to expand his counseling activities. He has been a natural counselor. A necessary prerequisite for being a good funeral director is a love of people, and love is a prime ingredient of good counseling. I can recall that my father and I were the professionals in our family funeral home, and my mother was always close at hand. She was outgoing, affable, and a warm friend to most of the families who called on us. On numerous occasions we three would be at the front door as the bereaved widow and family would arrive for the arrangement conference or first visitation. The widow would greet my father and me and then collapse in tears into my mother's arms.

Mother would take a widow aside and listen as she related everything, from past events in the life of her husband to the full narrative of his death. Relieved and composed, the widow would proceed with my mother, strengthened to face the events to come. Trust, love, patience, and a willingness to listen and share are the real ingredients necessary for helping people. Mother was an effective counselor, although she was never labeled as such. All that is needed to be a counselor is more of what is already being done but with a little more understanding of its goals and the use of improved skills.

Throughout the history of funeral service the funeral practitioner has identified needs and opportunities and has prepared himself to satisfy them. The early funeral functionary may have served as church sexton and undertaker or furniture maker and undertaker. He was the one in the community, whatever his calling, who undertook the care of the dead. Before long the undertaker identified other functions, services, and facilities that he could perform. In the process of recognizing these needs and then satisfying them, he established a unique business for himself. The funeral functionary of a more recent day has identified additional needs and in meeting them has further altered his professional services. This evolutionary process will continue as new needs are met. The funeral director must look beyond at-need services, as important as they may be, to the challenge of "before-need" and "after-need" service voids. Then he will be broadening the scope of his professional activities and raising the horizon of his service capacity. In the process he will be making himself more vital to his community life.

Today the funeral director's interaction with his community starts in the life of its young people when he is called upon as a resource person by schools to share in the teaching of courses on death and dying. Through his professional affiliations and organizations, curriculum materials are made available to schools and colleges, and the schools and colleges in turn call upon the funeral director to participate in classroom discussions. The funeral director is often invited to address church groups, service clubs, veterans and senior citizens, always as a primary community resource person, on the subjects of death, dying, bereavement, and the grief process. His professional image is recognized in parallel with that of other caregiving professionals in the community. It is important for the funeral director to earn this acceptance, for ultimately it will give him additional recognition as a counselor who can work to complement and supplement the work of other counseling professionals, including clergy, psychologists, physicians, social workers, and the like.

As equal professional status is gained, the funeral director is able to relate to other professionals during pre-need counseling sessions. Increasingly, families are coming to funeral directors in advance of death for a myriad of reasons, only one of which is to preplan and prefinance their funerals. The counseling funeral director has an opportunity to listen to his client, express his concerns, and learn to identify potential and real problems. He can then offer advice or help to solve those problems. He should also be prepared to refer the problem to other specialists who may be better qualified to help in a specific situation. Perhaps a visit to a clergyperson might appear necessary. Perhaps a visit to an attorney or some governmental office might be required, coupled with a followup counseling session to help solve a more chronic problem or to identify new problems that may develop as older problems are being resolved.

If the funeral director has been accepted as a resource person with counseling abilities and areas of expertise, individuals and families will be referred to him. An attorney might see the wisdom of advising a family to visit its funeral director to complete funeral arrangements. An elderly person might be referred to the funeral director by a clergyperson. Many older persons are given peace of mind by making their "arrangements" ahead of time and thus maintaining their independence and freedom of choice to the end. A primary goal is to cause the funeral director to become an even more important part of his professional community life and his funeral home to be more than just a place to conduct formal services. The opportunities for learning, showing, and growing are expanded for the benefit of everyone. The funeral director must be particularly attuned to his counseling responsibilities during the formal funeral process. It is imperative for the funeral director himself to be in attendance at the moments of greatest emotional stress, including the "first call," the arrangement conference, the first viewing, and, finally, the ceremony and committal. At each of these emotional and traumatic events, the funeral director needs to be available to offer his strength and loving concern. He should create quiet interludes to sit with the bereaved, listening to what they say and identifying their needs. Many of the bases for later psychological problems are readily perceived during these moments when the tragic reality of what has happened becomes apparent. It is imperative that the funeral director become a careful observer. He must not hide behind his desk, his busy work, or his pseudo-professionalism to insulate himself from the drama of death and its attendant stress. Too often we simply take out pencil and paper and begin asking questions rather than listen to what is said and adapt the assistance and the services to what is heard. Our at-need counseling techniques should be more sharply honed.

Pre-need and at-need counseling services by funeral directors are important, but an even more challenging opportunity exists for the funeral director in postfuneral counseling. Funeral directors are familiar with the symptoms of shock, numbness, and suffering exhibited by the bereaved. We have maintained that funerals help people through the early days of their grief, but even that knowledge does not make it any easier for them. We hold that "viewing" helps people face the reality of death, but even if it is good for us, like medicine, it does not make death any easier to endure.

Because people do suffer through a bereavement process, because the culture in which we live does create special bereavement problems, and because we are taught that many grieving people collapse emotionally or physically within six months, it is obvious that the funeral director has a continuing responsibility that began in before-need counseling, progressed during the funeral, and certainly does not conclude with the committal. Rather, it continues until final accommodation has occurred. Not accepting that fact would be an abdication of responsibility by the funeral service and forfeiture of an opportunity by the profession.

True, other trained professionals are available for assistance and support, but none is better positioned to render assistance during this entire experience than the funeral director. Nor is he usurping the prerogatives of other professionals, for he has purposeful, immediate, and continuing access to the grieving family. He does not need to wait to be invited or sought out. The day after the funeral he has practical reasons for visiting a widow who is often terribly alone when family and friends have departed. The funeral director in the course of his business can continue to listen, identify problems, and either assist or refer. If he has developed a good relationship during before-need and at-need counseling sessions, his presence and help will be welcomed by the bereaved family, as well as by the other caring community professionals. Other visits will follow logically as he routinely assists in the settlement of the estate, in the handling of government claims, insurance awards, and so on. Any number of counseling sessions, depending on need, may result. During each, the funeral director continues to listen, identify problems, and ultimately assist in their resolution or their referral to someone more specially qualified.

Some funeral directors who manage large funeral homes will say that, with their large staff, continuity of purpose is lost, for several directors may interact with each family. This need not be so; the largest funeral home may assign one director to one family and thus achieve the same "Mom and Pop" result. A team approach might even be used fruitfully, the best qualities of each team member being employed for specific assignments, but with a one-on-one principle maintained. To the funeral director who claims he is too busy to perform extensive counseling, I say, "Give it a try."

Some funeral homes engage a retired clergyperson as its counselor. This may or may not prove successful, but in any event it misses the point of developing the expertise and value of the funeral director. This in itself may not be important, but augmenting his front-line availability makes him a more indispensable member of the community of caregiving professionals. Once having carved out his professional niche as a member of this community's professional counseling team, the funeral director will find himself in a unique position. More and more, families will come to him or be referred to him in advance of need. He will provide all the customary, but enhanced, at-need services. He will then counsel the family through an extended postneed period, after which the family may be ready to preplan for the next family death. The family, ideally, will have gone full circle with the helping funeral director. The funeral director will have found himself in the middle of the family circle, occupying a very important place in the life of each family he serves. The funeral director will have emerged as the professional he has always sought to be and in the process everyone will benefit.

Index

List of Contributors

Arthur M. Arkin, M.D., Department of Psychology, Graduate School, City University of New York; Department of Psychiatry, Mount Sinai School of Medicine, New York, New York

Patricia D. Baker, R.N., M.S., Assistant Professor, School of Nursing, University of Colorado, Denver, Colorado

J. Robert Belmany, Funeral Director, Mobile, Alabama

James P. Carse, Ph.D., Professor of the History of the Literature of Religion, Faculty of Arts and Science, New York University, New York, New York

Daniel J. Cherico, Ph.D., M.P.H., Assistant Professor, Department of Health Care and Public Administration, Graduate School, Long Island University, C.W. Post Center, Greenvale, New York

Buell W. Dalton, D. Min., Ministry of United Methodist Church (retired); Funeral Director and Counselor, Fort Lauderdale, Florida

Bruce L. Danto, M.D., Clinical Associate Professor of Psychiatry, Wayne State University School of Medicine, Detroit, Michigan

Robert DeBellis, M.D., Assistant Professor of Clinical Medicine, College of Physicians and Surgeons, Columbia University, New York, New York

Wynetta Devore, Ed.D., Associate Professor, Syracuse University School of Social Work, Syracuse, New York

Kermit Edison, Funeral Director, Stoughton, Wisconsin

Jack Ferguson, Ph.D., Associate Professor of Sociology, University of Windsor, Windsor, Ontario, Canada

Tamara Ferguson, Ph.D., Adjunct Associate Professor of Sociology in Psychiatry, Wayne State University School of Medicine, Detroit, Michigan

Jeannette R. Folta, R.N., Ph.D., Professor and Chairperson, Department of Sociology, University of Vermont, Burlington, Vermont

Ralph A. Franciosi, M.D., Director of Laboratories, Director of Sudden Infant Death Center, Minneapolis Children's Health Center and Hospital, Minneapolis, Minnesota

Jerome F. Fredrick, Ph.D., Director of Chemical Research, The Dodge Chemical Company, Bronx, New York

Gertrude R. Friedman, M.S.S., Director, Human Ecology Program; Consultant, Minnesota Sudden Infant Death Center, Minneapolis Children's Health Center, Minneapolis, Minnesota

Carole E. Fudin, C.S.W., A.C.S.W., Adjunct Professor of Social Work, Rutgers University Graduate School, New Brunswick, New Jersey

C. Stewart Hausmann, Executive Director, New Jersey State Funeral Directors Association, Manasquan, New Jersey

Royal Keith, Past President, National Funeral Directors Association, Yakima, Washington

Ann S. Kliman, M.A., Director, Situational Crisis Service, The Center for Preventive Psychiatry, White Plains, New York

R. Jay Kraeer, Past President, National Funeral Directors Association, Pompano Beach, Florida

Austin H. Kutscher, President, The Foundation of Thanatology; Associate Professor, Columbia-Presbyterian Medical Center, New York, New York

Lillian G. Kutscher, Publications Editor, The Foundation of Thanatology, New York, New York

Otto S. Margolis, Ph.D., Vice President for Academic Affairs, American Academy McAllister Institute of Funeral Service, New York, New York

Rabbi Steven A. Moss, Coordinator, Jewish Chaplaincy Service, Memorial Sloan Kettering Hospital, New York, New York; Chaplaincy Supervisor, New York Board of Rabbis; Spiritual Leader, B'nai Israel Reform Temple, Oakdale, New York

Roy V. Nichols, M.A., Funeral Director, Chagrin Falls, Ohio

Carl T. Noll, Chief Memorial Affairs Director, Veterans Administration, Washington, D.C.

Clarence Novitzke, Past President, Wisconsin Funeral Directors Association, Park Falls, Wisconsin

Colin Murray Parkes, M.D., F.R.C. Psych., D.P.M., Senior Lecturer in Psychiatry, The London Hospital Medical College, London, England

Vanderlyn R. Pine, Ph.D., Associate Professor, Department of Sociology, State University of New York at New Paltz, New York

J. Bruce Powers, Funeral Director, Jamestown, New York

Joseph R. Proulx, R.N., Ed.D., Professor, School of Nursing, University of Maryland, Baltimore, Maryland

Howard C. Raether, Executive Director, National Funeral Directors Association, Milwaukee, Wisconsin

Calvin E. Schorer, M.D., Director of Education and Training, Lafayette Clinic; Professor of Psychiatry, Wayne State University School of Medicine, Detroit, Michigan

Irene B. Seeland, M.D., Associate in Clinical Psychiatry, College of Physicians and Surgeons, Columbia University, New York, New York

Irene Sullivan, M.S.W., C.S.W., Adjunct Professor, Mercy College, Dobbs Ferry, New York

Lee H. Suszycki, A.C.S.W., Department of Social Services, The Presbyterian Hospital in the City of New York, New York

William A. Tari, Dean, American Academy McAllister Institute of Funeral Service, New York, New York

Garfield Tourney, M.D., Professor of Psychiatry, The University of Mississippi Medical Center, Jackson, Mississippi

M. L. S. Vachon, R.N., Ph.D., Research Scientist, Social and Community Psychiatry Section, Clarke Institute of Psychiatry, Toronto, Canada; Assistant Professor, Department of Psychiatry, University of Toronto, Ontario, Canada

Rev. James P. Zimmerman, Christ Lutheran Church, East Northport, New York

Columbia University Press / Foundation of Thanatology Series

Teaching Psychosocial Aspects of Patient Care
Bernard Schoenberg, Helen F. Pettit, and Arthur C. Carr, editors

Loss and Grief: Psychological Management in Medical Practice
Bernard Schoenberg, Arthur C. Carr, David Peretz, and Austin H. Kutscher, editors

Psychosocial Aspects of Terminal Care
Bernard Schoenberg, Arthur C. Carr, David Peretz, and Austin H. Kutscher, editors

Psychosocial Aspects of Cystic Fibrosis: A Model for Chronic Lung Disease
Paul R. Patterson, Carolyn R. Denning, and Austin H. Kutscher, editors

The Terminal Patient: Oral Care
Austin H. Kutscher, Bernard Schoenberg, and Arthur C. Carr, editors

Psychopharmacologic Agents for the Terminally Ill and Bereaved
Ivan K. Goldberg, Sidney Malitz, and Austin H. Kutscher, editors

Anticipatory Grief
Bernard Schoenberg, Arthur C. Carr, Austin H. Kutscher, David Peretz, and Ivan K. Goldberg, editors

Bereavement: Its Psychosocial Aspects
Bernard Schoenberg, Irwin Gerber, Alfred Wiener, Austin H. Kutscher, David Peretz, and Arthur C. Carr, editors

The Nurse as Caregiver for the Terminal Patient and His Family
Ann M. Earle, Nina T. Argondizzo, and Austin H. Kutscher, editors

Social Work with the Dying Patient and the Family
Elizabeth R. Prichard, Jean Collard, Ben A. Orcutt, Austin H. Kutscher, Irene Seeland, and Nathan Lefkowitz, editors

Home Care: Living with Dying
Elizabeth R. Prichard, Jean Collard, Janet Starr, Josephine A. Lockwood, Austin H. Kutscher, and Irene B. Seeland, editors

Psychosocial Aspects of Cardiovascular Disease: The Life-Threatened Patient, the Family, and the Staff.
James Reiffel, Robert DeBellis, Lester C. Mark, Austin H. Kutscher, and Bernard Schoenberg, editors

Acute Grief: Counseling the Bereaved
Otto S. Margolis, Howard C. Raether, Austin H. Kutscher, J. Bruce Powers, Irene B. Seeland, Robert DeBellis, and Daniel J. Cherico, editors